LANGUAGES OF LIBERATION

WALTER KALAIDJIAN

Languages of Liberation

The Social Text in Contemporary American Poetry

Columbia University Press
New York

The Press acknowledges a grant from Mercer University toward the cost of publishing this book.

Columbia University Press
New York   Oxford
Copyright © 1989 Columbia University Press
All rights reserved

Library of Congress Cataloging-in-Publication Data

Kalaidjian, Walter B., 1952–
Languages of liberation : the social text in contemporary American
poetry / Walter Kalaidjian.
p.   cm.
Bibliography: p.
Includes index.
ISBN 0-231-06836-0
1. American poetry—20th century—History and criticism.
2. Literature and society—United States—History—20th century.
3. Social problems in literature. I. Title.
PS310.S7K35 1989
811'.54'09355—dc19
                                                88-30332
                                                CIP

Printed in the United States of America

Casebound editions of Columbia University Press books are Smyth-sewn
and are printed on permanent and durable acid-free paper

For My Family

Contents

Preface

RARELY HAS criticism of American poetry discussed the broad cultural issues that underwrite contemporary poetics. All too often critics who deal in contemporary literary and cultural theory simply overlook the historical and institutional limits of poetic discourse. The critical silence surrounding poetry's worldly contexts is symptomatic of the intrinsic reading habits long fostered by American New Criticism. Following Immanuel Kant's and Samuel Taylor Coleridge's insistence on art's remove from the world, John Crowe Ransom, the ideologue of American formalism, held that English studies need not address such extrinsic concerns as the life of the author, a work's cultural context, or its social milieu. In *The World's Body* (1938), Ransom decisively segregated communal life from "aesthetic forms" that "do not serve the principle of utility."[1]

Throughout the postwar decades, many critics followed Ransom in repressing verse writing's *social text*—that is, not merely poetry's inscription of historical events, but equally important, its social transactions with various interpretive communities, conglomerate and small press markets, the academy, and other spheres of cultural production.

Whereas the Fugitives divorced literature from its extrinsic bases and habitats, contemporaneous writings of the Frankfurt School offered detailed cultural readings of advanced capitalism's *Kulturindustrie*. Building on the work of Max Weber and Georg Lukács, for example, Theodor W. Adorno investigated how the logic of "exchange-value exerts its power in a special way in the realm of cultural goods."[2] "Today," he concluded in 1962, "every phenomenon of culture, even if a model of integrity, is liable to be suffocated in the cultivation of kitsch."[3] Given the spreading cultural domination of the commodity form, Herbert Marcuse for his part looked to the aesthetic dimension as a source of social emancipation.[4] Unlike the New Critics, the Frankfurt theorists did not elide history in seeking to preserve high culture. On the contrary, they were all too mindful of the failure of humanism in the face of German National Socialism, and later, the one-dimensional scene of advanced consumer capitalism in America. "No universal history," wrote Adorno, "leads from savagery to humanitarianism, but there is one leading from the slingshot to the megaton bomb."[5] But such pessimism, however sobering, did tend to curtail the prospects for a thoroughgoing aesthetic critique within advanced consumer society. Although Marcuse espoused various liberationist movements in the late 1960s, the Frankfurt School gave short shrift to the ways in which contemporary art fomented social change in postwar America.

Partially indebted to *and* critical of the Frankfurt project, *Languages of Liberation* looks at how contemporary American verse is both swept by and resistant to the commercial, institutional, and social pressures of our historical moment. My book's polemical shape is framed by three broad lines of investigation, taking into account lyric verse, long verse forms, and social modes of poetry. Within these movements, each chapter advances Frankfurt School theses into such areas as contemporary rhetorical criticism, feminism, and Afro-American aesthetics. This conversation with emergent theory confirms the Frankfurt critique of the commodity form as a pervasive, if not determining, motor force driving contemporary culture. At the same time, however, this dialogue also points up how the School's investment in high art blocks its theorizing of mass media, pop culture, and subaltern constituencies as sites oppositional to the one-dimensional spread of advanced capitalism in postwar America.

As a study of poetry and ideology, *Languages of Liberation* discusses the powers of *critique* offered by poetic form. Strong poems, I argue, not only disrupt the world outlooks of reigning ideologies but frequently resist incorporation by ruling narratives of literary criticism. Through such discursive force, verse writing serves politically to question and contest dominant modes of information that shape human subjectivity, institutional habitats, and the social field at large. Tempering my cultural argument, I offer close readings of seven major American poets: James Wright, W. S. Merwin, Charles Olson, James Merrill, Robert Bly, Adrienne Rich, and Gwendolyn Brooks. My choice of these particular writers is, of course, partly personal; obviously, I find their poetic visions compelling. But more importantly, this grouping permits certain strategic ends, enabling my discussions, for example, to cross and collapse disciplinary boundaries among contemporary poetics, poststructuralist theory, feminism, Afro-American studies, and cultural criticism generally. Moreover, working with figures who at once negotiate radical or marginal politics *and* command canonical authority calls attention to the ways in which academic criticism and other cultural industries routinely domesticate literature's powers of subversion.

I begin the book by tracing at some length the contemporary critique of lyric form, which since the romantic period has designated what Hegel called "intensely subjective and personal expression."[6] The romantic doctrine of expressive lyricism is still taken for granted in most discussions of contemporary poetry. "The conception of the *lyric* as the individual and personal emotion of the poet," observes C. Hugh Holman, "still holds, and is, perhaps, the chief basis for discriminating between the *lyric* and other poetic forms."[7] Such sanctions of personal lyricism, however, actually misconstrue the poet's role within the social networks that shape the contemporary verse canon. In my opening chapter I look at how lyric expression is, in fact, mediated by the review circuit, conglomerate publishing

firms and outlets, the academy, granting agencies, award committees, and other institutions of fame.

In chapter 2, my close readings of James Wright and W. S. Merwin show how the lyric's dubious status is inscribed in the rhetorical
makeup of these poets' minimalist verse forms. Wright longs for a
voiced and often pastoral lyricism even in the heartland of America's
industrial "rustbelt." In his verse, the valorized doctrine of the author's individual creativity, instead of serving as a fruitful source of
literary meaning, actually constrains poetry's verbal negotiations with
history. While Wright laments the loss of lyric expression, Merwin
exploits lyric failure in textual registers. Here he contests the standard notions that poetry finds its source in the author's intention and
should reflect a signified referential world. Moreover, Merwin does
not assume that the lyric voice either comes before writing or transcends other discourse. In his poetry of the 1960s through the 1980s,
Merwin reverses such "natural" givens. He decisively dethrones author, voice, and reference in favor of language, textuality, and writing. For Merwin, poetic discourse is radically inaugural: its language
bestows identity, not the other way around. The poet's erasures of
lyric presence part company with the existential confessionalism of
the so-called poetry of revolt. Significantly, Merwin's critique of the
self's expressive privilege clears the way for the second part of *Languages of Liberation,* where I consider the more explicitly textual resources of contemporary long poems. Like Merwin in the lyric mode,
Charles Olson and James Merrill pioneer a radically discursive poetics in the American long poem tradition.

Moving beyond past discussions of encyclopedic verse forms, my
readings of Olson and Merrill foreground the expanded possibilities
of political critique offered by the postmodern verse epic.[8] Throughout the book, I make guarded use of the term "postmodern." Ever
since Frederico de Oníz coined the label *postmodernismo* in 1934, its
increasing appeal for criticism has led to a certain terminological inflation. A password in cultural theory, architecture, the visual arts,
film, communications, music, and literature, it serves as a generic,
typological, period, and cultural designation. Not surprisingly, such
a popular usage is, for some, highly suspect on its face. Nonetheless,
I find strategic value in employing it here to mark what I see as
important formal and political differences distinguishing the contem-

porary long poem from the modern verse epic of the antebellum decades. The postmodernism of Olson and Merrill works rhetorically to oppose high modernism's leanings toward aesthetic elitism and hierarchic social orders. In different ways, Olson and Merrill both push the verbal character of their poetry beyond the epic's more "normal" didactic impulses. Anticipating the movement of post-structuralist theory, their poetics underscore moments of linguistic indeterminacy and ludic subversion in ways that Derrida would describe as being both "adventurous" and "strategic."[9] Although poetry has often been thought of as a mimetic enterprise—one that represents, copies, or imitates a prior referential ground—Derrida and others have shown that the authority of signified reference is itself subject to a certain slippage into the verbal displacements and deferrals of signification. Such linguistic supplementation is adventurous as it proliferates beyond the author's or reader's cognitive, epistemological, and ideological presuppositions. I use the notion of a postmodern, or what Olson called "post-humanist," style to designate such textual "otherness" and adventurous verbal excess. But more to the point, such linguistic moments, whether playful or disruptive, serve strategically to loosen and unravel the political closure of reigning ideological narratives.

Liberating the collage techniques of Eliot and Pound, Olson and Merrill open the modern verse epic to the nonliterary discourses of mass culture. Olson's magnum opus *The Maximus Poems* projects a dialogic zone of writing that both traverses formal generic boundaries and undermines poetry's conventional remove from worldly texts. Such verbal errancy is radically anarchic. But through his "post-humanist" style, the poet resists the ideological narratives underwriting modernism's desire for cultural hegemony. Just as Olson jettisons the self's "lyrical interference," Merrill also renounces lyric subjectivity to assume the role of textual "medium" in *The Changing Light at Sandover*. Composed, in part, at the Ouija board, Merrill's postmodern long poem presents a bizarre libretto—one that fuses high modernism with contemporary pop culture in an operatic pastiche. Working within the epic's elite aesthetic forms, he reduces them to objects of camp consumption. Beyond the trilogy's seemingly frivolous camp surface, its carnivalesque satire at once celebrates and unmasks the cultural authority of contemporary science. Although science would transcend its own discursive rhetoric—and thus lay claim to knowledge and truth—Merrill's dialogic textuality teases out science's grounding in fictive language games.

The poststructuralist insight that meaning rests on an undecidable linguistic base, not on foundational ideals, has important political consequences in Olson's and Merrill's writing. Both poets venture beyond a merely playful celebration of verbal indeterminacy. Instead, each actively employs poetic language to intervene in the discursive representations that shape America's social text. Outside the dominant Anglo-American tradition, other lines of theory also view poetic discourse as a social rather than "sullen" enterprise. For example, like Merwin, Olson, and Merrill, the Russian formalist critic Valentin Vološinov held that even our most private musings have a linguistic base. Consciousness itself, he claimed, depends on "some kind of semiotic material."[10] But such a semiotic theory of thought and perception should not be confused with the Continental linguistic tradition reaching back to Descartes and Leibniz, then through Saussure to Barthes and Derrida.[11] Instead of regarding language as an arbitrary system of signs, Vološinov conceived it first and foremost as a dialogic "contract between people." Since discourse is produced out of a social dialogue, it belongs neither to the author as a kind of private property, nor to some "transcendental" consciousness as in the phenomenological tradition. Rather, discursive form emerges from a contentious verbal praxis, underwritten by the "social ubiquity" of broader cultural, economic, and political forces. Beyond Vološinov, Adorno, in his benchmark essay "Lyric Poetry and Society," showed that over and above whatever social themes a lyric may express, its worldly context is rhetorically immanent in the makeup of its poetic form. He viewed the demand that lyric expression be isolated from society as itself a symptom of alienation, "a form of reaction against the reification of the world, against the rule of the wares of commerce over people." Thus, in Adorno's reversal, lyric subjectivity comes after the historical conditions of the personal, so that "neither the private person of the poet, his psychology, nor his so-called social viewpoint are to come into question here; what matters is the poem itself as a philosophical sundial of history."[12]

It is the poststructuralist writing of Michel Foucault that most propels the social understanding of linguistic form into sophisticated, theoretical registers. As is well known, after *The Order of Things*

Foucault probed language's strategic transactions with power. Discourse, he held, is hardly produced in a void, but in material settings that are culturally permitted.[13] Particular language formations (*epistèmes*) and fields of speech acts (*énoncés*) possess distinctive genealogies: they negotiate specific disciplinary boundaries, institutional domains, and regions of force. While power may serve repressive ends as in, say, Bentham's administrative Panopticon, it also flows through multiple sites of resistance to cultural domination.[14] Foucault's general observation that a "sphere of force relations" mediates all discourse sheds light on the formation and status of postwar "literary" culture. Until recently, most American readers accepted poetry's divorce from social life as a "natural" rather than political given. Moreover, few questioned the poet's expressive privilege as coming before language and at the end of ideology. Such norms were arguably the products of New Critical and existential theorists, however effaced their shaping roles. While W. S. Merwin debunks the sovereign self's private lyricism, Robert Bly, Adrienne Rich, and Gwendolyn Brooks open special lines of dialogue between poetic language and America's wider discursive scene. "Literature is intertextual," notes John Brenkman, "in the sense that literary practice actively responds to the entire set of discourses, symbolic formations, and systems of representation that define a particular society's cultural and political life."[15] Just so, the poetry of Bly, Rich, and Brooks "actively responds" to America's social text, at once reflecting, resisting, and remolding history. In this way, poetic form serves as critique in dialogue with society.

Robert Bly's early career is marked by the same emotive impulse that reigns in James Wright's colloquial verse. But responding to postwar American foreign policy in Central America and later Vietnam, Bly jettisons such personal lyricism. Throughout his middle career, the poet's political verse drives a discursive wedge into the official state rhetoric that props up American adventurism in the Third World. Drawing on the verbal resources of black humor, parody, and burlesque, his political satire subverts and dismantles bureaucratic propaganda. Bly's witty surrealism lampoons the administrative neologisms and jargon designed to provide what Orwell called "a defence of the indefensible." Less successful, however, is Bly's recent "feminist" poetics, based in the "deep" imagery of Bachofen, Jung, and Neumann. The poetry of Adrienne Rich, taken up in my sixth chapter, offers a more compelling feminist vision—one that is critically engaged with the political issues under debate in the women's movement. Her "re-visionary" images of feminine emancipation question the psychic, sexual, and cultural representations that make up women's place in contemporary America.

Like Rich, Gwendolyn Brooks retrieves powerful "re-memberings" of women's lives throughout her early formalist period. In my final chapter, I trace Brooks' progress beyond formalism toward a distinctively Afro-American aesthetic in the 1960s through the 1980s. Whereas Rich now writes mainly for a feminist audience, Brooks rests her verse on the rhetorical base of the black community, drawing from its long-standing folk traditions of black vernacular expression. Brooks has always been one of our more influential cultural leaders, at once a powerful celebrant and organizer of what Raya Dunayevskaya calls "masses in motion."[16] Her durable poetic forms have advocated black solidarity throughout the turbulent civil rights movement of the 1950s, the black aesthetic and power movements of the 1960s, the crisis of black cultural nationalism in the 1970s, and the unrelenting social cutbacks of the Reagan years. In the writing of Bly, Rich, and Brooks, the lyric self is decisively dispersed into transpersonal subject positions beyond and external to the conventional, humanizing range of introspective poetics.[17] Thus in their textual practice, poetic discourse, instead of standing outside of or above history, is actively aligned with the social field of intersubjective, group constituencies emerging from contemporary America's antiwar, feminist, and black power movements.

While *Languages of Liberation* advances beyond lyric and epic forms to consider the poetics of social critique, its general trajectory resists a totalizing thesis. Similarly, the book's historical frame is less constitutive than *destructive*: that is, critical of temporal narratives that ignore or willfully repress cultural difference. Moreover, my theoretical allegiances may well negotiate contested zones and regions of struggle on the contemporary map of critical reading. In working through some of the methodological controversies of my own moment, I have deliberately left in a productive tension the book's linguistic and social understandings of poetic form. This rift, I would like to think, will prove a fruitful opening for debate among my readers and other "figures of outward."

Acknowledgments

DURING THE writing of *Languages of Liberation,* I received much useful advice and criticism from several colleagues that I take pleasure in acknowledging here. To begin with, I am indebted to Cary Nelson, who read portions of the book. I am also grateful to J. Hillis Miller and Elaine Showalter, who read sections of the manuscript when I was a fellow at the 1986 School of Criticism and Theory at Dartmouth College. While an Andrew Mellon fellow at Vanderbilt University in 1984, I received helpful direction from William Richardson and John Sallis. I was also fortunate to have Roy Harvey Pearce clarify my understanding of the American long poem while I was an NEH fellow at the University of California at San Diego, La Jolla, in 1983.

Earlier versions of sections of chapter 2 concerning James Wright and W. S. Merwin were published, respectively, in *Boundary 2* (1981) and in Cary Nelson and L. Edwin Folsom, eds., *W. S. Merwin: Essays on the Poetry* (Urbana: University of Illinois Press, 1987). Parts of chapter 3 appeared in *Modern Poetry Studies* (1983). I am indebted to several colleagues who helped me refine portions of *Languages of Liberation* originally presented as papers at professional meetings of the Modern Language Association, the National Women's Studies Association, the Northeast Modern Language Association, the Society for Critical Exchange, the South Atlantic Modern Language Association, and the Twentieth-Century Literature Conference.

Special thanks go out to Jennifer Crewe and Ann Miller of Columbia University Press for their much-appreciated editorial advice. In addition, I would like to thank Mercer University for providing released time from my teaching duties and other support.

Finally, I gratefully acknowledge permission to quote from the following:

Reprinted from James Wright, *Collected Poems,* by permission of Wesleyan University Press: "To a Defeated Saviour" copyright © 1971 by James Wright (this poem first appeared in *The Green Wall,* published by Yale University Press); "At the Executed Murder's Grave" copyright © 1958 by James Wright; "Saint Judas" copyright © 1959 by James Wright; "Many of Our Waters: Variations on a Poem by a Black Child" copyright © 1969 by James Wright; "I Am a Sioux Brave, He Said in Minneapolis" copyright © 1968 by James Wright (this poem first appeared in *The Sixties*); and "The River Down Home" copyright © 1963 by James Wright. Excerpt from "One Last Look at the Adige: Verona in the Rain" from *To a Blossoming Pear Tree* by James Wright, copyright © 1973, 1974, 1975, 1976, 1977 by James Wright, reprinted by permission of Farrar, Straus and Giroux, Inc.

Reprinted from W. S. Merwin, with the permission of Atheneum Publishers, an imprint of Macmillan Publishing Company: excerpts from "The Counting Houses" and "Numbered Apartment" in *The Compass Flower,* copyright © 1977 W. S. Merwin; "Fear," "The Well," and "The Port" in *Carrier of Ladders,* copyright © 1970 W. S. Merwin; excerpt from "Sibyl" in *Writings to an Unfinished Accompaniment,* copyright © 1973 W. S. Merwin; excerpt from "The Black Jewel" in *Opening the Hand,* copyright © 1983 W. S. Merwin; excerpt from "The Child" in *The Lice,* copyright © 1967 W. S. Merwin; and from "The Cross Roads of the World Etc." in *The Moving Target,* copyright © 1963 W. S. Merwin. Excerpts from "The Mountains," "Green Island," "Summer Canyon," "Sheep Clouds," and "On the Mountain" in *Finding the Islands,* by W. S. Merwin, copyright © 1982 by W. S. Merwin, reprinted by permission of North Point Press.

Charles Olson, excerpts from *The Maximus Poems,* copyright © 1983 by Charles Olson, reprinted with the permission of the University of California Press.

James Merrill, excerpts from *The Book of Ephraim, Mirabell: Books of Number,* and *Scripts for the Pageant* in *The Changing Light at Sandover,* copyright © 1982 James Merrill, reprinted with the permission of Atheneum Publishers, an imprint of Macmillan Publishing Company.

Robert Bly, excerpts from "Poem Against the Rich," "Depression," and "A Man Writes to a Part of Himself" in *Silence in the Snowy Fields,* Wesleyan University Press, 1962, copyright © 1962 by Robert Bly, reprinted by permission of Robert Bly. Excerpts from *The Light Around the Body* by Robert Bly: "The Busy Man Speaks" copyright © 1962 by Robert Bly; "Come With Me" copyright © 1964 by Robert Bly; "Asian Peace Offers Rejected Without Publication" and "Johnson's Cabinet Watched by Ants" copyright © 1966 by Robert Bly; and "Counting Small-Boned Bodies" copyright © 1967 by Robert Bly, reprinted by permission of Harper and Row, Publishers, Inc. Excerpts from "The Teeth Mother Naked at Last" in *Sleepers Joining Hands* by Robert Bly, copyright © 1970 by Robert Bly, reprinted by permission of Robert Bly. This poem was first published by City Lights Books.

Lines from the poems from *The Fact of a Doorframe, Poems Selected and New, 1950–1984,* by Adrienne Rich, are used with the permission of W. W. Norton and Company, Inc., and the author. Copyright © 1984 by Adrienne Rich; copyright © 1975, 1978 by W. W. Norton and Company, Inc.; copyright © 1981 by Adrienne Rich. Lines from "The Images" from *A Wild Patience Has Taken Me This Far, Poems 1978–81,* by Adrienne Rich, are used with the permission of W. W. Norton and Company, Inc., and the author. Copyright © 1981 by Adrienne Rich. Lines from "Sibling Mysteries" from *The*

ACKNOWLEDGMENTS

Dream of a Common Language, Poems 1974–1977, by Adrienne Rich,
are used with the permission of W. W. Norton and Company, Inc.
 Gwendolyn Brooks, excerpts from "Riot," "A Welcome Song
for Laini Nzinga," and "The Boy Died in My Alley" in *To Disembark,* copyright © 1981 by Gwendolyn Brooks, reprinted by permission of Broadside Press. All other excerpts and poems from *Blacks.*
Copyright © 1987 by Gwendolyn Brooks. Reprinted by permission
of the David Company.

LANGUAGES OF LIBERATION

PART I

Lyricism in the Postwar Epoch

1.

Poetry's Institutional Settings

THE HISTORY of contemporary American poetry has typically been staged through critical narratives of dramatic struggle. On one side stands the New Critical verse tradition; on the other are massed its emergent adversaries: "projectivist," confessional, neosurrealist, "deep image," regional, feminist, Afro-American, and other local schools and movements. This founding opposition shaped two land-mark anthologies at the end of the 1950s: Donald Hall's *New Poets of England and America* (1957) and Donald Allen's *The New American Poetry* (1960). While Hall valorized the formalist aesthetics of the 1940s and 1950s, Allen welcomed the open form, anti-academic poetics of the 1960s. Both editors touted their choices as representative of the age. But not one of the "new" poets appeared in both collections.[1] Such a radical split in canon formation was a telling index of the polarized aesthetic tastes dividing the literary milieu of the 1950s. In the 1960s and 1970s, the struggle between these two camps was further promoted by poets' prose manifestoes and was reinforced by a second wave of critical reception.

From the hindsight of the post-Vietnam era, however, the lines of division that make up this standard critical opposition are highly suspect. In fact, their apparent differences conceal deeper ties that join New Criticism to the so-called poetry of revolt. While it is true that the reception of contemporary poetry has been shaped by the 1960s' challenge to New Critical strictures against the "intentional" and "affective" fallacies, this same critical line has largely erased poetry's dialogue with contemporary culture in favor of the author's private lyricism. The course of contemporary American poetry has actually reproduced, rather than contested, formalism's swerve from social change. Admittedly, my own leaning, which is hardly disguised here, is toward a social rather than "subjective" reading of contemporary American letters. Poetic "personalism," I contend, needs to be seen in the contexts of postwar history and, in particular, today's conglomerate publishing market. As we shall see, the habit of reading verse for intentional experience and introspective values has relegated poetry to the margins of America's cultural scene. Similarly, lyric solipsism has led to verse writing's professional domestication within the university. Arguing against these dominant tendencies, my opening chapter examines how recent advances in critical theory have both shed light on poetry's own critical dimension and opened its lyric closure to the social text of contemporary history.

The Critical Reception

DURING THE Great Depression and World War II decades, literary humanists all along the political spectrum were driven to the fringes of a spreading transnational consumer society. In America, the Fugitive movement resisted the New South's commercial tide. In their 1930 manifesto *I'll Take My Stand: The South and the Agrarian Tradition,* John Crowe Ransom, Allen Tate, and others harked back to more "classical," property-based, and agrarian modes of life that once shaped the old-line plantation order of the Deep South.

Although finding few political allies within the ranks of Dixie and New Deal Democrats, the Southern Agrarian agenda took hold nationwide in American universities through the successful New Criticism movement. Within the academy, the Fugitives promoted the cultural and political values espoused by high modernist precursors, most notably T. S. Eliot. "Literary" culture served as the ground for what Ransom, in the subtitle to his first prose volume, *God Without Thunder* (1930), called "An Unorthodox Defense of Orthodoxy."

Throughout the postwar years, the New Critics waged a tireless campaign to reverse the decline of English studies. In the twentieth century, lamented Cleanth Brooks and Robert Penn Warren, readers turned away from high aesthetic forms: "Instead, they listen to speeches, go to church, view television programs, read magazine stories, or the gossip columns of newspapers."[2] Beset by American mass culture, Brooks and Warren nonetheless enlarged the audience for verse with their popular book *Understanding Poetry* (1938; revised editions 1950, 1960, 1976). A forerunner to numerous other handbooks, primers, guidebooks, and anthologies, it packaged New Critical doctrine for the university classroom. Such "Understanding Literature" textbooks were shaped by critical works like Ransom's *The World's Body* (1938), R. P. Blackmur's *The Expense of Greatness* (1940), and René Wellek's and Austin Warren's *Theory of Literature* (1949), among others. New Critical method was further institutionalized in such influential journals as Brooks' and Warren's *Southern Review* of 1935–1942, the *Kenyon Review* under the editorial supervision of Ransom from 1939 to 1959, and the *Sewanee Review*, edited by Allen Tate and others in the 1940s; and it was eventually reproduced in the pedagogy of literature departments nationwide.

Although taking an active hand in fashioning the modern verse canon, New Criticism maintained that literature should have little truck with history. The Fugitives, of course, endorsed Eliot's resistance to romanticism, science, and the social sciences. They regarded poetry as an "objective" mode of knowledge ontologically distinct from all others. In 1946 W. K. Wimsatt's and Monroe Beardsley's critical admonitions against reading poems in terms of either authorial intent (the "intentional fallacy") or reader response (the "affective fallacy") followed Eliot's doctrine of poetic impersonality set forth in "Tradition and the Individual Talent." Regarding poems as autonomous and hermetically insulated verbal objects, Wimsatt and Beardsley restricted criticism to the technical art of close reading— explicating the poem's "organic system of relationships," its "essential structures" of irony, paradox, ambiguity, "extension," "intention," literary allusion, and so on. Thus, "the poem," wrote Wimsatt, "is an act." But, in critical reading, he added, it must be "hypostatized" or arrested and extricated from its biographical, social, and historical circumstances.[3] This delimitation of the *travail du text* served politically to close off the poem's dialogue with social forces.

Not incidentally, the New Critics also curtailed poetry's critical dimension by setting up rigid generic boundaries discriminating theoretical rhetoric from poetic discourse. Significantly, in "The Heresy of Paraphrase" (1947), Cleanth Brooks popularized the view that verse writing is ontologically prior to criticism. "The poem, if it be a true poem," he wrote, "is a simulacrum of reality—in this sense, at least, it is an 'imitation'—by *being* an experience rather than any mere statement about experience or any mere abstraction from experience."[4] Because poetry's aesthetic form ought to transcend historicity, Brooks dismissed any critical debate over "the use of poetry" as a "crippling form" of heresy (p. 185). Similarly, the poet's role came properly before the critic's and to confuse or reverse them was also heretical: "[The poet's] task is finally to unify experience. He must return to us the unity of the experience itself as man knows it in his own experience" (p. 194). Thus on the face of it, the poet's creative act rendered the more analytic discourse of the critic belated. But it was criticism, paradoxically, that conceived and enforced this privilege to begin with. Valorizing poetry as prior to its own theoretical discourse, New Criticism empowered verse ironically through a critical act.

Crucial to the formation of the contemporary verse canon, Don Allen's 1960 anthology *The New American Poetry* legitimated a strong counterpoetics to the New Critical formalism then dominating the American literary scene. As whetstone to his collection's polemical edge, Allen included prose manifestoes from its major contributors: Amiri Baraka (LeRoi Jones), Robert Creeley, Robert Duncan, Lawrence Ferlinghetti, Allen Ginsberg, Denise Levertov, Charles Olson, Jack Spicer, John Wieners, and others. But despite the provocative range of these poetics, the volume's aesthetic identity rested on a shared platform of anti-academic and counterformalist stances. Thus, Allen's introductory description of the anthology's "one common characteristic: a total rejection of all those qualities typical of academic verse" summed up the collection's oppositional *dependence* on the very traditions it repudiated.[5] However lodged "against" academic formalism, the confessional, regional, neosurrealist, "deep imagist," and other aesthetic schools and movements were surprisingly reticent about the broader, ideological investments and effects of their own formal choices. Like their academic counterparts, the "new" poets largely eschewed any overtly political commitments or affiliations in the wider social field.

Seldom, at first, did even the "projectivist" and Beat fringes launch serious cultural critiques. For example, in her position statement for *The New American Poetry*, Denise Levertov admitted: "I do not believe that a violent imitation of the horrors of our times is the concern of poetry. . . . I long for poems of an inner harmony in utter contrast to the chaos in which they exist" (p. 412). This apolitical stance arguably allowed Levertov to cross over from Allen's collection to Donald Hall's revised anthology in 1962. A disavowal of history similar to Levertov's also marked Allen Ginsberg's introduction to *Howl,* an otherwise stinging indictment of America's one-dimensional scene. "A word on the Politicians," he wrote for Allen's anthology, "my poetry is Angelic Ravings, & has nothing to do with dull materialistic vagaries" (p. 417). Poets throughout the 1950s and early 1960s did, of course, write on the state of postwar culture. Ginsberg's protests of cold war McCarthyism in "America," Robert Bly's and W. S. Merwin's protests of nuclear testing in the *Fifties* magazine and *The Nation,* Robert Lowell's reflections on the Cuban missile crisis in "For the Union Dead," and William Stafford's focus on nuclear escalation in "At the Bomb Testing Site" were all notable examples. But considering the collage of crises America faced throughout the postwar decades, the prevailing tendency to ignore history, common to most contemporary poets and their critics, is striking indeed.

Such discursive silence cries out as a telling symptom of resistance to the social text of the postwar years. Consider for a moment the turbulent events of the cold war decades: an era marked by foreign adventurism, unprecedented defense spending and weapons production, and a pervasive national atmosphere of fear and paranoia. In 1948, the year the Soviet Union blockaded West Berlin, it also annexed Czechoslovakia through staging a government coup. Two years later North Korean troops crossed the thirty-eighth parallel, invading South Korea and eventually leading to the United States' mobilization for possible war with the People's Republic of China. Meanwhile, the Eisenhower administration orchestrated its own CIA-backed military coup in Guatemala, overthrowing the land reform policies of Jacobo Arbenz Guzman in 1954 and installing the pro-American Colonel Carlos Castillo Armas. In 1956, Soviet tanks rolled into Hungary, at a time when British, French, and Israeli forces were invading Egypt during the Suez crisis. In 1959 Fidel Castro overthrew the Batista dictatorship in Cuba, to which the United States responded with its 1961 Bay of Pigs misadventure. That same year American advisers were deployed in South Vietnam. Such repeated crises were nothing less than traumatic given the possibility of their sudden escalation into global nuclear war.

An atmosphere of genuine national panic inaugurated the 1950s when it was disclosed in 1949 that the Soviets had detonated their own nuclear device. Cold war logic—initiated by Churchill's famous "iron curtain" speech in 1946 and the Truman Doctrine of Containment of World Communism (1947)—led to President Truman's 1950 decision to design and deploy the hydrogen bomb, and further to Secretary of State Dulles's massive retaliation doctrine of 1954. Under President Eisenhower, windfall defense budget increases accrued to the Strategic Air Command, commencing an era of incredible nuclear escalation.[6] By the end of his administration, defense expenditures had risen to an unprecedented $41 billion annually. America's huge investments in weapons development, however, did little to enhance national security. In fact, between 1960 and 1962 the United States military was put on nuclear alert twice: during the 1960 U-2 incident and the 1962 Cuban missile crisis. In 1964, when the United States was committing itself seriously in Southeast Asia, the People's Republic of China detonated its first nuclear device. Tom Hayden's 1962 "Port Huron Statement," inaugurating Students for a Democratic Society, summed up the 1950s' apocalyptic angst. "We may be," Hayden said, "the last generation in the experiment with living."[7]

Global tensions of the cold war era were further heightened by the Red Scare, McCarthyism, and the civil rights movement of the 1950s. In 1954, the year of McCarthy's Senate censure, the Warren Court's landmark desegregation ruling in *Brown v. the Board of Education of Topeka* struck down as unconstitutional the "separate but equal" doctrine condoning racial segregation in the public schools. This decision ushered in an era of progressive legislation and assertive grass-roots movements for racial equality, particularly across the South. In 1955 Martin Luther King's Montgomery Improvement Association waged a successful campaign for integrated seating on local buses that triggered other gains in black voter registration, urban development, and in the desegregation of housing, transportation, and education. The following year witnessed the establishment of a bipartisan Civil Rights Commission under the 1957 Civil Rights Act. But these were also years of violent racial backlash, notably in the federal and state clashes over desegregation in Little Rock, Arkansas (1957), Anniston, Alabama (1961), and Oxford, Mississippi (1962). The push for civil rights through freedom rides, lunch counter sit-ins, and high school and university actions culminated in the success of King's civil disobedience campaign in Birmingham and his March on Washington in August of 1963.

Despite their differences, Americans in the postwar decades were increasingly drawn together into a common national drama and fate. The urban "massification" of American culture was fostered by the growth of print journalism and the spread of television during the 1950s and 1960s. By 1960, Americans had bought an average of one TV per household—over 45 million sets. Framing the imagery of the cold war era as media spectacle, television moved to the heart of postwar American culture. There, its centralized networks promoted what Jean Baudrillard has described as a "speech without response," nurturing habits of consumerism and passivity before television's own imaginary, one-dimensional scene.[8] Faced with these tremendous shifts in national mood, opinion, and culture, most contemporary poets and their critics succumbed to a kind of inward emigration. In their writing, America's rich, contentious history was reduced and contained in personal narratives of private existential angst.

By thus hoping to transcend history, poetry found itself increasingly driven to the obscure and eccentric margins of cultural life. Cutting across the grain of America's cloistral poetics, Charles Olson's trenchant manifesto "Projective Verse" (1950) sought to open verse to a broader social text. Olson's assault on lyric formalism, however, was not seriously taken up in American criticism until the 1970s. Instead, critics following the emergence of confessionalism in the careers of Berryman, Lowell, and Roethke, and later, Plath, Sexton, and Snodgrass, took aim against New Criticism's doctrine of the "intentional fallacy." While Olson flouted "the lyrical interference of the individual,"[9] criticism of the 1960s valorized lyric expression. Poetry's social text was largely silenced throughout the 1960s. Verse writing tended to be viewed as an intentional act of the private lyric self removed from the transpersonal difficulties of contemporary political history.

Thus, Stephen Stepanchev in *American Poetry Since 1945: A Critical Study* (1965) opposed the "personally tested facts" of contemporary poetry to the "aesthetic distance" of modernism.[10] Stepanchev's critical survey repeated the guiding assumptions of precursors such as David Ossman (*The Sullen Art*, 1963) and Anthony Ostroff (*The Contemporary Poet as Artist and Critic*, 1964). Moreover, his study looked forward to standard approaches of the late 1960s. Ossman's collection of critical interviews took its title from Dylan Thomas. The choice of "sullen"—whose etymological root is the Latin "solus," alone—foregrounded the private, lyric self. Despite his rejection of the "intentional fallacy," Ossman followed the standard New Critical separation of poetry from history. He merely shifted the site of closure from the poem's verbal artifice to the author's subjective life: "These poets," he said "and all poets, despite their contacts with the world, are ultimately alone. One creates after all by one's *self*."[11]

The following year Anthony Ostroff leveled his volume's eight symposia of poets and critics to a single intentional theme: "all the contributors take as a principle: that experience is individual—and that communication of experience, therefore, must always in some measure be personal, intimate."[12] Ostroff's critical stance was lodged within the 1960s' critique of the intentional fallacy, but like the New Critics he took for granted that experience is individual rather than social. M. L. Rosenthal's *The New Poets* (1967) endorsed the "subjective" readings of Ossman and Ostroff. Like Ostroff, Rosenthal

repressed poetry's social base by subordinating history to the subjective life of the author. "Our poetry of political and cultural criticism," he said, "centers on the individual as the *victim*."[13] Despite
the buffetings of history, the drama of the individual self still held
the center of Rosenthal's critical discourse. The next year Paul Carroll's
The Poem in Its Skin (1968) used a bodily metaphor to valorize contemporary verse as lyric utterance. "Every good poem," he said, "is
like a person: it has its own skin."[14] Using an approach not unlike
Carroll's, Ralph J. Mills, Jr.'s 1969 essay "Creation's Very Self: On
the Personal Element in Recent American Poetry," later reprinted in
Cry of the Human (1974), viewed poetic form as a bodying forth of
the confessional self: "[Poets] seek a personal mode of utterance to
embody perceivings and intuitions very much their own." "The poet,"
Mills asserted, "voluntarily stands exposed as 'creation's very self'
before us."[15] Yeats' phrase was an apt rubric for poetry's critical
reduction to lyric incarnation.

Throughout the 1970s, major studies and anthologies of contemporary poetry upheld the lyric self as the source of poetry's emotive
power. Thus, Robert B. Shaw's preface to his critical anthology
American Poetry Since 1960: Some Critical Perspectives (1973) reproduced the 1960s' "intentional" bias. Unlike the "modern school,"
"academic formalism," and the "cult of impersonality," the contemporary poet, Shaw said, offers an "unvarnished portrait of himself."[16] Moreover, he argued for the solipsistic character of contemporary American long poems, defining them as "epics of self" (pp.
12–13). Shaw's grounding in a subjective aesthetic also typified the
approach of Robert Phillips in *The Confessional Poets* (1973) and guided
the writing of George S. Lensing and Ronald Moran, whose *Four
Poets and the Emotive Imagination* (1976) was a central text in the reception of the deep image writers during the 1970s. The following
year, David Kalstone tempered the critical edge of confessional poetics; his *Five Temperaments* (1977) considered "the revisions of the
self that come through writing verse: how this happens, its resources, its limits."[17] The theme of lyric subjectivity persisted well
into criticism of the mid-1980s in works such as *Introspection and
Contemporary Poetry* (1984) by Alan Williamson and *Style and Authenticity in Postmodern Poetry* (1986) by Jonathan Holden. Williamson's aim was "to examine the images of self—or the nature and

quality of subjective experience—in contemporary American poetry."[18] Harking all the way back to Allen's polemic, Holden retrieved the "intentional" split from modernism. The contemporary poet, he argued, must choose "whether to trust one's vision and presume to impose upon the world, by sheer force of character, an individual aesthetic and ethical order, or to continue the modernist hegemony of Eliot and Pound."[19]

Criticism's fascination with the lyric self not only underwrote poetry's reception in the postwar era, but also guided its formation in major anthologies for popular and academic readerships. Summing up the lyric impulse of the 1960s, Mark Strand argued in *The Contemporary American Poets* (1969) that postwar writers made "a lifetime's work of the self."[20] Following Allen and Strand, Al Poulin repeated this dominant critical narrative in each printing of his *Contemporary American Poetry* anthology (1971, 1975, 1985): "One of the major differences between modernist and contemporary poetry is that the latter—at least seemingly—is more intimate and personal."[21] This powerful theme abided as a "natural" given well into the 1980s. Thus, anthologists Stuart Friebert and David Young in *The Longman Anthology of Contemporary American Poetry, 1950–1980* (1983) asserted that "our primary emphasis is on the poets as individual artists."[22] Likewise, in *The Morrow Anthology of Younger American Poets* (1985), editors Dave Smith and David Bottoms valorized the poet's (tellingly male) persona: "In his poems the younger poet tends to be himself, an invented version of himself."[23]

Buttressing lyric subjectivity, criticism often read the poet's voiced experience through the standard themes of existential writers such as Dostoevsky, Kafka, Sartre, and Camus. In these studies, poets were seen as enacting a certain ontological unease in the face of God's absence as theorized by Kierkegaard and Tillich. Many writers themselves took up this critical line as in, say, Robert Lowell's comments on "Skunk Hour": "My night is not gracious, but secular, puritan, and agnostical. An Existentialist night. Somewhere in my mind was a passage from Sartre or Camus about reaching some point of final darkness where the one free act is suicide."[24] Encountering what Stanley Romaine Hopper described in *The Crisis of Faith* as "the palpable reality of Nothingness," poets felt challenged, in the idiom of Sartre, to "become" rather than "be."[25] Similarly guided by the existential dictum that "existence precedes essence," Richard Howard in *Alone with America* (1969) presented contemporary poets as writers "who address themselves to the current, to the flux, to the process of experience rather than to its precepts."[26] The poet's unmediated vision of experience likewise informed J. Hillis Miller's *Poets of Reality* (1965) during his early association with the Geneva phenomenologists. Existential phenomenology's struggle with New Criticism was a major critical narrative throughout the 1960s and 1970s. Although opening this existential line to cultural studies, Charles Molesworth's *The Fierce Embrace* (1979) still portrayed contemporary American poetry as "increasingly immersive in its strategy . . . an embrace not only of the raw and chaotic energies of contemporary life, but also of the interior life of individual subjects."[27] Five years later, Anthony Libby's study *Mythologies of Nothing* (1984) joined the "secular mysticism" of this "immersive aesthetic" to the tradition of American romanticism—what Harold Bloom described as the Orphic strain of Emerson and Whitman.[28]

A telling irony, however, belies much of American existential criticism. Critics such as Howard, Lensing, Mills, Moran, and Stepanchev and editors such as Allen, Poulin, Strand, and the rest did quarrel with New Critical formalism. But by tying poetry to authorial intention, they reproduced New Criticism's own close readings of the poet's representative sensibility, as in Randall Jarrell's readings of Auden and Lowell during the 1940s and 1950s.[29] Despite the outpouring of rhetoric dubbing postwar verse a "poetry of revolt," its reception was marked by the foundational oppositions of New Critical doctrine: poetry enjoys an aesthetic autonomy from its institutional infrastructures; the "ideal reader" transcends heterogeneous interpretive communities; and the private lyric voice dwells apart from history's social text. Traditionally such binary habits of thought, as Derrida has argued, tend politically to valorize one member of the paired notions, concepts, or ideas in a hierarchic position of power and authority over the other. The very meaning and identity of such privileged signifieds, however, rests structurally on the signifying exclusions, distanciations, and deferrals of nominal opposites.[30] Similarly, in each case poetic autonomy, "disinterested" reading, and voice dominated the center of the New Critical enterprise by marginalizing history, audience, and textuality. The poetry of revolt did contest the intentional fallacy. But throughout the 1960s, poets and critics failed to interrogate the vestiges of New Critical thought that persisted in their own continuing blindness to America's social field.

From our vantage point in the 1980s, this theoretical failure can be mapped as the period's political limit: one that actively led readers to invest in ideologies of bourgeois individualism. Seldom in the 1950s and 1960s would writers speculate on the social foundations of poetic form. Throughout the "subjective" discussions of these decades one looks in vain for the kind of social poetics that once flourished in American letters of the prewar years. Whereas it seemed natural in the early 1960s to think of poetry as a personal idiom, for a 1930s writer such as, say, Isidor Schneider it was just as evident that "poetry is, by its nature, a social art. . . . It was only under capitalism that poetry, attempting to adapt itself, began to attempt individualistic forms, especially the lyric . . . [which] had the further effect of withdrawing poetry from the masses. It made of poetry a 'mystery,' gave it an unworldly standard."[31] From this earlier, historicizing perspective, the poetics of personal lyricism—instead of serving as the vital source of poetry's creative expression—can now be reread as *the* symbolic form par excellence of the more recent American impulse to contain and repress the social text of contemporary history.[32]

The Conglomeration of the Word

CONFESSIONALISM'S FASCINATION with the emotive self led to a poetic solipsism at the end of ideology and "beyond" politics. Such resistance to social forces was a vestige of New Criticism's provincial denial of history. Cleanth Brooks' definition of the poem as "a hierarchy subordinated to a total and governing attitude" ("The Heresy of Paraphrase," p. 189) revived the cultural conservatism of Matthew Arnold and T. S. Eliot. For his part, John Crowe Ransom openly espoused their old-line values. Advertising himself as being "in manners, aristocratic; in religion, ritualistic; in art, traditional," he followed Eliot's earlier authoritarian platform: "classicist in literature, royalist in politics, and Anglo-Catholic in religion."[33] The

New Critical industry, promoted in Ransom's 1937 essay "Criticism, Inc.," had little to say about the socialist writers of the 1930s. Instead, the New Critics sought in theory to elevate literature as an autonomous and ideal discourse above and beyond social forces. But hardly disinterested, they actively campaigned for a formalist agenda. New Criticism's effort to shape the modernist canon is plain to see in the awarding of the first Bollingen Prize to Ezra Pound.[34] The 1949 Bollingen Prize incident underscored New Criticism's push for the apolitical status of literature. Similarly, throughout the 1950s social issues were largely excluded as criteria from the Yale Younger Poets Series Awards.[35]

Despite the ahistorical rhetoric of American New Criticism and its ephebes in the 1960s, contemporary poetry was as much a business as a "sullen" art. There is a telling irony in W. H. Auden's Yeatsian description of poetry as an art that "survives / In the valley of its making where executives / Would never want to tamper."[36] Today, poetry's pastoral valley resembles less a "sacred wood" than a resort condo community. In fact, much executive tampering enters into the decisions about where and under what circumstances poets will be published, what awards will accrue to them, which organizations and performing circuits will underwrite their public readings, and how critics will cultivate their audiences.[37] Verse writing in the postmodern era, it is plausible to claim, is less a visionary or sacramental art than a highly competitive industry.

But very few poets reflect openly on the market forces that underwrite their careers. Charles Olson, however, is one of our major postwar poets whose work unrelentingly lodges such institutional critiques. Emerging as the major theorist of "projective verse" in Donald Allen's anthology, he arguably had access to the major publishing houses and influential academic journals. But he deliberately avoided them, choosing instead to publish with alternative outlets such as Jonathan William's Jargon Press and small independent periodicals like Robert Creeley's *Black Mountain Review* and Cid Corman's *Origin*. Olson deployed his writing against the mainstream publishing organs of the 1950s and 1960s. The tactic was part of his larger struggle against what he referred to as "pejorocracy"—literally, "worse rule." Olson liberated the term from Pound, employing it as a rubric for monopoly capitalism's accelerating corporate mergers that feed today's giant conglomerates. Olson's refusal to publish with the big publishing houses followed his assault on the dehumanizing absentee ownership of the major transnationals. In particular, his magnum opus *The Maximus Poems* indicted the corporate takeover of Gloucester's locally owned fishing industry by Gorton and Morton Pew. These giant mills, Olson charged, reified Gloucester's traditional cultural values and community heritage, leveling them to a homogeneous scene of commodification. Olson's protest against the spread of American consumer society proved a prophetic stance. Indeed, his suspicions about the imminent conglomeration of publishing soon became reality.

In 1960, the same year that Olson appeared in Allen's Grove Press anthology, Bennett Cerf, then president of Random House, set his firm's agenda for the coming decade. In a speech delivered to the New York Society of Security Analysts, Cerf reached Olson's same conclusion but from a managerial perspective totally at odds with the poet's politics. "It is my belief," Cerf said, "that within the next few years, some five or six great publishing combines will dominate the publishing scene, much the way that a handful of companies today dominate steel, automobiles, and other truly big industries. We intend that Random House will be one of these larger companies."[38] In 1977 Random House emerged as one of the giant "combines" Cerf envisioned, leading the field as a publisher of adult and juvenile hardcovers and trade paperbacks. But ironically, the handful of companies Cerf envisioned in the industrial sector are now the same conglomerates controlling America's mass communication industry. RCA is not only the parent company of Random House but also of NBC; it ranks in the upper thirty of *Fortune's* list of one thousand top manufacturing companies. Even more disturbing, by 1982 five parent companies owned half of the mass publishing market, while the top ten managed 85 percent.[39] Merger mania in the 1980s was fostered by the relaxed antitrust atmosphere of the Reagan White House. Such domestic mergers, coupled with a weakening U.S. dollar, fueled foreign investments in the lucrative $10 billion American book sales market. In 1986, for example, the West German communications giant Bertelsmann bought Doubleday and Company for $500 million, making it the second largest book publisher after Simon and Schuster. Other European entities such as the

Holtzbrinck Group, Elsevier, and Penguin Books of Britain have taken over Henry Holt and Company, Praeger, New American Library, Viking, and E. P. Dutton.

In addition to their holdings in industrial and manufacturing economies, giant conglomerates such as Time, Gulf + Western, CBS, MCA, Times Mirror, and Westinghouse wholly control the diversified sectors of America's mass culture industry. Publishing is now a centralized business in large part because greater profits accrue to established presses than to emergent publishing ventures. The big houses dominate the market. They command editorial staffs with ties to established authors and production jobbers, as well as marketing channels for distributing and merchandizing literature. Most large publishing houses are owned, in turn, by even bigger parent companies with subsidiaries in other mass media (newspapers, magazines, book clubs, pay and cable TV, broadcast networks, motion picture companies, video disc and cassette industries). Consider Time, Inc. With its acquisition of the Book-of-the-Month Club in 1977, Time became an industry leader in book publishing, along with CBS, Reader's Digest Association, McGraw-Hill, and Doubleday. Time is the parent company of Little, Brown; Time-Life Books; Book-of-the-Month Club; The Atlantic Monthly Press; and The New York Graphic Society. But it is also a diversified conglomerate that manages such magazines as *Fortune, Life, Time, People, Money,* and *Sports Illustrated.* In addition, Time is a major parent company for the cable TV industry, owning Home Box Office, Telematon, and American Television and Communication Corporation. As Time demonstrates in the conglomerate market, the distinction between private ownership of mass communication networks and their "objective" content is blurred. As the mass media is increasingly bureaucratized and centered in a literal handful of giant service conglomerates, the likelihood of a diverse, heterogeneous national culture grows increasingly remote.

Contemporary poets, as a result, are fated to write either for an audience largely oriented to the homogeneous representations of a monolithic culture industry or for fringe readerships pushed to the edge of America's cultural scene. But more troubling, poets live with the reality that they are bought and sold by the same conglomerates that marginalize their art. Resisting the mass publishing market, many poets start up their own small presses and alternative magazines, often moving into desk-top publishing through the laborsaving advances of laser printing and computer technology.[40] The inception of Paul Carroll's *Big Table* typifies the institutional formation of such avant-garde ventures. In the late 1950s, Carroll edited the *Chicago Review*, funded by the University of Chicago. In 1958, however, after he published controversial writings of the Beat poets, the university began to exert budgetary pressure over editorial decisions by threatening to withhold its support funds. As a result, Carroll quit his position to found *Big Table*. This move allowed him to continue to publish poets such as Burroughs and Corso, who both won Longview Poetry Awards for their work in *Big Table* 1.

Often the projects of aesthetic schools and sociopolitical movements, small presses and little magazines publish on the fringes of America's culture industry. Nonetheless, they provide important sites for the emergence of avant-garde aesthetics and polemical counter-statements to the dominant publishing outlets. These cultural critiques, however, are frequently incorporated by the very institutions they challenge. For example, Robert Bly at first promoted his international deep image surrealism in 1958 as editor of his home-grown *Fifties* magazine and through other deep image publications such as George Hitchcock's *Kayak*. In 1962 Bly was picked up by Wesleyan University Press's poetry series and in 1967 by Harper and Row; this led in 1968 to a National Book Award for *The Light Around the Body*. Dissenting from *within* the dominant organs of mass culture, Bly's National Book Award speech lodged a sweeping indictment against America's academic, scholarly, and publishing communities that fueled his political leadership of the 1966 American Writers Against the Vietnam War movement. "What has my own publisher, Harper and Row, done to help end the war?" he asked:

> Nothing. In an age of gross and savage crimes by legal governments, the institutions will have to learn responsibility, learn to take their part in preserving the nation, and take their risk by committing acts of disobedience. The book companies can find ways to act like Thoreau, whom they publish. Where were the publishing houses when Dr. Spock and Mr. Goodman and Mr. Raskin—all three writers—were indicted? It's clear they *can* have an editorial policy: they can refuse to pay taxes.[41]

Despite Bly's critique, the mainstream conglomerates still invest in his work, exploiting the very stances and position statements intended to unseat their authority. Bly publishes with such giant houses as both Harper and Row—parent company for J. B. Lippincott, A. J. Holman, Basic Books, and T. Y. Crowell—and Dial Press, a subsidiary of Doubleday, which is the parent of Dell, Delacorte, Laidlaw Brothers, J. G. Ferguson, and the Literary Guild.

As big as it is, Harper and Row was itself the object of a $300 million buy-out by media czar Rupert Murdoch in 1987. Now merged with Murdoch's other ventures, Harper and Row is part of a $3 billion empire spanning three continents, with holdings that include the *Times* (London) the *New York Post,* the *Boston Herald, New York Magazine,* 20th-Century Fox Corporation, *New Woman* and *Star* magazines, Salem House, Ltd., Times Books London, William Collins and Sons, John Bartholomew, and Bay Books. Well known for his sensationalist journalism, Murdoch set out to merge and shake up the editorial staffs of Harper and Row and William Collins. For his part, Harper and Row's chairman and CEO Brooks Thomas summed up the merger, offering a telling insight into the commercialization of today's publishing market: "As the players in the publishing game get bigger and bigger we couldn't go out and acquire another college textbook publisher, the way they could. But Rupert has deep pockets, and he's shown a willingness to back up his convictions with cash."[42]

Now writing within the mass market, Bly, of course, continues to enjoy a certain aesthetic distance from such rampant corporate buy-outs. Yet this structural autonomy among the levels of the publishing mode of production cuts both ways. Ironically, the force of his anti-establishment polemic has been commodified by the very infrastructures he set out to contest. Whether such oppositional aesthetics will at all change the institutional base supporting Bly's writing is also a crucial challenge for Adrienne Rich's revisionary cultural feminism. Gwendolyn Brooks, of course, took more radical steps than either Bly or Rich by severing her ties to Harper and Row in 1971, publishing thereafter with outlets native to the Afro-American community such as Dudley Randall's Broadside Press, Haki Madhubuti's Third World Press, and, in the 1980s with her own Brooks Press and David Company. Nevertheless, whether dissenting from within America's mass culture industry or choosing more subaltern sites of aesthetic opposition, each of these poets undertook political risks that others of their generation could not face.

Professional Poets Within the Postwar University

THE 1960s critical establishment endorsed the poet's private self, sullen at the end of ideology, and thereby rendered verse writing acceptably apolitical for the university, which served as its main institutional base of support. The nexus between academe and poetry writing is vital to the formation of the postwar verse canon. The same one-dimensional ethos driving contemporary mass communication and publishing markets has also shaped American institutions of higher learning—poets' other main access to their readerships. Higher education's dramatic expansion in the postwar epoch was commensurate with the rapid growth of information management in corporate America. The 1950s' high-growth economy financed the emergence of what has been described as a managerial "new class" that now oversees today's business, government, university research, and social service sectors.[43] In the early 1950s, sociological explorations such as David Reisman's *The Lonely Crowd* (1950), C. Wright Mills' *White Collar* (1952) and *The Power Elite* (1956), William Whyte's *The Organizational Man* (1956), and John Kenneth Galbraith's *The Affluent Society* (1958) considered the dehumanizing effects of homogeneous corporate models. Galbraith, in particular, discussed the role of the communication industry in fabricating mass consumer demands and perceived needs. This project was further illuminated in Vance Packard's *The Hidden Persuaders* (1957). Packard's classic exposé of corporate advertising's subliminal seduction paralleled the work of postwar Frankfurt theorists in America. Herbert Marcuse's *One-Dimensional Man* (1964) surpassed sociological studies of the 1950s with a more theoretical and sophisticated critique of corporate bureaucracy. The increasingly specialized and technical nature of the corporate apparatus managing the production and distribution of goods, services, and information, Marcuse argued, could not be separated, as a simple set of functional means, from its social and political effects. On the contrary, instrumental reason had become an end in itself, governing the consumer's needs, attitudes, desires, and sources of personal fulfillment.[44]

Such one-dimensionality also reached into the postwar university. During the intense high-growth years of the 1950s' technostructure, universities and colleges also witnessed a mushrooming of federal and corporate support services, as well as an enrollment boom that fueled the expansion of higher learning.[45] Given the sudden glut of liberal arts students and the institutional urgency of certifying their careers, the corporate world provided irresistible models for managing the expansion of university humanities and social science programs. Influenced by early Frankfurt School theory, C. Wright Mills pointed to the university's growing bureaucratization in the early 1950s. The spread of special disciplines and graduate programs, he argued in *White Collar* (1953), meshed with the narrow technical and vocational niches of the corporate machine. Little by little, the institutional structure of higher education reproduced the technical specialization of the postwar corporate apparatus.[46] Such professional models had the appeal of divorcing knowledge from power. The university's ivory tower served in many cases to insulate American intellectuals from political history. Endorsing the myth of disinterested scholarship, the academy resisted the rising tide of political controversy that swept the postwar welfare/warfare State. In the 1950s, Mills predicted the university's conservative swerve from social commitment throughout the next three decades:

> As a group, American professors have seldom if ever been politically engaged: the trend toward a technician's role has, by strengthening their apolitical professional ideology, reduced whatever political involvement they may have had and often, by sheer atrophy, their ability to grasp political problems. . . . This vacuum means that the American scholar's situation allows him to take up the new practicality—in effect to become a political tool—without any shift of political ideology and with little political guilt. (*White Collar*, p. 136)

Mills' account of the academy's apolitical status quo helps explain the appeal of New Criticism's own repression of social history. Moreover, within the academy the myth of disinterested scholarship allowed power to flow to an increasingly centralized managerial class of school administrators. Higher education's pedagogical ideal of participatory democracy was steadily eroded by principles of organizational theory and techniques of business administration imported from America's corporate sphere.

Increasingly, however, some American critics, faced with the social turmoil of the 1960s, began to question their professional lives. Richard Ohmann's autobiographical reflections in *English in America* (1976), for example, describe how the logic of specialization often undermined the humanistic mission of American universities. He recalls how in 1963 his own professional identity became unmanageably absurd. Having contracted to review the year's critical offerings in modern British and American literature, Ohmann's task entailed an exhaustive account of nearly one hundred books. Little by little, the critic was overwhelmed by the sheer glut of scholarly publication—embodied in the well over 30,000 citations annually listed by the MLA. Moreover, such textual proliferation, for Ohmann, was compounded by the rapid institutional growth that he oversaw as a university administrator. Gradually, his image of the university as a humane community of scholars was eroded by the daily struggle he adjudicated among departments lobbying for elite doctoral programs and smaller service loads across the curriculum. His dismay with academe was futher clarified in the 1968 struggle within the Modern Language Association over America's escalating involvement in the Vietnam War.[47] Vietnam deepened his critique of the largely instrumental role English studies serves in today's society. The war left Ohmann possessed by doubts that even now shake the foundations of liberal education in America. "Why," he asked, "were these institutions unable to have the critical impact that their ideologies claimed for them? Why were universities unable to resist a government that was crushing the values of human freedom and of pursuit of truth, values that are the primary allegiance of the liberal university? Why couldn't literature professors enact the values we found in literary culture?"[48]

Academia's apolitical conservatism was a continuing problematic for critics and poets in the 1980s. Edward Said, for example, in "Opponents, Audiences, Constituencies, and Community" (1982) indicted the university's failure to question its own ties to corporate America. "The particular mission of the humanities is, in the aggregate," he wrote, "to represent *noninterference* in the affairs of the everyday world." Contemporary humanism's silence, he argued, obscures "the hierarchy of powers that occupy the center, define the social terrain, and fix the limits of use functions, fields, marginality and so on."[49] Said's point concerning humanism's laissez faire non-interference in politics reinforced Richard Ohmann's earlier argument that the postwar university values knowledge which serves the dominant power interests of bourgeois America: "Knowledge, like culture and production, has a social base, but we middle-class people like to think of knowing as an individual adventure, which mysteriously and indirectly benefits society" (*English in America,* p. 316).

Said's and Ohmann's points shed light on how academic criticism erased both the political shaping of literary culture and, for our purposes, the formation of contemporary poetry. Criticism of the 1960s espoused the solipsistic closure of contemporary lyric verse by claiming that such privacy was therapeutic. But in the postwar decades, emotive confessionalism was merely a harmless negation of the sources of its unease. Like other academic practices, contemporary poetry's staging of the private self—along with the critical industry that recruited a readership for it—proved a bourgeois aesthetic: one that was blind to the social foundations of its own anxious malaise. Endorsing a subjective poetics, critics were decidedly silent about the social forces that enter into verse writing. Such reticence was not entirely innocent but was arguably symptomatic of underlying power relations. Not surprisingly, the culturally permitted notion of introspective lyricism neatly coincided with the dominant class interests of bourgeois individuality. Moreover, by spreading the pedagogical ideal of poetry as a sullen art, criticism successfully concealed the ensemble of institutional mechanisms and disciplinary practices that sustained its existing canons of literary power and fame. Thus, in fostering the habit of reading poetry as lyric expression, critics nurtured what Pierre Bourdieu would describe as a durable "habitus" for reproducing their own cultural authority.[50]

Ironically, the careers of most "sullen" poets accommodated the very academic bureaucratization that, on the face of it, they sought to escape. In seeking simply to elide their institutional lives, most poets were incorporated into the very university technostructure they set out to dismantle. Although insisting on poetry's ontological difference from institutional life, most practicing poets pursued their craft in the creative writing mills of the postwar university. Glancing quickly through any of the representative poetry anthologies of the last two decades one sees that for most poets writing verse goes hand in hand with an academic career. Even the more radical so-called anti-academic poets of the 1950s and 1960s became, in some cases, the university's most distinguished academics.[51] Consistently, however, postwar poets and critics chose to repress poetry's institutional base. Most followed New Criticism's segregation of lyric verse from other modes of writing that might possibly reflect on how poetry negotiates a wider social text.[52]

Editors Stuart Friebert and David Young typify how the nominal boundaries between poetry and criticism are blurred in practice. Like Cleanth Brooks, they privileged verse over criticism, bemoaning the disappearance of the critic who will dutifully "follow" the creative writer. Theoretical readings of poetry, they argued, are written "in institutional settings where only the critics have been doing the watching and the defining," while poets have somehow managed to elude and transcend such coercive, disciplinary scenes.[53] But in fact, their collection itself was the product of an NEA writers-in-residence program housed at Oberlin College, whose institutional settings, no doubt typify those of academia nationwide. Similarly, the New Critical given that the poet is somehow "beyond" the critic guided the playful but anti-intellectual stereotypes of David Bottoms' and Dave Smith's *The Morrow Anthology of Younger American Poets*. According to Bottoms and Smith, the younger poet "seems to jog more than to write literary criticism" (p. 19).

Today, however, the standard opposition between poetic and critical rhetoric is viewed with suspicion. In fact, most of our representative poets have always served as willing contributors to critical anthologies that blend their institutional roles. Volumes such as Paul Engle's and Joseph Langland's *Poet's Choice* (1962), Anthony Ostroff's *The Contemporary Poet as Artist and Critic* (1964), Howard Nemerov's *Poets on Poetry* (1965), William J. Martz's *The Distinctive Voice* (1966), Stephen Berg's and Robert Mazey's *Naked Poetry* (1969), and William Heyen's *American Poets in 1976* (1975) looked forward to Donald Hall's recent successful series with the University of Michigan Press entitled *Poets on Poetry*.

Among the institutional criteria that make poets visible candidates for large conglomerate presses, their ties to the critical community and the academy are arguably vital to their success. The ensemble of practices that constitutes a viable career—journal and book publication, prestigious awards and fellowships, professional readings and conference presentations, and so on—cannot be wholly divorced from one's "creative" life. In contemporary America, the integrity of the career rather than the quality of the poetry often dictates the terms of a poet's endurance. Take the career of, say, Laurence Lieberman: a poet whose reputation is at once impeded and sustained by his work as a reviewer for influential poetry journals such as *American Poetry Review, The Hudson Review, Poetry,* and *The Yale Review,* among others. Lieberman is a university poet; his criticism no doubt secured his academic position and gave him national visibility as a scholar. Not surprisingly, his professional role as a reviewer within the university system has decisively molded his identity as a creative writer. "Though I felt, consistently," he has said, "that my work in poetry was dominant, the criticism subordinate— if complementary—to my verse, at intervals, my critical prose seemed to usurp a disproportionate share of my primary creative resources. I found, to my surprise, that I was becoming wholly preoccupied by exploring the *mode* of the short review-essay."[54] Similarly, this hybrid institutional role has marked the career of Robert Pinsky, whose influential book *The Situation of Poetry* (1977) combined with his position as poetry editor of *The New Republic* were instrumental in building an audience for his poetry. Arriving as one of our major poets in the 1980s, Pinsky has also published criticism in such premier theoretical journals as *Critical Inquiry.* Moreover, his prestige as a critic enabled him in 1986 to have a hand in poetry's critical reception through directing a NEH Summer Seminar for College Teachers at his home institution, the University of California at Berkeley.

Given the postwar inflation of practicing poets, their publishing outlets, award committees, and so on, academic prestige is now crucial to a writer's fame. By the late 1970s, the *International Who's Who in Poetry* recorded 5,500 biographies of practicing poets. Moreover, in 1986 Judson Jerome's *Poet's Market* listed 1,300 American publishers of poetry. In *The Fierce Embrace,* Charles Molesworth provides a telling commentary on the recent spread of "creative" writing: "A small magazine of modest reputation, *Poetry Northwest,* considers forty thousand poems a year, though the magazine has fewer than one thousand subscribers. Grim quip that it is, it is true: more people write poetry than read it" (p. 5). That verse writing now far outstrips its readership creates a legitimation crisis for critics who must define career status and form the canon. Given the sheer glut of poets and their press organs, neither the volume of one's published writing nor the number of prizes determine a writer's stature. In America today there are hundreds of grant and prize awarding agencies, with several bestowing multiple awards annually.[55] Certain awards, of course, are crucial to the emergence of our most important poets. For example, James Merrill, one of Atheneum's best-selling poets and judge for the Yale Younger Poets series, has won two National Book Awards, a Pulitzer Prize, a Bollingen Prize, and a National Book Critics' Circle Award, among numerous others. While this kind of professional recognition is impressive, it is not always the final measure of one's reputation.[56]

Book publication, favorable reviews, prizes, and so on ultimately promote poets into the canons of the anthology market. "In a sense, every poem of every new book," writes James Dickey, "is presided over and judged by an imminent Anthology."[57] Even more than prizes, anthologies build poets' readerships and reputations. In addition to standard teaching anthologies and surveys, a host of secondary collections saturate today's poetry market.[58] Anthologies decide who will survive from decade to decade in contemporary letters. The kind of attention a poet enjoys from publishing one or two poems alongside, say, 199 other contributors, as in David Ray's 1981 Swallow Press anthology *From A to Z: 200 Contemporary American Poets,* obviously does not approach the kind of exposure one receives from having over 20 pages of verse and an essay appear with the work of only 18 other poets, as in Philip Dow's 1984 Harcourt Brace volume *19 New American Poets of the Golden Gate.* The professional accreditation poets solicit, however, has not gone unchallenged. Richard Kostelanetz, for example, in a review of Daniel Halpern's *The American Poetry Anthology* (1975), fulminated against the literary nepotism that often supplants aesthetic values.[59] Kostelanetz's complaint is symptomatic of the legitimation crisis now facing contemporary English studies.

Today literature's humanizing rhetoric is often belied by its actual disciplinary formations and institutional limits. This tension continues to be most deeply felt by academics, whose everyday professional lives deny the consoling models of community that humanism traditionally espouses. For better or worse, most of our enduring verse writers are academics whose poetry typically seeks to repress and transcend their institutional lives. Often reproducing the professional regimen and bureaucratic functioning of the corporate world, academe has a hand in defining the writer's role, mixing its discourse little by little with poetry's lyric rhetoric. Alienation has value, however, when it leads to powerful "re-visionary" poetics. But the subjective impulse common to many academic poets often lapses into a romantic solipsism that ultimately impoverishes the "giant forms" of high romanticism. All too often, postwar confessionalism has reduced the kind of cultural criticism offered in Blake's "America, A Prophecy" or Wordsworth's *The Prelude* to a narrow introspective rhetoric. Since the 1970s, however, this "romantic persistence," as Robert Pinsky described it, has been the target of an emergent group of American critics and poets whose writing comes out of the new wave of political movements and critical theory of the 1970s and 1980s.[60]

Practicing Critics and Practicing Poets in the Space Age

DATING FROM the late 1960s, American criticism has pioneered new theoretical frontiers that have opened fresh directions for contemporary poetry. In the 1970s, criticism's traditional belatedness in relation to poetry underwent a kind of reversal. The practicing critic little by little began to redefine both the role and the rhetoric of the practicing poet. During this time, Afro-American, feminist, and other ethnic and minority critics mounted cultural rereadings of the traditional canon. Writing from the margins of the New Critical industry, they challenged literature's cloistral remove from social experience. Quarreling with New Criticism and bourgeois confessionalism alike, black and feminist critics questioned the history and status of what constitutes "literary" culture. In defending the aesthetics of black verse against a traditionally white, European canon, Stephen Henderson's *Understanding Black Poetry* (1973) as-

serted that "what is meant by 'beautiful' and by 'forms' is to a significant degree dependent upon a people's way of life, their needs,
their aspirations, their history—in short their culture."[61] Henderson's focus on the social base of canon formation was aligned with
the black aesthetic, black power, and black cultural nationalism
movements of the 1960s. Throughout the next two decades, critics
such as Houston A. Baker, Jr., Barbara Christian, Henry Louis Gates,
Jr., Addison Gayle, Jr., Barbara Smith, Robert B. Stepto, Mary Helen
Washington, Susan Willis, and others took earlier studies in the black
vernacular tradition in more sophisticated and theoretical directions.

The Afro-American assault on New Critical formalism was reinforced by the new wave of feminist criticism in the 1970s. In ways
similar to Henderson's focus on the social foundations of aesthetic
judgment, feminists took up cross-disciplinary investigations of how
gender's cultural inscription negotiates a distinctively sexual politics
in the social field. In her inaugural editorial statement to *Signs* (1985),
Catharine R. Stimpson asserted that the new scholarship on women
"tends to question the social, political, economic, cultural, and psychological arrangements that have governed relations between females and males, that have defined femininity and masculinity. It
even suspects that those arrangements have been a source of the er-
rors that must be corrected."[62] Following in the tracks of such re-
visionary feminist theory, a new generation of feminist critics conceived powerful rereadings of contemporary American poetry, as in
Suzanne Juhasz's *Naked and Fiery Forms* (1976), Janet Sternberg's *The
Writer on Her Work* (1980), Alicia Ostriker's *Writing Like a Woman*
(1984) and *Stealing the Language* (1986), Wendy K. Martin's *American
Triptych* (1984), Jean Gould's *Modern American Women Poets* (1984),
Rachel Blau Duplessis' *Writing Beyond the Ending* (1985), and others.
On the vanguard of such rereading, Sandra Gilbert, for example,
surpassed standard existential readings of the 1960s, arguing that the
"confessional genre . . . may be (at least for our own time) a distinctly female poetic mode."[63] Increasingly from the late 1960s on-
ward, those on the margins of literary culture have interrogated the
race, sex, and class exclusions of the traditional canon. Since the early
1970s, such refusals of the mainly Caucasian and male "mind of Europe" have been affiliated with other bodies of emergent interpretive
theory.

Although Jacques Derrida arrived as a central figure on the Continental intellectual scene in 1967 with the publication of *La Voix et le phénomène, L'écriture et la différence,* and *De la grammatologie,* he was not widely translated into English until the mid-1970s. By then, of course, the writing of Derrida, Barthes, and Foucault had already penetrated American criticism through the various projects of the so-called Yale Critics—Harold Bloom, Paul de Man, Geoffrey Hartman, Barbara Johnson, and J. Hillis Miller—and others such as Jonathan Culler, Fredric Jameson, and Edward Said. Throughout the 1970s, several emergent methodologies—reader response, Lacanian psychoanalysis, structuralism, feminism, neo-Marxism, and deconstruction—decisively changed critical practice in America, as seen in de Man's *Blindness and Insight* (1971), Jameson's *The Prison House of Language* (1972), Norman Holland's *Poems in Persons* (1973), Wolfgang Iser's *The Implied Reader* (1974), Culler's *Structuralist Poetics* (1975), Bloom's *Poetry and Repression* (1976), Terence Hawkes' *Structuralism and Semiotics* (1977), Judith Fetterley's *The Resisting Reader* (1978), and Sandra Gilbert's and Susan Gubar's *The Madwoman in the Attic* (1979), to name only a few. During these years, several notably innovative journals espoused the new thinking of such interpretive theory: *New Literary History: A Journal of Theory and Interpretation* (1969), *Diacritics: A Review of Contemporary Criticism* (1971), *Boundary 2: A Journal of Postmodern Literature* (1972), *Critical Inquiry* (1975), *Signs: Journal of Women in Culture and Society* (1975), and *Glyph: Johns Hopkins Textual Studies* (1977). Each embraced cross-disciplinary and cross-cultural investigation and critique. *New Literary History*— founded the year after the MLA's 1968 crisis in political mission— reflected on the irresistible pressure of history reshaping literary studies in America at the end of the decade: "As our own investigations forced historical inquiries upon us and led us to a reconsideration of historical questions from quite different perspectives," wrote editor Ralph Cohen, "we found that the idea of history formed a point of intersection."[64] Underscoring literary historicism as the nexus of textual studies, Cohen's interpretive stance was not unlike the theoretical pluralism of *Critical Inquiry.* "It was clear to us from the outset then," wrote Chicago School editor Sheldon Sacks, "that the journal should not derive its unity from the limits of any single subject."[65] During the 1970s, these editorial policies responded directly to the critical intervention of Continental theory in American letters.

Led by theory, practical criticism in the 1970s overcame the limits of personal lyricism that had dominated poetry throughout the previous decade. Critical reading actively ramified the structure and questioned the status of the lyric self. Karl Malkoff's *Escape from the Self* (1977), for example, read contemporary poetry through the existential themes of the early Sartre, synthesized with the theology of Paul Tillich, the communications theory of Marshal McLuhan, the eclectic poetics of Stanley Burnshaw, and the revisionary neo-Freudianism of Norman O. Brown. Increasingly, others began to interpret contemporary poetry variously as a dialectical exchange, transaction, struggle, or play between the author and the available discursive codes of his or her linguistic moment. Thus, Joseph Riddel, in his ground-breaking study *The Inverted Bell: Modernism and the Counterpoetics of William Carlos Williams* (1974), tied the American tradition of close reading to Continental phenomenology and deconstruction. The 1970s witnessed something of a rapprochement in American letters between poststructuralist theory and applied close reading. This alliance of theory and practical criticism shaped the careers of a generation of American scholars of postmodern literature. For example, William V. Spanos' and Paul Bové's writings on Heidegger, Derrida, and Foucault culminated in powerful rereadings of poets such as Charles Olson.[66] Similarly, Evan Watkins' essays on W. S. Merwin and Charles Tomlinson appeared in a revisionary poststructuralist study, *The Critical Act* (1978). In the interim between Charles Altieri's two books on contemporary poetry—*Enlarging the Temple* (1979) and *Self and Sensibility* (1984)—he published *Act and Quality* (1981), a critical volume employing Wittgenstein and Anglo-American speech act theory as a challenge to deconstruction. Significantly, Cary Nelson's essays, such as "Reading Criticism" for *PMLA*, led to a theoretical critique of contemporary American verse. In *Our Last First Poets: Vision and History in Contemporary American Poetry* (1981), Nelson brought phenomenology into dialogue with cultural studies. In contrast to New Critical method, Nelson investigated how history is inscribed in poetic and critical languages:

> Like other modes of analysis that tend to undermine the still common New Critical assumptions about the reader's objectivity and the independence of poetic creation, such as Marxist or deconstructive criticism, the kind of historical phenomenology offered

POETRY'S INSTITUTIONAL SETTINGS

here may seem unsettling and unresolvable. . . . Because it can
address its own permanent verbal tradition, its own history of formal choices, poetry is not always tied in obvious and unavoidable
ways to social forces. Even though such ties are inevitably present,
a poet can disguise them, deflect his readers' attention from them,
or even deceive himself about their significance, by seeming to
contend with a tradition exclusively literary.[67]

Nelson sought to disclose the social forces that are disguised and
deflected in poetic discourse. Leading critical theory into dialogue
with poetry, his study anticipated the work of a new group of poststructuralist writers and theorists that reconsidered poetry as a medium for cultural critique.

During the 1980s the so-called L=A=N=G=U=A=G=E poets—
Charles Bernstein, Clark Coolidge, Tina Darragh, Lyn Hejinian, Bob
Perelman, and Ron Silliman, among others—undermined conventional generic differences dividing critical and poetic discourses. Inspired by theory, their poetics questioned and resisted crucial aesthetic assumptions underlying bourgeois culture: the unified identity
of the expressive lyric subject, poetry's transcendence of historical
reference, and the dominance of signified meaning over the play of
the signifier. "It's a mistake," said Charles Bernstein, " . . . to posit
the self as the primary organizing feature of writing. As many others
have pointed out, a poem exists in a matrix of social and historical
relations that are more significant to the formation of an individual
text than any personal qualities of the life or voice of an author."[68]
Dethroning the expressive privilege of the lyric self, Bernstein's avant-
garde project deployed poetic language so as to interrupt and estrange commodified discourse, thereby contesting the normalizing
reading habits that reflect and reproduce advanced consumer culture.[69]

Similarly, *Languages of Liberation* considers verse writing as a so-
cioaesthetic praxis: at once shaped by and resisting the broader discursive forces that make up our historical moment. On the one hand,
poetic language enjoys only a relative autonomy from the textual
and institutional networks that mediate lyric expression. On the other
hand, an author's poetic forms and a poetic text's linguistic techniques exist in a critical relationship to other literary and cultural

discourses. As we turn to close readings of the careers of some of our foremost postwar American poets, we shall see how challenges to poetry's survival in the age of advanced capitalism compel poets to jettison traditional assumptions about the lyric self and poetic autonomy, thus aligning verse with the social text of the contemporary American scene.

Two Versions of Lyric Minimalism: James Wright and W. S. Merwin

HERALDING CONTEMPORARY cultural studies, Walter Benjamin's landmark essay "Some Motifs in Baudelaire" (1939) noted both a decline in the lyric mode under advanced capitalism and the loss of the poet's traditional social role as storyteller. Significantly, Benjamin's reading of Baudelaire foretold the degradation of experience itself in the face of big-city life and modern mass communication. Benjamin admired Baudelaire's critique of the pastoral lyricism prized by nineteenth-century German *lebensphilosophie*. Rejecting any romantic nostalgia for a "natural" pre-industrial past, Baudelaire boldly inscribed the emergent social forces of mass society in new motifs. The romantic figure of lyric bard gave way, in his work, to the *flaneur:* the errant man of the streets, who is everywhere jostled by the city's "crowd of clients." The poet too had to contend with an industrial scene whose perceptual shock effects little by little eroded the aura of intimate, personal life—the traditional hallmark of the lyric mode. Not incidentally, Baudelaire looked forward to changing notions of self and society occasioned by modern advertising, print journalism, photography, and other mechanically reproduced media. Such a poetics shook the ground of lyric expression. The poet's cutting gibe—"How much do they give in the pawnshop for a lyre?"[1]—summed up the lyric's dubious relevance to the modern age.

Writing in the 1960s, Adorno was even more skeptical about poetry's survival amid the spreading one-dimensional organization of postwar culture. A witness to the propaganda campaigns of German National Socialism, Adorno decried the modern state's bureaucratic management of culture. "The more total society becomes," he warned, "the greater the reification of the mind and the more paradoxical its effort to escape reification on its own. Even the most extreme consciousness of doom threatens to degenerate into idle chatter." Adorno's dire judgment that "to write poetry after Auschwitz is barbaric" alluded, in part, to poetry's reification as "literature."[2] Similarly, Martin Heidegger's brief but fateful tenure as Rector of the University of Freiburg led him to resist literature's complicity with state power.[3] Heidegger's late critique of mass culture argued that its burgeoning institutional, academic, and commercial organs together shaped the "talking, writing, and broadcasting of spoken words" for public consumption. "One of its functionaries," he concluded, "at once driver and driven—is the literature industry. In such a setting poetry cannot appear otherwise than as literature."[4]

The precarious literary status of contemporary poetry, detailed in my opening chapter, further casts lyric verse into jeopardy. To begin with, the recent conglomeration of American mass culture—now saturated by a dense semiotic barrage from the print media, pop music, video, TV, computer graphics, and other electronic outlets—is hardly congenial to the poet's "sullen art." Indeed, as Jean Baudrillard has argued, today's advanced consumer society not only dispenses culture as sheer spectacle, but more radically levels experience itself to "the smooth operational surface of communication," "a pure screen, a switching center for all networks of influence."[5] In this postindustrial scene, according to Baudrillard, what were once "authentic" sites of resistance to the commodity form—nature, the body, the pastoral life of things; the public sphere of constitutional democracy and trade unions; the cultural spaces of the gallery, concert stage, the lecture hall, and so on—are all systematically drained of their oppositional power. Reprogrammed through contemporary communication networks, such signs of "real" personal and community life gradually lose their moorings in traditional sources of value and now simply float in the domain of the hyper-real, to be exchanged there as weightless simulacra and bouyant signifying elements within a totalizing habitus of consumption.

Moreover, the poet's vocation, largely housed in the postwar university, has been domesticated little by little by the disciplinary pressures and professional regimen of the academy. As a group, however, contemporary American poets are surprisingly silent about today's commercial verse market. By and large, they are reluctant to think of poetry as a verbal praxis. Yet not only is lyric utterance detoured through a maze of institutional mediations, but since the 1970s, contemporary criticism has challenged the lyric's long-standing generic privilege as the voice of the private self. Personal writing is never entirely divorced from language's broader social contexts. Recent theorists of the lyric have both questioned the poet's "expressive" privilege and gone beyond New Critical formalism.[6] Profiting from recent advances in semiotics, psychoanalysis, Marxism, feminism, gender theory, cultural anthropology, and Afro-American aesthetics, much of American criticism through the 1980s reads lyric poetry as cultural discourse in dialogue with other literary and nonliterary discursive modes.

Not insignificantly, such shifts in the lyric's critical reception shape the careers of James Wright and W. S. Merwin. Like most postwar poets, Wright and Merwin brood anxiously over the status and fate of the lyric self. But more importantly, the failure of emotive lyricism itself is decisively inscribed in the rhetorical makeup of their minimalist verse forms. The poetics of Wright and of Merwin offer two representative versions of the lyric's contemporary decline.

Like Benjamin, Adorno, and Heidegger, Wright grapples with the leveling forces of advanced consumer society as they reify subjectivity, lyric expression, and culture at large. In postwar America, the pervasive logic of the commodity form infiltrates the discourse of the state, the academy, literature, and popular culture with a common managerial rhetoric. Wright is understandably dismayed by this linguistic erosion. Not surprisingly, he regresses back to the self's mythic privacy before industrial capitalism. Turning away from America's alienated public milieu, he retreats into a subjective poetics. There his verse rests on an "expressive" phenomenology of voice—one that finds poetry's authentic source in the author's colloquial idiom, private life, and "deep" personal myths. But such a neoromantic poetics, instead of retrieving some rich plenitude of being, merely saps the poet's discursive critique of American consumer society. W. S. Merwin's later career, however, offers a cogent counterpoetics to the drawbacks of Wright's confessional aesthetic. Like Adorno, Merwin accepts the lyric's cultural bankruptcy, but resists Wright's pastoral nostalgia. Instead, Merwin lodges a powerful critique of lyric subjectivity within what is properly a linguistic register. Merwin eludes the trap of solipsism that ensnares Wright by teasing out the textual resources underwriting lyric expression. Like much of contemporary critical theory, Merwin's recent writing aims to deconstruct the lyric rhetoric of the bourgeois self.

The Cultural Fate of the Lyric

AN ACADEMIC poet, James Wright first apprenticed to the modernist tradition under the exacting formalist tutelage of John Crowe Ransom at Kenyon College. Following his graduate studies with Theodore Roethke at the University of Washington, Wright wrestled with the influence of New Critical instructors, succumbing, in time, to a profound disenchantment with postwar America and its literary establishment. According to his *Paris Review* interview, Wright's first volume, *The Green Wall* (1957), envisioned a contemporary *felix culpa*. "I tried," he says, "to weave my way in and out through nature poems and people suffering in nature because they were conscious."[7] From the very beginning, the poet's social vision is couched in a certain pastoral nostalgia, a vestige of New Criticism's agrarian agenda. Nonetheless, Wright's depiction of what W. H. Auden called his "social outsiders" offers a radically pessimistic critique of postwar America.[8] Fugitives, mental patients, murderers, alcoholics, prisoners, prostitutes, and exiles everywhere loiter on the margins of Wright's world. In early works such as "A Poem About George Doty in the Death House," "To a Fugitive," "Morning Hymn to a Dark Girl," and "Sappho," Wright's derelict personae belong to a distinctively American tradition. This sorrowful polis recalls earlier modern figures such as Luke Havergal, Richard Cory, Miniver Cheevy, and the rest of Edwin Arlington Robinson's Tilbury Town misfits. Wright found in Robinson "one of the great poets of the dark side of American experience."⁹ Similarly, he was struck by Robert Frost's "profound, terrifying, and very tragic view of the universe" (PR, 46). In the 1950s, Wright revived Robinson's and Frost's existential despair in a decidedly social critique of the contemporary American scene.

Thrown into what Robert Lowell describes as the "ditch" of postwar history,¹⁰ Wright finds himself radically alienated from the romantic consolations of expressive lyricism. Instead, the poet fails to "dare" redemptive acts of human sympathy and care, as in "To A Defeated Saviour":

> The circling tow, the shadowy pool
> Shift underneath us everywhere.
> You would have raised him, flesh and soul,
> Had you been strong enough to dare;
> You would have lifted him to breathe,
> Believing your good hands would keep
> His body clear of your own death:
> This dream, this drowning in your sleep.¹¹

Reflecting back on "Saviour" in a 1972 interview, Wright linked its theme of human failure to language's public degradation:

> It seems that all of our great ethical ideals always come to grief because, at least in part, our public figures take our language away from us, erode its meaning, so that we can't tell whether or not to trust other people when they make some public gesture in language. We're left sort of scrambling around in the dark, trying to help one another, and yet, being afraid to. As people are afraid to help one another on the streets. (SHR, 135)

Wright's early worries about the linguistic decay of America's public milieu arguably responded to the rhetorical excesses of the Red Scare orchestrated by Wisconsin Senator Joseph McCarthy. In 1948, the year Wright matriculated at Kenyon College, former Soviet agent Whittaker Chambers testified before the House Un-American Activities Committee concerning alleged Soviet espionage by former State Department official Alger Hiss. Subsequent spy trials of Judith Coplon of the Justice Department, in 1949, and Dr. Fuchs of the Manhattan Project, in 1950, climaxed in the 1951 trial and 1953 execution of Ethel and Julius Rosenberg for conspiring to share atomic weapons secrets with the Soviet Union. Such public spectacles were further orchestrated by McCarthy's charges of extensive Communist infiltration of government. Throughout the early 1950s until his censure in 1954, McCarthy directed a kind of grotesque national theater of slander and intimidation. An aspiring academic at the time, Wright witnessed firsthand the denial of teaching positions to alleged Communists, a common policy vigorously endorsed in 1953 by the Association of American Universities, the National Education Association, and the American Federation of Teachers.

As the social text of "Saviour" and Wright's other drowning poems shows, the erosion of a credible public rhetoric also entails the general degradation of America's political and cultural spheres. In these works, Wright's anxiety about language's public decay repeats Martin Heidegger's critique of the "fallen," "idle talk" *(Gerede)* of administrative speaking indicted in *Being and Time*.[12] The poet's personae continually struggle against alienating undercurrents that engulf such rustbelt settings as Bridgeport, Wheeling, Moundsville, Belaire, Martins Ferry, Steubenville, and the other Ohio Valley mill towns. The "circling tow" of America's cultural "suckhole," to borrow Wright's Ohio slang, dooms the contemporary American everyman to anonymity, as in "The River Down Home": "Under the enormous pier shadow, / Hobie Johnson drowned in a suckhole. / I cannot even remember / His obliterated face. / Outside my window, now, Minneapolis / Drowns, dark" (CP, 164–65). Similarly, such erasures of identity befall the nameless victims of "The Poor Washed Up by the Chicago Winter" and the drowned fathers "who have no names" (CP, 140) in "The Minneapolis Poem."

Not surprisingly, in the estranging cultural milieu of McCarthyite

witch hunts and executions, Wright came to identify little by little
with *The Green Wall*'s "social outsiders." In "At the Executed Murderer's Grave," a telling self-portrait from his second volume, *Saint
Judas* (1959), he tries to exorcise the ghost of *The Green Wall*'s death-
row murderer George Doty:

> Doty, if I confess I do not love you,
> Will you let me alone? I burn for my own lies.
> The nights electrocute my fugitive,
> My mind. I run like the bewildered mad
> At St. Clair Sanitarium, who lurk,
> Arch and cunning, under the maple trees,
> Pleased to be playing guilty after dark.
> Staring to bed, they croon self-lullabies.
> Doty, you make me sick. I am not dead.
> I croon my tears at fifty cents per line.
>
> (CP, 83)

Summing up Wright's divorce from both his poetic vocation and,
more broadly, America's public scene, these lines fissure the politically disinterested façade of New Critical aesthetics. Not insignificantly, in 1959 Wright thought of *Saint Judas* as his last book, his
poetic career having reached the end of the road. "I tried to come
to terms in that book," he said, "with what I felt to be the truth of
my own life, which is that of a man who wants very much to be
happy, but who is not happy" (PR, 47). As it happened, Wright
revised "At the Executed Murderer's Grave" while traveling by train
to Minneapolis, having just defended his doctoral dissertation in Seattle.[13] Driven by the academy's professional regimen, Wright be-
moans the lyric's present commodification. "I croon my tears," he
writes, "at fifty cents per line."

Symptomatic of the poet's alienated institutional role in postwar
consumer society, Wright's complaint echoes the angst of Roethke's
"The Lost Son" (1948), written while he too was an aspiring aca-
demician: "I have married my hands to perpetual agitation, / I run,
I run to the whistle of money."[14] But unlike Roethke, who throve
on dickering his way into the Republic of Letters, Wright actively
resisted literature's cash nexus. "Saint Judas" (CP, 84–85), in par-

ticular, indicts "the whistle of money" as a kind of cosmic taint. Wright describes the title piece of *Saint Judas* as an exemplum of "the desolation of the spirit" (SHR, 149). Patterned on Robinson's "How Annandale Went Out," it stands, he says, as a "summary stylistically and thematically, of everything I was trying to do in the book" (SHR, 149).

The sonnet's octave plunges us into Judas' desperate guilt over having "bargained the proper coins, and slipped away." The sestet unravels the fall of the exiled disciple, now "banished from heaven" for having sold his salvation. In the poem's epiphany, Judas attempts to aid the victim of "a pack of hoodlums": "Dropping my robe / Aside I ran, ignored the uniforms." Peter Stitt views this ethical turn as a reversal that redeems the otherwise damned disciple.[15] But such a happy reading ignores the sestet's devastating return of the language of commercial exchange. The "bargain" persists despite Judas' attempts to expunge it:

> Then I remembered bread my flesh had eaten,
> The kiss that ate my flesh. Flayed without hope,
> I held the man for nothing in my arms.

"Saint Judas" hardly canonizes the one-time disciple. Marked by the telling phrase "for nothing," read "free of charge," Wright's bathetic pieta is radically suspect. Fatefully inscribed with a commercial subtext, its sacrament of communion fails, without hope.

Wright dubbed Judas "the ultimate lost betrayer" (PR, 46)—one who "had placed himself beyond the moral pale" (SHR, 148) through an ultimate cash transaction. Encoded by the language of the commodity form, "Saint Judas" looks forward to Wright's later poems on the erosion of humane and socially progressive modes of life under advanced capitalism. Like the Frankfurt School theorists, Wright also fulminated against the pervasive logic of contemporary capitalism. His grim lament—"There are men in this city who labor dawn after dawn / To sell me my death" (CP, 141)—speaks to the same cultural reification analyzed by Benjamin, Adorno, and Marcuse. But sustaining such a bleak social critique finally proved too demoralizing even for Wright, who steeped himself in the pessimism of Frost and Robinson. Instead, he sought to transcend the cultural bankrupcy of American consumer society by celebrating a more humanizing pastoral myth.

Poetry and Authenticity

WRIGHT'S LYRIC career survived its initial debts to the Fugitives and moved through a dark period of social alienation to arrive at a hopeful vision of regional place. Not insignificantly, the poet lays out this very trajectory in the essay "The Delicacy of Walt Whitman." Here he reads Whitman's own poetic journey through a revealing quest narrative: Nietzsche's parable of the spirit's metamorphosis from a camel to a lion and, finally, a child:

> The spirit that truly grows, says Nietzsche, will first be a camel, a beast of burden, who labors to bear the forms of the past, whether in morality or art or anything else; then he will change into a lion, and destroy not merely what he hates but even what he loves and understands; and the result of this concerned and accurate destruction will be the spirit's emergence as a child, who is at last able to create clearly and powerfully from within his own imagination.[16]

Reading Whitman in this way, Wright projects the growth of his own poetics. At first, Wright's poetry labors like Nietzsche's camel under the influence of past writing: the New Critical formalism of *The Green Wall* and *Saint Judas,* as well as the deep image poetics of *The Branch Will Not Break* (1963). As a result, his early work suffers from a certain stylistic excess as he works with the surrealism of Theodore Roethke and Robert Bly.[17]

Roethke's own struggle with modernist precursors—documented in essays such as "Open Letter" (1950), "How To Write Like Somebody Else" (1959), and "On Identity" (1963)—led to an innovative poetics based variously in formal lyricism, confessional surrealism, and the long, Whitmanesque open forms of "North American Sequence." As Wright's mentor at the University of Washington in the 1950s, Roethke served as a significant model of both formal and experimental lyricism. "The significant thing [about Roethke],"

Wright has said, "was that he had not only the ability but the imaginative courage to chance moving in another stylistic direction to its very ends, or as far as he could possibly go" (SHR, 138). Roethke's regressive journey ended up in "the marsh, the mire, the Void," where, improbably, he found "a splendid place for schooling the spirit."[18] Such surrealistic forays at once plumbed the psychic depths of the unconscious and pioneered America's scenic expanse.

Published the year Roethke suffered a fatal heart attack, Wright's third volume, *The Branch Will Not Break* (1963), not only turned toward Roethke's late pastoralism but also borrowed from Robert Bly's deep image lyricism. In the late 1950s, Wright's translations of poets such as Georg Trakl, Pablo Neruda, Cesar Vallejo, and Juan Ramon Jimenez paralleled the internationalist leanings of Robert Bly. After corresponding, the two poets struck a professional and personal alliance, with Wright first publishing his new "subjective" lyrics in Bly's *Fifties* magazine in 1959. In his campaign against the Fugitives' closed forms and elaborate syntax, Bly showed Wright the resources of free verse, colloquial speech rhythms, vernacular diction, and the associative surrealism of the "deep image." "[Bly] made it clear to me," Wright said, "that the tradition of poetry, which I had tried to master, and in which I'd come to a dead end, was not the only one. He reminded me that poetry is a possibility, that, although all poetry is formal, there are many forms, just as there are many forms of feeling" (PR, 49). In *The Branch* Wright tries to temper Bly's wild leaps of surrealistic imagery with the poetic parallelism he valued in Georg Trakl and Whitman.[19] *The Branch's* eclectic style, however, often disrupts the controlling parallelism of image, lapsing into verbal pastiche, as in "Spring Images."[20]

But more than either Roethke or Bly, Wright questioned the fate and survival of poetic speaking in contemporary America. In the second stage of his career, inaugurated with *Shall We Gather at the River* (1968), he pursues an even more personal idiom—a speaking poised "between order and adventure." In a 1968 review of Pablo Neruda's *The Heights of Macchu Picchu,* Wright says that "great poetry folds personal death and general love into one dark blossom."[21] Like Neruda, Wright chances a radically negative poetics in pursuit of the "pure clear word" (CP, 208). He aims "to move from death to resurrection and death again, and challenge death finally" (PR,

52). But often dissatisfied with his Midwestern idiom, Wright's prosaic confessionalism comes to a dead end in a kind of verbal breakdown. "To speak in a flat voice," he admits, "is all I can do" (CP, 149). Moreover, he is anxious to purge his verse of other writing, as in the "New Poems" section of his Pulitzer Prize–winning *Collected Poems* (1971): "All of this time I've been slicking into my own words / The beautiful language of my friends. / I have to use my own, now" (CP, 212). His next volume, *Two Citizens* (1973), enacts the necessary labor of Nietzsche's lion, who must "destroy not merely what he hates but even what he loves and understands."

Wright's destructive poetics resembles the positive work of destruction in Heidegger's *Being and Time.*[22] In the jacket notes to *Two Citizens,* Wright says he came to affirm his love for America, ironically, through a savage attack on his native country: "*Two Citizens* is an expression of my patriotism, of my love and discovery of my native place. I never knew or loved my America so well, and I begin the book with a savage attack upon it." The epigraph from Hemingway's "The Killers" sets the tone for Wright's aggressive pessimism: "Hell, I ain't got nothing. / Ah, you bastards, / How I hate you" (TC, 7). Probing the violence of the American idiom, he jettisons the Latinate rhetoric of his Fugitive period. Most of Wright's critics find little to applaud in the book's stylized gestures of illiterate rage.[23] But however bleak, *Two Citizens* serves as a necessary catharsis—one that leads the poet to a phenomenological poetics of place.

In the midst of profoundly alienated landscapes, Wright undertakes an Orphic quest. Turning away from America's industrial scene, he pursues a poetics of lyric disclosure, not unlike Heidegger's later understanding of poetic language. "Poetry," writes Heidegger, "is the saying of the unconcealedness of what is."[24] This phenomenological moment opens a clearing (*a-letheia*) that bestows revolutionary modes of life. Heidegger describes such poetic disclosures as taking place through a fourfold process. A mutual appropriation or luminous gathering together (*Ereignis*) of earth, sky, mortals, and divinities: "In saving the earth, in receiving the sky, in awaiting the divinities, in initiating mortals, dwelling occurs as the fourfold preservation of the fourfold."[25] Toward the end of his career, Wright seeks out such moments of fourfold dwelling even in the wake of

America's commercial tide. For example, his long poem "Many of Our Waters," delivered as a Phi Beta Kappa address to the College of William and Mary, devotes seven sections of verse to celebrating "our waters in our native country" (CP, 212). Section 2, "to the Ohio," would reclaim and preserve a primordial knowledge of place by way of language's etymological past: "My rotted Ohio, / It was only a little while ago / That I learned the meaning of your name. / The Winnebago gave you your name, Ohio, / And Ohio means beautiful river." (CP, 207). Discussing D. H. Lawrence's "The Spirit of Place," Wright endorses native Americans' sacred respect for regional locales. Such reverence persists even now, and "is, for some writers," he says, "an important way of participating in the life around them. . . . It appeals to me very much" (PCW, 6).

Yet Wright's nostalgia for a primitive *participation mystique* can only seem at best romantic and at worst somewhat patronizing compared to his earlier, more critical images of contemporary American Indians. For example, his poem "I Am a Sioux Brave, He Said in Minneapolis" more trenchantly notes the loss of native traditions to today's urban midwest: "He is just plain drunk. / He knows no more than I do / What true waters to mourn for / Or what kind of words to sing / When he dies" (CP, 144). Wright's last poems, however, forgo such critical negations, lapsing instead into pastoral optimism. "Beautiful Ohio," the final poem of Wright's posthumous volume *To A Blossoming Pear Tree* (1977), dwells on the original meaning of Ohio, affirming that "those old Winnebago men / Knew what they were singing" (BPT, 62). Mindful of both the contemporary fate of the earth and the industrial decay of the Midwest's rustbelt, Wright pines for the "beautiful river" of his native state. Similarly in "One Last Look at the Adige: Vienna in the Rain," he tries to summon the original harmony of the Ohio River's native places:

> The Ohio must have looked
> Something like this
> To the people who loved it
> Long before I was born.
> They called the three
> Slim islands of willow and poplar
> Above Steubenville,

They, they, they
Called
The three slim islands
Our Sisters.

(BPT, 5)

The local place names of "mill and smoke marrow" (CP, 160) return in Wright's last poems, but now wholly drained of their industrial history. Not insignificantly, the poet's stammering prosody betrays a telling unease with such fourfold celebrations of today's Steubenville, Ohio. Such a divided speaking typifies much contemporary writing. Many poets find it distressing to think about American consumer culture and thus, symptomatically, swerve from history into various brands of utopian poetics.

Wright's pursuit of authentic lyric expression ends in a dubious phenomenology of place. He trades Nietzsche's destructive lion for the spiritual child who, as a metaphor for the poet, can "create clearly and powerfully from within his own imagination." At issue here ultimately is this third stage of Nietzsche's parable of the spirit. The success or failure of Wright's poetry turns on whether an existential poetics rooted in a fourfold vision of place can contend with the history and material culture of postwar America. Unlike the high modernism of, say, T. S. Eliot—who writes for the "mind of Europe"[26]—Wright stakes his career on an "authentic" style of sheer lyric assertion. Fleeing from America's public rhetoric, Wright risks what Roland Barthes describes as a "zero-degree" writing.[27] Wright's forays into nothingness and his witnessing to *a-letheia* assume that Being and poetic language are equiprimordial. He is nostalgic for a poetry of unmediated transparence—one that communicates the emotive life of the personal lyric voice.

Employing regional vernacular, Wright wants to preserve the privacy of voiced lyricism before social experience and textuality. Quite simply, he seeks to salvage "the pure clear word" from its infiltration by other writing. Wright's dependence upon an academically valorized model of personal lyricism bears out Michel Foucault's contention that the myth of the author's creative individuality, instead of celebrating some ideal inner life of the mind, can actually interrupt and constrain literature's verbal productivity.[28] Of course, within the Continental linguistic tradition of Saussure, Barthes, and Derrida, the poet's faith in phenomenological utterance seems woefully naive. By reducing poetic discourse to the "subjective" lyric, Wright represses the linguistic presuppositions and intertextual networks that mediate personal expression, literature, and culture at large.

Lyricism and Textuality

ALTHOUGH SHARING Wright's reservations about contemporary America, W. S. Merwin is suspicious of any ideal myths of selfhood. Unlike Wright's poetry, Merwin's does not depend on registering authentic authorial presence. Instead, he speaks to an absence at the heart of language, thereby reducing lyric expression to a merely rhetorical effect. Resembling Wright's experiments with colloquial idiom, Merwin's poetry moves beyond Roethke's subjective surrealism toward the same minimalist dialogue with silence that ultimately stifles Wright's verbal inventiveness. Merwin courts absence, however, in a different way. Calling Wright's phenomenological poetics into crisis, Merwin effects the closure of voiced presence in the contemporary American lyric.

Merwin's first poems, like those of Roethke and Wright, were in highly crafted closed forms—works that won him the Yale Younger Poets Award in 1952 for *A Mask for Janus*. This early recognition gave Merwin an entrée into a literary establishment whose aesthetics were fashioned a decade earlier by Eliot and the American New Critics. Merwin, Rich, and Wright all emerged as promising young poets in the 1950s by tailoring their formidable verbal talents to suit New Criticism's demand for technically difficult, learnedly allusive, and ironic formal lyrics. By the 1960s, of course, all three had abandoned this early formalist style, turning instead to the "deep" confessional surrealism that enabled Roethke and Bly to adopt a more emotive poetics. But beyond the work of these poets, Merwin's writing, from *Moving Target* (1963) to *Opening the Hand* (1983), turns toward textuality to undercut the authority of voiced poetic utterance. "My words," he writes in a famous simile, "are the garment of what I shall never be / Like the tucked sleeve of a one-armed boy."[29] As vestments of loss, such lines are severed from any referential meaning beyond the brief drama of their own unraveling. Words fail to embody the poet's phenomenological encounters with Being. Instead, as in Jacques Derrida's metaphor, language is a "fabric of signs" tucked back on its own absence of signified meaning. Merwin's later project enacts the failure of language's phenomenological function.

Nonetheless Merwin sometimes gestures toward an almost Heideggerean vision of language's humanistic role, while he resists what Heidegger describes as the inauthentic, everyday use of language as an instrument of public communication.[30] In contrast, the poet's more indeterminate syntax "destroys" his imagery's decidable meaning. Such poetic destructions preserve an uncanny quality of otherness in Merwin's strongest poems. Evoking the unfamiliar, the ambiguous, the strange, Merwin's aesthetic resembles Heidegger's phenomenology of disclosure as *a-letheia*—a temporal process that brings beings into an openness of illumination *and* concealment:

> Truth is un-truth, insofar as there belongs to it the reservoir of the not-yet-uncovered, the un-uncovered, in the sense of concealment. In unconcealedness, as truth, there occurs also the other "un-" of a double restraint or refusal. Truth occurs as such in the opposition of clearing and double concealing. Truth is the primal conflict in which, always in some particular way, the Open is won within which everything stands and from which everything withholds itself that shows itself and withdraws itself as a being.[31]

In Heidegger's terms, the poet (as a "messenger," "shepherd," "neighbor," or "guardian" of Being) leads us authentically into language, the "house" of Being, a "dwelling" that is also a "region" of thought—a "coming into the nearness of distance."[32] Derrida, of course, sees a substantial vestige of metaphysics in this model. "With respect to the metaphysics of presence and logocentrism," Derrida writes, Heidegger's work "is at once contained within it and transgresses it."[33] Derrida would complete (and so displace) Heidegger's "transgression" of Western metaphysics by supplementing "destructive" thinking with "deconstructive" writing—a textual practice Derrida describes as *l'écriture*, trace, *différance, supplement,* and hymen. Derrida's critical turn toward textuality, moving beyond

Heidegger's identification of language with *a-letheia,* parallels Merwin's later poetics. Merwin often undermines his phenomenological landscapes by exposing their grounding in fictive textual production. His aesthetic reaches the threshold where such lived experience is appropriated by language. There the world is transfigured by the word's symbolic order—its self-referential system of differential signs.[34]

Merwin stages his double vision of language—as either a medium of phenomenal disclosure or a wholly structured system of linguistic codes—through two traditional metaphoric locales. To begin with, the postmodern metropolis is the site of the word's secular traffic in material signification; there "ciphers wake and evil / Gets itself the face of the norm / And contrives cities" (L, 34). The city is a modern Babel where "Division, mother of pain" (MT, 53) proliferates in infinite verbal differences. This vision of the word's fall from ideal presence into an inscribed text of division recalls Saussure's argument that "in language there are only differences *without positive terms.*"[35] Instead of being a privileged origin, signified meaning is merely the product of a systematic relation of signifiers. Poetry is just one more echo in the endless feedback of "tongues being divided" (CL, 107). As a consequence, the poet's identity is called into radical crisis. No longer prior to language, the experience of selfhood is displaced by the divided word and can only be possessed as a site of verbal transaction. Mediated by a cultural matrix of colliding messages, subjectivity is reduced to a metaphoric contraption. "I am the son of division," the poet writes, "but the nails the wires the hasps the bolts / the locks the traps the wrapping that hold me together are / part of the inheritance" (CL, 95).

Within language's labyrinth of division, however, Merwin seeks pastoral enclaves where words bestow an improbable grace. "This must be what I wanted to be doing," he realizes in one such moment, "Walking at night between the two deserts, / Singing" (MT, 50). To utter this song despite language's division is to imagine dwelling within a pastoral myth that harmonizes self and world. Like Eliot's Tiresias, Merwin wanders "between two lives"—one of fragmentation, the other of mythic unity. However transient, ironic, or mute, Merwin's pastoral makes devotional gestures toward a purged landscape where "the grass had its own language" (L, 5).

Yet that other, more "natural" language can only be uttered as negation, through its difference from the rhetoric of the city. Constituted by that linguistic tension, Merwin's poetry rigorously resists
any phenomenal transcendence of language.

Similarly, Merwin disagrees with the view that the self's emotive
experience comes before language:

> Once once and once
> In the same city I was born
> Asking what shall I say.
>
> (L, 32)

Throughout the later poetry this image of birth as a kind of aphasia
before language's city of words recurs as an estranging rite of passage. "I would never have thought I would be born here," he writes,
in "Memory my city . . . / With my grief on your bridges with my
voice / In your stones what is your name" (MT, 62). The desire to
name, to master reality through the word, has already been claimed
by language, into whose history we are born too late. Entering language, the poet is inscribed by discursive forces already set in motion. In *The Lice* (1967), Merwin represents the assault of that
"memory of tongues" with the myth of "The Hydra": "The Hydra
calls me but I am used to it / It calls me Everybody / But I know my
name and do not answer" (L, 5). The dilemma here is unresolvable,
for offering his name as a rejoinder to the hydra only gives it another
mouth.

No longer a point of origin for or bearer of spiritual essence, the
poet's personal voice dissolves into a sedimented, textual history,[36]
as in "The Counting Houses":

> Where do the hours of a city begin and end
> among so many
> the limits rising
> and setting each time in each body
> in a city how many hands of timepieces
> must be counting the hours
> clicking at a given moment
> numbering insects into machines to be codified

calculating newsprint in the days of the living
all together they are not infinite
any more than the ignored patience
of rubber tires day and night
or the dumbness of wheels or the wires of passions

where is the horizon the avenue has not reached it
reaching and reaching lying palm upward
exposing the places where blood is given or let
at night the veins of the sleepers remember trees
countless sleepers the hours of trees
the uncounted hours the leaves in the dark
by day the light of the streets is the color of arms kept covered
and of much purpose
again at night the lights of the streets play on ceilings
they brush across walls
of room after unlit room hung with pictures
of the youth of the world

(CF, 29)

This disorienting poem advances the Blakean critique of the city as a wholly "chartered" locale. For Merwin, the production, quantification, and encoding of the world into cultural limits is a hellish spectacle. The hours of the metropolis, "numbering insects into machines to be codified," are not infinite but fallen. Merwin's personification of inanimate things—"the ignored patience / of rubber tires," "the dumbness of wheels,"—subverts such Cartesian binary pairs as subjectivity / objectivity, the inwardness of consciousness / the outwardness of things, spiritual essence / material substance, and the mind / the body. The surreal city disrupts the poet's mimetic grounding in signified reference by exposing such divisions as culturally produced fictions—categories within the text of bourgeois capitalism's myth of the individual. Writing in this way, Merwin undermines what he calls "habitual and customary referentiality which is dulled and blunted and exterior."[37] The poet's seemingly emotive experience of the city follows from his linguistic transactions with its codified symbolic systems.

Stanza 2 personifies the "ignored patience" of this verbal metropolis. "Reaching and reaching lying palm upward," the urban landscape strains toward some transcendent horizon of the *civitas dei*. Yet that gesture only reopens the wounds of its mortality, "exposing the places where blood is given or let." That collective crucifixion, however, yields a redemptive vision of the "countless sleepers the hours of trees/the uncounted hours the leaves in the dark." Merwin's pastoral dream cannot be embodied, of course, except in such provisional textual pleasures. Even then his phenomenal utopia amounts to little more than a fleeting linguistic difference bounded by the language of the street. Moreover, the irony of Merwin's final lines immobilizes any privileged world of beauty and truth. In the poem's closing metaphor, aesthetic representation itself suspends the youthful immediacy of the image—the duration of its "uncounted hours"— by reducing art to artifact. The unregenerate space of the avenue returns as the architecture of the counting house now opens onto the cryptic gallery of art. Here, ghostly street lights "brush across walls/of room after unlit room hung with pictures/of the youth of the world." Any romantic faith in a world of ideal meaning prior to language is radically suspect. Youth here is merely a text.

Merwin's later verse, like the half-illumined labyrinth of "The Counting Houses," describes a chiaroscuro of indeterminacy. His mature work resembles an extended web of fragments or a palimpsest, where what can be read is either never entire or a dialogic effect of other utterances it simultaneously reveals and effaces.[38] Yet if Merwin's later work possesses integrity, it resists the symbolic depth of the high modernism of Yeats or Eliot. Unlike Yeats' reliance on *A Vision*'s esoteric myth of history or Eliot's Christian orthodoxy, Merwin's project rejects the closure of master narratives. Although individual images can catalyze extended readings of other poems, his textuality invites a plural, anarchic play of meanings. In addition to his ambiguous syntax and his abandonment of punctuation,[39] he conceives the form of the later poetry against a background of what critics have described either positively as silence, transparence, and numinous presence, or negatively as void, abyss, distance, death, failure, and apocalyptic chaos.[40] However hopeful or despairing past readings of Merwin's "otherness" have been, most mystify and valorize his work through an appeal to phenomenal experience.[41] Yet Merwin often invokes his characteristic diction, or the silence of his lacunae and erasures, not so much to create a mystified world of natural presence, but more to exploit a compositional resource. His strategy is to bracket out the final status of his poetry's otherness in order to exploit it discursively. Merwin's authorial mastery is precisely that uncanny, verbal deployment of silence, nothingness, and distance to render invisible, paradoxically, any trace of linguistic determination.[42]

The romantic hope, of course, is that a luminous spirituality will inspire the poet's words with an ideal transparence, yet for Merwin that plenitude is merely rhetorical. Though Merwin might want to efface his medium to voice the immediacy of experience, poetic discourse is never wholly spontaneous: "it never is the experience, it is something else."[43] That admission, however, need not be a source of regret. That there are no exits from Merwin's city of signifiers to a pastoral world of ideal meaning is at once pathetic and liberating. Merwin discovers a tragic joy in overcoming the burden of the word's history through momentary acts of verbal displacement. Because his poems are willed in spite of the word's fall from unmediated presence, their vistas at times seem to disclose landscapes that possess a kind of phenomenal grace. But each one is, finally, a linguistic mirage.

Unraveling the Logos

ONE CAN, of course, invest Merwin's later aesthetic with lyric optimism, but only by ignoring his poignant understanding of poetry's linguistic base. In Carol Kyle's reading of "The Child," for example, Merwin's trope of the thread represents the connection between self and environment. Surrealism, for Kyle, is Merwin's way of spinning a unified vision out of the apparent fragments of modern experience: "Surrealism in Merwin's poetry is much more than a technique: it is a large, affirmative vision, optimistic in the connections among all things."[44] In Kyle's reading, the technique of discourse, again, is in the service of some larger, disembodied vision of experience. But Merwin's surrealism is inscribed with the omnipresent division of language itself, which in "The Child" is consistently distanced from that kind of absolute appeal to visionary experience:

> Then there are the stories and after a while I think something
> Else must connect them besides just this me
> I regard myself starting the search turning
> Corners in remembered metropoli
> I pass skins withering in gardens that I see now
> Are not familiar
> And I have lost even the thread I thought I had
>
> (L, 37)

In memory's metropolis the search for meaning leads only deeper into a narrative labyrinth of loss and bewilderment. The city's stories unravel withering skins whose ciphers, as in "The Counting Houses," are "not familiar," but wholly estranged. The thread in "The Child" leads only endlessly through the decentered maze of discourse.

Merwin's return to this trope in "The Thread," from *The Carrier of Ladders* (1970), traces even more darkly the poet's passage through the archives of the word:

> Unrolling the black thread
> through the tunnel
> you come to the wide wall
> of shoes
> the soles standing
> out in the air you breath
> crowded from side to side
> floor to ceiling
> and no names
> and no door
> and the bodies
> stacked before them like bottles
> generation upon
> generation
> upon   generation
> with their threads
> asleep in their hands

and the tunnel is full
of their bodies
from there
all the way to the end of the mountain
the beginning of time
the light of day
the bird
and you are unrolling
the Sibyll's song
that is trying to reach her
beyond your dead

(CL, 121)

Unrolling the Sibyl's song, the poet is hopelessly detoured among history's dead. His Orphic quest out of the tunnel's underworld is thwarted by the sheer density of time's victims. Such a radically unsettling vision of mortality invokes a claustrophobic image of time as Holocaust.[45] Even the thread of language, which might connect him to the descending dove of the Holy Ghost, belongs to the Sibyl—a grotesque reminder of Petronius' Sibyl at Cumae. Merwin's muse "beyond your dead" is herself the personification of the unregenerate word—an immortal yet decrepit spinster.

In "Sibyl" the poet addresses his muse with the same sense of tragic irony: "Your whole age sits between what you hear / and what you write." Contending against the moment's fateful unraveling, the poet races to outdistance memory: "the same wind that tells you everything at once / unstitches your memory / you try to write faster than the thread is pulled" (WA, 53). Inspired by that divine wind, that *ruach,* one would envision a world wholly transparent. Yet for Merwin the clarity of that correspondent breeze does not disclose an absolute presence, but an omnipresent nothingness. Moreover, the poet's verse must be manufactured in the sweatshop of language, whose history is a random tapestry of discourses. Often, for Merwin, writing itself is alienated labor whose verbal "stitching" everywhere seems to violate experience. At these times, the city is the locale for the poet's urgent sense of crisis in vocation: "the nine village tailors fear / their thread if not their needles if not / their needles in everything and it is / here this is New York" (CL, 83–84).

Merwin has called New York the archetypal city, where he works through his anxiety about language's mediation of "everything."[46] By unraveling the world's fabric of signs, he achieves an ecstatic vision of the city's linguistic transformations:

> the stone city in
> the river has changed and of course
> the river
> and all words even those unread in
> envelopes
> all those shining cars vanished
> after them entire roads gone like kite strings
> incalculable records' print grown finer
> just the names at that followed by smoke of numbers
> and high buildings turned to glass in
> other air oh one clear day
>
> (CF, 33)

This Heraclitean affirmation of "all words" assumes a kind of pastoral grace even as it invokes an infinite semiotic transaction quite void of human agency.

That vision of linguistic free play is openly bucolic in "The Well":

> Under the stone sky the water
> waits
> with all its songs inside it
> the immortal
> it sang once
> it will sing again
> the days
> walk across the stone in heaven
> unseen as planets at noon
> while the water
> watches the same night
>
> Echoes come in like swallows
> calling to it
> it answers without moving
> but in echoes

> not in its voice
> they do not say what it is
> only where
>
> It is a city to which many travellers
> came with clear minds
> having left everything even
> heaven
> to sit in the dark praying as one silence
> for the resurrection
>
> (CL, 37)

One could never expect to master the patience of this strange, linguistic landscape. The stone sky and waiting water endlessly reflect one another in a scenic *mise en abyme*. For Merwin, the infinite regress of that mutual regard is totally "other" as language, the voice of the well's dark pool. The well is pregnant with "all its songs" and there is the assurance that "it sang once / it will sing again." Yet the desire to possess its lyricism is infinitely refracted and deferred because the well answers "but in echoes / not in its voice." Here, of course, we have come full circle to Merwin's initial depiction of Babel's "memory of tongues." Now he enters the city of language as a pilgrim to a New Jerusalem. Like the many travellers who have "left everything even / heaven / to sit in the dark praying as one silence," the poet has abandoned desire for experience unmediated by language. Yet the city's redemptive dwelling is infested, ultimately, by the unfulfilled irony of messianic hope—an all-too-human anticipation that Merwin, like Beckett, finds absurd.

The poet's later verse fuses images of lyric plenitude and discursive absence so as to subvert and undermine their conventional differences. Here the mobility of water and words describes a significant confluence of pastoral and urban settings. Woven into the fabric of each country scene is the same verbal trace that shuttles through the urban tapestry. To step into this urban world is to enter the dark flux of its "words flowing under the place of the avenue" (OH, 51). But that Orphic descent allows the poet to return to a new dwelling within the "known music" of the city's urban voices: "most beautiful / of cities and most empty / pure avenue behind the words of friends / and the known music" (OH, 51). The music of Merwin's latest two volumes, *Finding the Islands* (1982) and *Opening the Hand* (1983), is known in the same terms as in the earlier volumes—through its double mediation of the poet's experience.

In either its urban or pastoral mode, Merwin's recent verse can at once disclose a dwelling of phenomenological plenitude, one hospitable to human desire, and systematically fragment it. In *Finding*, plenitude takes precedence. Here, the poet's names offer entrances to everything language had failed to provide or merely promised in *The Moving Target, The Lice, Writings,* and *The Compass Flower.* The frank, erotic lyrics of *Finding* depict a love conceived in a language of assured simplicity. No longer hollowed by division, the poet calls forth an intimate unity. "We tell each other a language and it breathes / between us" (FI, 51). At times his words lead his readers into that shared life: "Our names surrounded / by a heart / entwine in the dark" (FI, 55). More often, though, they become entirely elusive: "If I were to talk to you / how would anyone know what the words meant" (FI, 66). Indeed, *Finding* aims to possess a voice that moves beyond language into a wholly ineffable world, yet, paradoxically, abides there, uttering its name. "For each voiceless flower," the poet promises, "there is a voice among / the absent flowers" (FI, 7). Again, Merwin's pastoral mode gestures toward a threshold of presence just beyond the poet's words:

> In your voice the rain
> is finding its way to the stream
> above the sea
>
> (FI, 62)

> Gray voice
> nuthatch after sunset
> nothing to call it
>
> (FI, 10)

> Some of the mayflies
> drift on into hot June
> without their names
>
> (FI, 5)

> Once you leave
> you have a name
> you can't remember
>
> (FI, 34)

Each of these short three-line lyrics, Merwin has said, embodies a discrete poetic form: "complete as a small, if not the smallest unit." Together they exist "in relation to each other" (Fact, 44). What draws them into a larger continuity, however, is not a conscious authorial intention, which Merwin rejects, but precisely that unknown source of forceful otherness—what he has called "the teacher who is not dead, the world of silence" (Fact, 43). That paradox of Being, residing in all creation as an invisible Other, *is* the poet's forgotten name—an absence that reminds him of the world's "islands" of phenomenal plenitude. In *Opening the Hand* the silence of that "one word for all the trees ever seen / and their lifetimes" (FI, 11) becomes deafening, just as the poet's need to speak its name becomes more insistent: "if I could take one voice / with me it would be / the sound I hear everyday" (OH, 24). That omnipresent sound—what Heidegger would describe as the "call" of Being—summons the poet to a more authentically conceived world.[47] Yet its communication lacks message or judgment; its clearing is obscure. The "one word" of silence teaches us of the authentic only by resisting the threshold of meaning. Consequently, Merwin's dialogue with that voice has led him to a kind of attentive passivity. Hearing, wondering, looking are the representative terms of Merwin's witnessing here.

Opening the Hand and *Finding the Islands,* as the titles' syntax suggests, probe an ongoing phenomenological process—an unfolding gesture of commitment to the Other. But while love's fulfillment was Merwin's subject in *Finding,* time, aging, and death qualify the pastoral optimism of *Opening,* particularly in the troubled ruminations of section 1 that work through the loss of the poet's father. The dream images of the father in "The Oars" and "Sunset Water," the psychic presentiments of his death in "The Waving of a Hand" and "Strawberries," the play of imagination and memory in "Sun and Rain" and "The Houses" culminate in "Apparitions." There, simply "opening the hand" reminds the poet of the past's uncanny persistence in the present, of his bodily inheritance of a familial likeness.

If Merwin, like Keats in "This Living Hand," were to open his hand to us in a final blessing, he might offer the volume's last poem, "The Black Jewel":

> In the dark
> there is only the sound of the cricket
>
> south wind in the leaves
> is the cricket
> so is the surf on the shore
> and the barking across the valley
>
> the cricket never sleeps
> the whole cricket is the pupil of one eye
> it can run it can leap it can fly
> in its back the moon
> crosses the night
>
> there is only the one cricket
> when I listen
>
> the cricket lives in the unlit ground
> in the roots
> out of the wind
> it has only the one sound
>
> before I could talk
> I heard the cricket
> under the house
> then I remembered summer
>
> mice too and the blind lightning
> are born hearing the cricket
> dying they hear it
> bodies of light turn listening to the cricket
> the cricket is neither alive nor dead
> the death of the cricket
> is still the cricket

in the bare room the luck of the cricket
echoes

(OH, 83)

In "The Black Jewel" Merwin pursues the same unnamable syllable
that he has struggled to voice as early as "The Child" and as recently
as "Summer Canyon," "Green Island," "Dark Side," "After a Storm,"
and "Hearing." Yet here the *logos* bespeaks an alienating universal.
Merwin's black crystal reflects the same mediating role of figurative
displacement that he presents in language's demonic incarnation as
"Division." The poem's metaphoric chain of associative images—
"south wind in the leaves," "surf on the shore," "barking across the
valley"—mobilizes a process of verbal substitution that is devoid of
meaning precisely because it is conceived against the cricket's un-
fathomable dark.

In stanza 3 the poet's entire experience, which is "only the sound
of the cricket," endures as the vigilance of an estranged consciousness. The unity of the "whole cricket" stands as a radically anti-
Platonic version of God's omniscient witnessing. Unlike earlier, romantic mystifications of this visionary image—for example Emerson's "transparent eyeball" in "Nature," or Shelley's "Hymn to
Apollo"—Merwin's omnipresent "pupil" reflects a more Diony-
sian, earthbound spectacle, reminiscent of Yeats in "Tom the Lu-
natic." The cricket's eye, through which Merwin would imagine a
plenitude of phenomenological presence, resists that visionary drive
to become, instead, sheer surface. Crystallized in "The Black Jewel"
is Merwin's sense of the void behind each of the world's surfaces.
The poet dilates his imagery to engulf us in an unsettling distance:
"in its back the moon / crosses the night." Hearing the "one cricket,"
Merwin enters its subterranean dwelling "in the unlit ground / in the
roots." There, the poet's journey "under the house" leads him into
a deeper listening to that "one sound" whose unity permeates the
night's black jewel. That omnipresent silence is discharged as "blind
lightning"—Merwin's oxymoron for the cricket's dark word. Although lightning traditionally signals spiritual liberation, here it collapses the poem's entire scene into the same abyss. There, the poet
discovers the source of his own speaking to be deathless: "the cricket
is neither alive nor dead / the death of the cricket / is still the cricket."

The cricket's voice echoes beyond life and death in the "breathless mouth" of language itself.

Although Merwin's volumes in the 1980s gesture toward a pastoral vision of phenomenal experience, each line is, finally, a black jewel compressed from the discursive sedimentation of other texts. Not even *Finding*'s most candid and spontaneous love lyrics escape that rhetorical grounding. Indeed, Merwin has known this truth about language throughout his career: every seemingly essential utterance is already split by the word's polysemy. "It would be very difficult and very rare," he has said, "to make a poem out of pure anger, or out of pure anything. Even love poems are seldom made out of pure love. Actually, they're made out of words, so all of the paradoxes that are built into any phrase come into it. Pure anger would just be a scream" (Fact, 41). It is this divorce of the word from both essential meaning and authorial determination that makes the poet wary of language's representational function. Merwin's verbal medium, even in his pastoral love lyrics, threatens the phenomenological dwelling he would envision:

> Across the mountain I see you
> across the crater
> we live on
>
> You avoid the words
> about you
> like a mountain goat
>
> (FI, 57)

Words are redemptive for Merwin as they open ways leading to the phenomenological disclosure of the world. Yet such linguistic powers can also reify visionary experience as a wholly codified text. Just as Merwin's pastoral "island" is bombarded by the urban present—"Young deer standing in headlights / in ditch below cliff / cars coming both ways" (FI, 10)—the poet's "other" life is often in the way of the word's more mobile and mechanistic autonomy, "in the way of language":

> Something continues and   I don't know what to call

it though the language is full of suggestions
in the way of language
                    but they are all anonymous
                                        (OH, 67)

Merwin always finds himself "in the way of language" in a dual
sense: both led to encounter a subjective, pastoral life and named as
object by the city's text. Moreover, this double conception of writing advances his poetry beyond both the more romantic aesthetics of
place in a poet such as Theodore Roethke and the "subjective" imagery of phenomenological surrealism in James Wright's emotive verse.

In these urban and pastoral moments we could easily oversimplify
Merwin's complex play of landscapes by reducing them to a rigid
binarism. We could group, on the one hand, images describing natural innocence, seasonal renewal, and a subjective phenomenology
of bucolic presence. On the other hand, we could set off locales marred
by industrial apocalypse, determined by a totalitarian quantification
of time and space, and blighted by the loss of a genuine cultural and
communal inheritance. We could assign each setting a particular idiom. Indeed, Merwin himself, in "Notes for a Preface," sets in opposition what he calls "the great language itself, the vernacular of
the imagination" and "the voice of the institution" in which "the
person and senses are being lost in the consumer, who does not know
what he sees, hears, wants, or is afraid of."[48]

The problem in such an essentialist reduction, however, would
be the temptation to resolve that tension by privileging the voice of
imagination as an empowering term lending a transcendent aura to
Merwin's writing. In fact, his poetics resists that kind of romantic
synthesis. Because Merwin is mindful of language's mediation of all
imaginative vision, he allows pastoral utterance and the discourse of
the city to coexist and to become reversible idioms within one continuous text. This kind of fusion happens not only in the final, urban
image in "The Well," for example, but also at the end of "In Autumn." There, nature's arbor blossoms as a New Jerusalem: "The
lights are going on in the leaves nothing to do with evening / Those
are cities / Where I had hoped to live" (L, 41).

It is within the word's symbolic order, finally, and not in some
ineffable phenomenology of numinous experience, that Merwin crafts

a forceful, postmodern aesthetic. Moreover, his text's dialectical exchange of country and city landscapes bespeaks the poet's fundamental ambivalence toward writing. On the one hand, he is wary of the trap of linguistic representation, as in "Words from a Totem Animal." "I stumble when I remember," he writes, "how it was / with one foot / one foot still in a name" (CL, 17). On the other hand, the poet finds himself led, like Orpheus, into language's redemptive "other" life:

> it is true that in
> our language deaths are to be heard
> at any moment through the talk
> pacing their wooden rooms jarring
> the dried flowers
> but they have forgotten who they are
> and our voices in their heads waken
> childhoods in other tongues
>
> (CL, 56)

If Merwin is possessed by a vision of apocalypse—what one reviewer has called "the agony of a generation which knows itself to be the last"[49]—he also speaks from what Auden, in his preface to *A Mask for Janus,* named "the other side of disaster."[50] In almost any of the later poems we can trace the poet's imaginative shuttle between these two landscapes. Indeed, individual images oscillate rapidly between these two alternatives, and whole poems enact their fusion. Both moments coalesce into a single discursive practice, a landscape of verbal differences whose settings are reversible. The double edge of Merwin's faith in and suspicion of that linguistic dwelling cuts through each of his powerful images. His paradoxical understanding of language and its landscapes informs each utterance with both an assertion of the word's "strange land" and a questioning of its "heaven" of tongues:

> the prophecies waking without names in
> strange lands on unborn tongues those syllables
> resurrected staring is that heaven
>
> (CL, 87)

Merwin's lyric project serves as a powerful foil to the existential and phenomenal aesthetics that shaped Wright's career. Merwin has less faith than Wright in language's "pure clear word." As far as he is concerned, even the most personal utterance is always already infiltrated by other discourse. Opening what is traditionally the most intimate and private of literary genres to issues of textuality, Merwin releases the lyric into transpersonal expressive registers. Considering poetry as a distinctively linguistic rather than emotive medium, Merwin's lyricism advances beyond the ideological constraints of the imperial self.

PART II

Poetic Discourse and the American Long Poem

3.

Mapping Historical Breaches:
The Maximus Poems of Charles Olson

Cᴏɴᴛᴇsᴛɪɴɢ ᴛʜᴇ academically valorized model of lyric voice, W. S. Merwin's textual poetics serves as a minimalist counterpart to Charles Olson's transpersonal epic poetry. Like Merwin, Olson anticipates the poststructuralist recognition that personal identity, and indeed all cognitive and epistemological understanding, rests on an undecidable linguistic base. But moving beyond Merwin's textual lyricism, Olson's long encyclopedic verse forms employ such a "posthumanist" vision of language in a decidedly cultural critique of the contemporary social field. Olson, like Ezra Pound, was a highly influential broker of the avant-garde. As rector of Black Mountain College in the early 1950s, he played a key role in shaping the so-called poetry of revolt of the 1960s. Not insignificantly, his "projective" poetics kept open a vital line of critical exchange between on the one hand the imagist, vorticist, and objectivist aesthetics of Pound, Williams, and Zukofsky, and on the other hand the emergent poetics of such postwar writers as Creeley, Dorn, Duncan, and Levertov. Moreover, in the 1980s, he emerged as an important precursor for the $L = A = N = G = U = A = G = E$ poets and other poststructuralist writers. But mainstream American criticism, however supportive of Olson's role as a modern theoritician, has had a good deal of trouble deciding just what to make of his poetry.

Typically, Olson is viewed as a kind of *il miglior fabbro* of contemporary poetics. Thus, Robert von Hallberg admits, "I am concerned primarily with Olson's understanding of poetry and only secondarily with individual poems."[1] Predictably, the strategy of empowering Olson's poetics has led several critics to harp on his poetry's alleged shortcomings. Charles Altieri, for example, admires Olson's criticism but has little use for the poetry. "Olson's tragedy," he writes, "is that his poems rarely fulfill the promises held out by his prose."[2] Perhaps Olson's severest critic, Marjorie Perloff is highly suspicious of his poetic style, charging that it is "a clever but confused collage made up of bits and pieces of Pound, Fenollosa, Gaudier-Brzeska, Williams, and Creeley."[3] Even those who have tried to take the heat off such charges and carried water for Olson in academia tend to read the poems as serving the didactic impulse of his prose. Michael Bernstein, despite his close attention to the verbal character of the verse, nevertheless valorizes Olson's role as *lecteur,* placing *The Maximus Poems* in the modern verse epic tradition, as a tale of the tribe. Olson's magnum opus, he argues, draws its unity and authority from the poet's "dominant voice" that communicates "an element of instruction."[4] Each of these critics, whether siding with or against the poet, resists what Olson called his "post-humanist" style. Reading him for signified meaning, each curtails the play of his "projective" signification.

But Olson, who never aspired to the clarity and decorum of a poet-critic such as, say, T. S. Eliot, was anything but a methodical theoretician. Following Whitehead, Heisenberg, and others, he "projected" a radically "prehensive" poetics, valuing linguistic moments of uncertainty, indeterminacy, and serendipitous error. Moving beyond the scholar's art, Olson's later essays verge on sheer verbal collage. Such literary disruptions undermine the conceptual ground of Western humanism that, since Plato, has placed language at the beck and call of the life of ideas. Beginning with his 1950 "Projective Verse" manifesto, Olson argued for writing as a "kinetic" flow of material forces:

> (projectile   (percussive   (prospective
>
> *vs.*
>
> The NON-Projective
>
> *(or what a French critic calls "closed" verse, that verse which print bred and which is pretty much what we have had, in English & American, and have still got, despite the work of Pound & Williams*[5]

The opening of "Projective Verse" recalls such early modernist aggressions as Wyndham Lewis' and Ezra Pound's *Blast* advertisements heralding the "vorticist movement." Embodying Olson's dictum that "FORM IS NEVER MORE THAN AN EXTENSION OF CONTENT" (SW, 16), the essay's parenthetical typography brackets "thought" as afterthought—here, as the random accretion or assemblage of the signifier's alliterative play. In Olson's verbal game, the "percussive" shock wave of his critical "projectile" is "prospective," looking ahead to the ephebes of Black Mountain even as it levels the formalist milieu of the 1950s. Olson's assault on "closed" poetry comes a decade before similar polemics collected in Don Allen's 1960 anthology, *The New American Poetry*.

Not incidentally, "Projective Verse" also jettisoned what Olson called "the lyrical interference of the individual" (SW, 24). He understood, as early as 1950, that postwar confessional poetics could only come to a dead end in bourgeois solipsism. But more importantly, Olson's resistance to contemporary "talk" poetry was part of a broader cultural critique that foresaw the entire poststructuralist drive to debunk the grand narratives underwriting Western culture. Olson rejected conventional narration that, like Freytag's Pyramid, straightforwardly rises toward a climax and unravels a falling action. Such storytelling simply expresses an imaginary relation to social life that reproduces the "realistic" habits of thought of a distinctively bourgeois world outlook. Ideological narratives, whether Eliot's version of Christian humanism or the foundational story of bourgeois individualism, interfere with language's signifying play to reflect some more normal, regular, or natural order of things.

Olson subverted such colonized discourses by "projecting" his writing into the web of linguistic and cultural signs that bestow sense and meaning on social life. Narrative interference, Olson thought, begins with the casual use of personification, simile, metaphor, and so on. Such figurative rhetoric fosters the habit of misreading purely linguistic signs as natural fact. The poetic line, instead of mirroring signified ideas, should act as a productive unit of verbal exchange. "There is a whole flock of rhetorical devices," he wrote, "which have now to be brought under a new bead, now that we sight with the line. Simile is only one bird who comes down, too easily. The descriptive functions generally have to be watched, every second, in projective verse, because of their easiness, and thus their drain on the energy which composition by field allows into a poem" (SW, 19–20). Thus, starting with the smallest unit of a given word, Olson launched his poetic discourse as a critique of the powers of ideology.

Less freighted with ideological baggage than either Eliot or Pound, Olson released their collage style from high modernism's narratives of cultural domination. From the start, he turned away from lyric formalism, moving into a dialogic horizon or "field" of other writing.[6] The textuality of *Maximus* sprawls across a vast discursive network that fuses Heraclitean and other pre-Socratic philosophy; Keats' romantic theory of negative capability; Whitehead's "prehensive" model of process; and a metaphorics of relativity and uncertainty based in the post-Newtonian physics of Einstein and Heisenberg. Resting on massive textual strata grounded in anthropology, geology, linguistics, traditional myth, sea narratives, and other historical chronicles, Olson's eclectic "field" poetics flouted the seemingly natural boundaries separating literature from nonliterary discourses. He thus called into question the whole history and status of "literary" culture. But more importantly, his verbal ruptures produced new symbolic forms of action that served as catalysts for social change. Olson's radically projective style, in the 1950s, decisively subverted the narrative reproduction of American consumer society.

Epic Verse in the Age of Advanced Capitalism

IN *Maximus*, Olson launched his critique of advanced capitalism under the rubric of "Pejorocracy," a neologism meaning "worse rule" that he liberated from Pound's Canto 79. There Pound borrowed the social credit economics of Clifford Hugh Douglas to fulminate against "usury," his term for the "incentive to produce useless or superfluous articles."[7] Olson, however, employed the term "pejorocracy" somewhat differently, to focus not so much on the production of useless things as on spreading patterns of consumption. In decrying the culture of the commodity form, Olson repeated Georg Lukács' basic notions about reification. "The essence of commodity-structure," Lukács wrote, "is that a relation between people takes on the character of a thing."[8] Moreover, like the Frankfurt School theorists, Olson viewed such reification as installed across the total fabric of postwar media, journalism, advertising, and corporate life.

The poet's symbol for the ideological web of commodity fetishism stems from his clever pun on the *Muzak* service industry: "musick (the trick/of corporations, newspapers, slick magazines, movie houses" (M, 14). Lamenting America's one-dimensional scene, Olson asks, "where shall you listen/when all is become billboards, when, all, even silence, is spray-gunned? . . . /when even you, when sound itself is neoned in?" (M, 6). American consumer culture, Olson notes in the 1950s, is driven by the all-embracing medium of money that has literally "invaded, appropriated, outraged, all senses/including the mind" with

> colored pictures
> of all things to eat: dirty
> postcards
> And words, words, words
> all over everything
> No eyes or ears left
> to do their own doings (all
>
> invaded, appropriated, outraged, all senses

> including the mind, that worker on what is
>   And that other sense
> made to give even the most wretched, or any of us, wretched,
> that consolation (greased
>   lulled
> even the street-cars
>
> song
>   (M, 17)

The commodification Olson indicts here in "The Songs of Maximus" was actually planned out three decades earlier. Throughout the 1920s, America's corporate managers set out to package consumerism as *the* way of life. Borrowing from *art decoratif* and Bauhaus styles, advertising lavished an aura of glamour and modernity on products that at best possessed only a marginal utility.[9] Prophetically, the trade journal *Advertising and Selling* predicted in the 1920s that "by 1950 men will have learned to express their ideas, their motives, their experiences, their hopes and ambitions as human beings, and their desires and aspirations as groups, by means of printed or painted advertising, or of messages projected through the air" (CC, 74). In the 1950s, the total orchestration of the print media, photography, film, and television reached its zenith. By fostering the habit of passivity before its own imaginary spectacle, American advertising triumphed in the conspicuous consumption of suburban living. Corporate America's futuristic vision in the 1920s, ironically, shaped the brave new world that trapped Olson in the 1950s. "Where / shall we go from here," he asks in "The Songs of Maximus," "what can we do / when even the public conveyances / sing? / how can we go anywhere, / even cross-town / how get out of anywhere" (M, 17).

While Olson bemoaned advertising's commercial sprawl of billboards and "colored pictures," Martin Heidegger's late essay "The Age of the World Picture" (1952) similarly probed modernity's fascination with the spectacle of visual form. The world view of the modern age, he claimed, is shaped by representational thinking *(vorstellen)*, cast in a pictorial mode: "The fundamental event of the modern age is the conquest of the world as picture. The word 'picture' *(Bild)* now means the structured image *(Gebild)* that is the creature of man's producing which represents and sets before. In such producing, man contends for the position in which he can be that particular being who gives the measure and draws up the guidelines for everything that is."[10]

Like Heidegger's ontological questioning of the modern *scene,* Olson's writing also subverts the culture of the visual image. He not only puns on the commodification of "musick" but playfully subverts what Guy Debord has called the "society of the spectacle":[11] "Tell-A-Vision, the best / is soap. / The true troubadours / are CBS" (M, 75). In 1950, the year Olson published "Projective Verse," Ed Sullivan started up his "Toast of the Town" vaudeville show that later would evolve into his widely watched TV weekly, "The Ed Sullivan Show." Reflecting the burgeoning growth of TV, the cost of prime-time advertising took a tenfold jump from $45,000 an hour in the late 1940s to $150,000 by the mid-1950s. By 1952 over 2,000 stations nationwide were broadcasting shows sponsored mainly by the giant monopoly conglomerates: "*Texaco* Star Theatre," "*G.E.* Theatre" (hosted by Ronald Reagan), "*Ford* Theater," "*Bell Telephone* Hour," "*Kraft* Theater," "*Alcoa* Theater," and "*Colgate* Comedy Hour."[12] Such single corporate sponsors in effect shaped TV imagery and content to reflect the rapidly spreading ideal of consumerism. Fueling the suburban life-style, popular situation comedies such as "The Life of Riley" with William Bendix and game shows such as the Goodson-Todman production "The Price is Right" arguably provided an ideological safe-haven from cold war angst and Red Scare paranoia in the early 1950s.[13]

Such a carefully orchestrated and centralized network of communication had the effect of leveling cultural difference to the one-dimensional scene Adorno indicted in his landmark essay "Television and the Patterns of Mass Culture." "The more stereotypes become reified and rigid in the present setup of cultural industry," Adorno argued, "the less people are likely to change their preconceived ideas with the progress of their experience. The more opaque and complicated modern life becomes, the more people are tempted to cling desperately to clichés which seem to bring some order into the otherwise ununderstandable."[14] For his part, Olson viewed TV as symptomatic of a deeper impulse to reduce the world to the specular one-dimensionality of the commodity form. Before Debord, Olson actively responded to the cultural spectacle of advanced capitalism: "the moment when the commodity has attained the *total occupation* of social life" (SS, 42). Writing against the scene of American consumer society, he employs poetic discourse to fissure the representational ground of the modern world picture. Mindful that "the word does intimidate" (M, 15), Olson empowers his language with a disruptive force. The poet, he says, must actively labor to resist those "who advertise you/out" (M, 8).

The movement of Olson's political "forwarding" is subtle and wayward in its governing paradoxes. The only state he espouses is an America "born of yourself" (M, 7)—a native country conceived out of your very estrangement. Only too aware that "Limits/are what any of us/are inside of" (M, 21), Olson goes to the margins of "pejorocracy." His opening address in *Maximus* beckons the reader "Off-shore, by islands hidden in the blood" (M, 5), into the knowledge of a wholly other body politic. This more errant passage follows in the wake of Olson's earlier reading of *Moby Dick* in *Call Me Ishmael*. There, he personifies the desire for "landlessness" in Bulkinghorn, "who by 'deep, earnest thinking' puts out to sea, scorning the land, convinced that 'in landlessness alone resides the highest truth, shoreless, indefinite as God'" (CMI, 57). Olson also sought out the highest truth of landlessness beyond the culture of the visual image. Like Heidegger, he found that shoreless domain, finally, in the "groundless ground" *(abgrund)* of the word. In "Language" (1959), Heidegger contrasts inauthentic discourse—the "idle talk" of the quotidien, "they" world analyzed in *Being and Time*—with language which "speaks" Being. For Heidegger, authentic dwelling resides in the groundlessness of a linguistic abyss *(abgrund)*. Similarly, Olson holds that language frustrates our desire to get to the bottom of things. Instead of being anchored in any fixed foundations of meaning, language opens up and "hovers" over its own *abgrund*.[15]

Heidegger's theory of language's groundlessness parallels the landlessness of Olson's poetics in *Maximus,* what he variously describes as forwarding, newing, going, migrating, making passage, and so on. Not insignificantly, it is through such metaphors for the word's projective waywardness that Olson resists the cultural domination of ideological narration. Such adventurous linguistic voyaging, Olson writes in "The Present Is Prologue," moves "forward into the post-modern, the post-humanist, the post-historic" (AP, 40). Olson's own desire for "deep, earnest thinking" is akin to the psychic impulses of the deep image writers. But unlike Bly or Wright, and parting company with Heidegger, Olson is more skeptical about language's phenomenological disclosures. The word, for him, is not necessarily one with the world, as some of his critics have argued.[16] Quite the contrary, in "Maximus, to himself" (M, 56–57), the poet finds himself exiled from such phenomenological dwelling. Olson wrote this somewhat confessional lyric in April 1953, after the "destructive" tirades against pejorocracy that Paul Bové reads in the earlier letters from 1950 to January 1953. Significantly, Olson's troubled ruminations in 1953 deny Bové's claim that phenomenological destruction leads the poet into a primordial harmony with things themselves. "The sea was not, finally, my trade," Olson complains. "But even my trade, at it, I stood estranged/from that which was most familiar."[17]

In "Maximus, to himself" Olson's divided loyalties compromise his poetic vocation. He would emulate those authentic seamen of Gloucester "who do the world's/businesses,/and who do nature's." Yet the poet's craft is belated. Having, finally, no sense of that "first" world, Olson confesses to a more modest occupation: "I have made dialogues,/have discussed ancient texts/have thrown what light I could, offered/what pleasures/doceat allows/But the known?/This, I have had to be given." A poem such as "Maximus, to himself," in contrast to the self-confident tirades of Olson's early cultural critiques, projects a more anxious openness. It registers a new tone of uncertainty. Olson's unease stems from the same romantic division between world and ancient texts that splits the early careers of Wright and Bly. Insofar as language in this world/text hierarchy marks a falling away from nature's immediacy, the poet's art, of necessity, is compromised. Olson is unsure whether poetry's "undone business" will ever allow him to dwell authentically in the world of Gloucester as a "wind/and water man" (M, 57). Yet such estrangement, as a kind of negative capability, provides Olson passage though the depths of language's *abgrund,* allowing him to reverse and displace the word's reflection of the world.

Moving beyond the failure of modernism in Pound and Williams,

Maximus enters the horizon of what Olson called "post-human-ism."[18] Here, the pressure to evade high modernism's cultural elitism, to escape history through the sheer presence of the lyric voice, seduces less inventive poets into the emotive imagination, often stifling the play of their language. Finding rhetorical strategies that will finesse emotive lyricism is the challenge to which the poetics of Bly and Wright respond with mixed success. Faced with the same dilemma, Olson turns toward a more radical textuality. He becomes Gloucester's "first" poet by recognizing, before Derrida and other poststructuralists, that the world is always already inscribed by an omnipresent network of signification.

Olson's "newing" emerges nearly a decade after his "Projective Verse" essay. In "Letter to Elaine Feinstein" (1959), he describes a historical "double-axis," crossing the "classical-representational" epoch of modernism with the vertical depth of historicity. In *The Special View of History* (1956) and the 1963 essay "On History," he contrasts the "scientific" chronicals of Thucydidean history with the more mythic narrative *('istorin)* of Herodotus. 'Istorin, literally "finding out for oneself," resists the static periodization of the past imaged as world picture. More to the point, in "Letter 23" of *Maximus* I, Olson defines 'istorin ("finding out for oneself") as *muthos* ("what is said"), thus returning history to verbal process. Muthos, he explains in *Special View,* is what is both invented and discovered. Quoting Jane Harrison's theory of myth in *Themis,* Olson says: "The primary meaning of myth in religion is just the same: it is the spoken correlative of the acted rite, the thing done . . . (things said are things done)" (SVH, 21–22). Significantly, Olson's borrowing from Harrison—"things said are things done"—lays stress on the agency of the word. Poetic discourse, as a performative speech act, is in a radical way for Olson a verbal *praxis*. Poetry "does" something to us: it produces meaning and our experience of the world, not the other way around. Moreover, it would be a mistake to limit muthos—what is said and done—to the spoken performatives intended by the lyric poet. On the contrary, consistent with Olson's early rebuff of "lyrical interference," the author's role is not subjective.

For Olson, the "forwarding" of muthos as a performative is not understood as simply the spoken communication or transport of the author's thoughts, ideas, or intention. Looking forward to, for example, Derrida's critique of "ordinary language" theorists such as J. L. Austin, Olson "finds out for himself" that what muthos says and does rests on language's discursive base. "This is my thought," he writes, "that form as an extension of content will only get far if we recognize, and then investigate, how much language is the root and branch of content as well as it is patently the leaf that form is."[19] What does it mean, however, to think the form/content of muthos as flowering from language itself? For muthos to signify, to be readable, its word, whether spoken or written, must be rooted in a linguistic code that functions regardless of the author's or addressee's presence or absence. As a mark governed by a verbal structure, muthos is thus repeatable or, as Derrida would have it, "iterable": subject to citation or textual grafting beyond its immediate context.[20] Things said and done, then, can be voiced otherwise and inscribed elsewhere beyond one's original word. Subject to repetition and always already based in prior citation, language is never the transparent bearer of meaning but is itself rhetorically mediated.

The Via Rupta of Projective Inscription

IN THE 1960s, Olson's understanding of textuality looks forward to the deconstructive turn Derrida would make beyond Heidegger's final thinking of the equiprimordiality of Being, temporality, and language. Following Saussure's notion of "the arbitrary character of the sign," its "differential character," Derrida insists that signified meanings, referents, concepts, things—everything that claims the plenitude of presence for which the sign stands—come after language's differential order. "Essentially and lawfully," Derrida announces, "every concept is inscribed in a chain or in a system within which it refers to the other, to other concepts, by means of the systematic play of differences" (Margins, 11). Différance, of course, is Derrida's term for "the movement according to which language, or any code, any system of referral in general, is constituted 'historically' as a weave of differences" (Margins, 12). Significantly, Derrida's view of history as an inscribed weave of differences is anticipated in the postmodern historicism of Maximus.

Olson writes a "history" of Gloucester, yet one which the poet describes as "post-historical." The strategy is to resist offering either a chronological narrative of Gloucester's past or a thematic account of its heritage. Instead, the poet's authentic muthos, as Olson describes it in "Bibliography for Ed Dorn," "will disclose the intimate connection between person-as-continuation-of-millenia-of-all-past-persons, places, things and actions-as-data (objects)" (AP, 7). This shorthand definition of Olson's "historicism" deconstructs the discrete signified concepts of person, place, thing, action, past, present, reality, stressing how such notions are generated out of the differential weave and signifying chains of 'istorin/muthos. Understanding that tradition is constructed through the active repression of difference, Olson sees that its authority is arbitrary and subject to change. Consequently, he opens Gloucester's "history" to error, misreadings, gaps, breaks, and indeterminate, even unreadable, narratives.

Maximus' posthistoricism subjects Gloucester's chronology to its own eccentric weave of historical citation. "Letter 15," for example, opens with one of Olson's better-known corrections to his own text. Here he returns to the story of Nathaniel Bowditch's last voyage on Christmas Day 1803, which Olson earlier misread in "Maximus, to Gloucester, Letter 2." Supplementing the popular tale he was told as a boy with the documented account of H. Bowditch, Nathaniel's son, Olson opens "Letter 15" with this rambling admission:

> It goes to show you. It was not the "Eppie Sawyer". It was the ship "Putnam". It wasn't Christmas morning, it was Christmas night, after dark. And the violent north-easter, with snow, which we were all raised to believe did show Bowditch such a navigator, was a gale sprung up from W, hit them outside the Bay, and had blown itself out by the 23rd.
>
> (M, 71)

In revising the ship's name, time of day, wind directions, and weather of *Maximus* I, "Letter 2," Olson does not so much correct his earlier letter as embrace errancy in a more gracious acceptance of muthos—the sum of what is said. "Letter 15" draws out this wayward historiography, jumping back to Olson's correspondence with Paul Blackburn during 1951: "He sd, 'You go all around the subject.' And I sd, 'I didn't know it was a sub-/ject.' He sd, 'You

twist,' and I sd, 'I do'" (M, 72). Blackburn's "twist" metaphor is
an apt trope for Olson's eccentric "forwarding." The twist Olson
gives to history folds the present back onto the past, collapses time,
identity, prose documents and lyric poetry. But the poet's rejoinder
takes this errancy toward a more textual horizon: "I sd, 'Rhapsodia'
. . . " (M, 72). As a technique of Homeric epic, "rhapsodia" literally means "songs stitched together."[21] Olson employs it as a rubric for the narrative twists, warps, and textual patchwork that con-
stitute *Maximus'* posthistoricism. Rhapsodia stands for Olson's
posthumanist vision of the inscribing thread of language everywhere
"stitching together" the world, which "is sewn / in all parts, under
/ and over" (M, 343).

Significantly, Olson's major tropes for the word's productive
agency—its forwarding, newing, navigating, voyaging, migrating,
and so on—look ahead to similar metaphors for writing in Derrida's
"Freud and the Scene of Writing," his revision of Freud's "Note on
the Mystic Writing Pad," and also in his well-known critique of
Lévi-Strauss, "The Violence of the Letter." In both essays, Derrida
depicts the play of *différance* as a "breaching" (*Bahnung,* or "pathbreaking," in Freud's "Note") and a *picada,* the beaten path or *via
rupta* of the Nambikwara tribe. Derrida uses "pathbreaking" as a
metaphor for the word's necessary violence: "Breaching, the tracing
of a trail, opens up a conducting path. Which presupposes a certain
violence and a certain resistance to effraction. The path is broken,
cracked, *fracta,* breached."[22] Thus, the *via rupta* stands as the active
mark of a textual difference from other breaches. Such discursive
tensions, jostlings, clashes, and violent erasures escalate Heidegger's
struggle to dwell even in the midst of language's groundless depth.

Derrida's metaphor sheds light on Olson's poetics as it describes
writing as a web of forces. Ultimately, Olson understands the "forwarding" of Gloucester's "first men" as a kind of discursive pathbreaking. But more than Derrida, Olson presents such linguistic
breachings as passages into America's social text. While he views
history as figural, Olson also leans toward Bakhtin's notion that language's symbolic forms are founded on distinctively social forces:

> Instead of the virginal fullness and inexhaustibility of the object
> itself, the prose writer confronts a multitude of routes, roads and

paths that have been laid down in the object by social consciousness. Along with the internal contradictions inside the object itself,
the prose writer witnesses as well the unfolding of social heter-
oglossia *surrounding* the object, the Tower-of-Babel mixing of languages that goes on around any object; the dialectics of the object
are interwoven with the social dialogue surrounding it.[23]

Navigating Gloucester's verbal passages, Olson's rhapsodia joins him,
finally, to the Heraclitean flux of the familiar—the primordially
communal world of the wind and water men celebrated in "Maximus, to himself." Olson's understanding that writing negotiates such
a densely inscribed social habitat satisfies his desire for landlessness.
Maximus compels social change by a "newing" or breaching of history's discursive depths.

One of the many places where Olson stages the inaugural powers
of poetic discourse is "Maximus to Gloucester, Letter 27 [with-
held]." Here he recalls an image of the poet's high office in archaic
Celtic culture, gleaned from Robert Grave's *The White Goddess*. During the pitch of battle between warring kingdoms, poets (Druids)
would intervene in the fight and through their songs determine the
outcome of the struggle. Olson was attracted to this ritual as a metaphor for how the word might possibly generate history. He was
fascinated by the linguistic force "that can stop Enyalion," the char-
ismatic divinity of war (Guide to Maximus, 140). Earlier in *Maximus*
I, in "Letter 22," Olson used the same Celtic drama to retrieve the
poet's cultural authority: "And what I write / is stopping the battle"
(M, 101). There, however, poetry merely possesses mimetic powers
to reflect and record the doings of Enyalion. In "Letter 22" Olson
is still in the service of nature's "first men." Belated, the poet rushes
"to get down, right in the midst of / the deeds, to tell / what this one
did, how, / in the fray; he made his play, did grapple / with that one,
how / his eye flashed" (M, 102).

But borrowing its idiom from Whitehead's *Adventures of Ideas,*
"Letter 27 [withheld]" closes the gap dividing history's material
events—Whitehead's "antecedant predecessions, the precessions"—
from the poet's text. Whitehead provided Olson with an important
critique of the kind of Platonic mimesis that bound poetry to the
slavish representation of the world. Not insignificantly, Whitehead

displaced "determinate entities," static "things," signified ideas, and here, in Olson's allusions, "abstract form," with "events" in process:

> This, is no bare incoming
> of novel abstract form, this
>
> is no welter or the forms
> of those events, this,
>
> Greeks, is the stopping
> of the battle
>
>   It is the imposing
> of all those antecedent predecessions, the precessions
>
> of me, the generation of those facts
> which are my words
>
>   (M, 184)

In "Letter 27 [withheld]" the heroic past returns now as a linguistic moment. As poet, Olson oversees "the generation of those facts/ which are my words, it is coming/ from all that I no longer am, yet am" (M, 184). Still resisting the poet's "lyrical interference," Olson envisions the world that verse writing bestows as a "complex of occasions" (M, 185), having "no strict personal order" (M, 184): at once belonging to and exceeding his authorial identity.

Throughout *Maximus,* Olson is challenged by the ideological baggage of Gloucester's narrative heritage. The burden of that cultural past threatens to entomb the poet's word as a "dead letter" in its deep discursive sedimentation. "No wonder," Olson writes in "The Vindland Map Review," "poets care for finding a better sort somewhere lower, and deeper, and in more careful zones and strata, than their quite recent counterparts" (AP, 68). As a writer, Olson survives the vertical depth of history's textual geography through his writing's *via rupta.* The poet negotiates the *abgrund* of language's landlessness through fracturing the ground of tradition. Thus, he asserts "that forever the geography/ which leans in/ on me I compell/backwards I compell Gloucester/to yield, to/change" (M, 185). Moreover, such a "forwarding" joins the poet to Gloucester's "first men," those "who do the world's/businesses" (M, 56). Reversing writing's belatedness to history, Gloucester's wind and water man gives way to the cartographer, the textual navigator who inscribes the primordial world of the familiar in the portulans of his *via rupta*. In *Maximus,* Juan de la Cosa, Columbus' "Chief Chart Maker" and captain of the Nina in 1493, draws the first authentic mappemonde—one that charts modern representations of New World geography.

La Cosa's mappemonde is the prototype of Olson's own textual twists that join geographic accounts of the waters "offshore" Cape Ann to the voyages of Odysseus, Pytheus, Hercules-Melkaart, Martin Behaim, Hakluyt, St. Brendan, Hieronymus da Verrazano, Gaspar and Miguel Cortereal, John Cabot, and John Lloyd, among others. La Cosa's primordial act of mapping, "what he drew who drew Hercules/going by the Bear off from Calypso" (M, 82), achieves an authentic portulans: a graphic version of 'istorin. Such textual soundings cross the conventional boundary dividing empirical from mythic representation. Similarly, Olson's muthos joins the calculated measurements of Bowditch's fifth voyage across Gloucester's shoals to what past mariners knew as Cape Raz, Tierra de Bacalaos, emerging beyond Pytheas' Ultima Thule and St. Brendan's Judas Land: Terra Nova sive Limo Lue, or "Land of the Cod-Fish" (Guide to Maximus, 121). Each of these graphs has the same claim to textual authority; each traces a *via rupta,* a breached periplus, through the differential field of all other voyages.

The Text of "Post-Humanism"

THE POET'S formidable archive, collected by George Butterick at the University of Connecticut Library, is telling evidence that Olson wrote from an immense palimpsest of secondary material that far outstripped the bibliography he sketched for Ed Dorn. Even the walls of Olson's Fort Square apartment in Gloucester were papered with a dense collage of citations. His writing was literally a linguistic breaching of other texts, so much so that even the volumes of his personal library are covered thick with marginalia, a complex scribbling in pencil and up to four colors of ink. That he came to consider such inscription as an actual navigation of Gloucester's "first" world is clear in this little-read self-portrait, "3rd letter on Georges, unwritten" from *Maximus* II:

> [In this place is a poem which I have not been able to write—or a story to be called the Eastern End of Georges, about a captain I knew about, as of the days when it was important to race to market—to the Boston market, or directly in to Gloucester, when she had fresh fish, and how this man had such careful charts of his own of these very shallow waters along the way to market if you were coming in from the Winter Cod Grounds on the Eastern End—the point was to cut the corner, if you were that good or that crazy, though he was as good as they come, he even had the charts marked in different colored pencils and could go over those rips and shoals dug out in a storm, driving a full-loaded vessel and down to her deck edge, across them as a wagon might salt licks or unship her wheels and ferry across—it is a vision or at least an experience I make off as though I have had, to ride with a man like that—even have the picture of him sitting on his cabin floor following those charts like a race-sheet while taking the calls down the stern passageway and if it sounds more like Henry Ware & Paul Cotter in the Eyes of the Woods, it could be so, for I've looked & looked for the verification, and the details of sail at a time when there were no engines—and I went to James Connolly expecting to be able to depend upon him, but somehow he hasn't come across, or it's all prettied up, and it was either Bohlin or Sylvanus Smith or it may have been someone as late as Marty Callaghan but the roar of this guy going through the snow and bent to a north easter and not taking any round about way off the shoals to the north but going as he was up & down dale like a horseman out of some English novel makes it with me, and I want that sense here, of this fellow going home] (M, 277)

This "poem" typifies the difficulty of reading *Maximus* as well as the whole work's problematic relationship to American epic tradition.[24] To begin with, any generic coding of this writing as poem, note, letter, marginalia, and so on is suspended by the poet's own typographical bracketing of its status. As a textual parody of a speech act, the poem presents a virtual context that is repeatedly qualified: "it is a vision or at least an experience / I make off as though I have had . . . / it could be so." By both presenting the poem and adding the proviso that it is "unwritten," Olson's double narrative jogs the reader out of the habit of reading verse for any straight, mimetic rendering of experience. Such equivocation resists conventional realism even as it eludes interpretation. Olson sought to undermine the division between poetry and prose, von Hallberg argues, in order "to destroy the category of Poetry itself."[25] Yet in touting Olson's ideas about poetry, von Hallberg ignores the risks such a verbal subversion negotiates. Olson compels his textuality to navigate a zone of literary inscription to test the limits of aesthetic form. His passage is, in Derrida's terms, both "strategic" and "adventurous"—strategic as it solicits and disrupts traditional generic boundaries, and adventurous in embracing textual effraction as an end in itself (Margins, 7). Yet as the troping of the "3rd letter" illustrates, such a "going" is at once ecstatic and hazardous.

The "3rd letter on Georges, unwritten" of *Maximus* II alludes to a thick sheaf of other texts both glossed and "unwritten" within the poem. It demands the same vertical stance of the reader that Olson takes as poet. The "3rd letter" moves "off-shore" into the domain of other poems that twist and warp about the "geography" of Georges Bank, located about 190 miles east of Cape Cod. We have already been there in Nathaniel Bowditch's fifth voyage, in "Letter 15" and "On First Looking Out Through Juan de la Cosa's Eyes" in *Maximus* I. The wealth of the Bank's fishing grounds makes it one of Gloucester's exemplary locales—at once a place of profit and legendary heroism. That abundance, however, is won only by running the tremendous risks which test the "first" men of *Maximus*. The first and second letters on Georges of *Maximus* I twist about narratives of hazard and ill fate. Olson first relates a disaster that befalls a Gloucester fishing fleet of over one hundred ships in 1862. There, gales drive fifteen vessels off their anchors and onto the rocky shoals, killing one hundred twenty men during one harrowing day. The second story, dating from 1905, relates Johnny McKenzie's drowning, told to Olson by Ben Frost, who sailed on the *Ella M. Goodwin* at the time. Running beneath the ecstatic passage of Olson's "good"

and "crazy" captain in the "3rd letter' is the same violent seascape
whose history of disasters is commemorated in Gloucester's annual
memorial service of "Maximus, to Gloucester, Sunday, July 19."

In Olson's "On First Looking Out Through Juan de la Cosa's
Eyes," that proving ground challenges another of America's "first"
men, Christopher Columbus: "It was the teredo-worm / was 1492:
riddle a ship's hull / in one voyage ('pierced / with worm-holes / like
a bee-hive, / the report was" (M, 84). The teredo-worm—the Car-
ribean coral reefs—tests Columbus' "forwarding" with a rite of passage offering at once the potential for disaster and triumph. But
through their reserves of negative capability, Olson's explorers survive such primordial encounters with America's New World, thereby
becoming "men of achievement." Moving among those "very shallow waters," Olson writes that "the point was to cut the / corner,
if you were that good or that crazy." Unlike Captain Moulton's
folly in "Tyrian Businesses," this captain's bold navigation succeeds
through his scrupulous craft: "this man had such careful charts of
his / own . . . / . . . he even had charts marked / in different colored pencils and could go over those / rips and shoals dug out in a
storm."

This "first" eccentric navigator is, of course, a doppelgänger. He
retraces his portulans with the same rainbow of colors that marks
the passages of Olson's marginalia. "Sitting on / his cabin floor following those charts like a race- / sheet," he is a mirror image of Olson the poet. Both negotiate landscapes of resistant and shifting forces
by means of primordial inscription. Olson's captain must "cut the /
corner" of shoals that would gut his vessel. Likewise, the poet's
challenge is to navigate a *via rupta* among prior texts threatening his
poem's "newing." Olson's "3rd letter on Georges, unwritten" is that
breached passage which both resides in and differs from letters 1 and
2 on Georges, and the historical narratives which inform them: Proc-
tor's *The Fisherman's Memorial and Record Book,* the *Boston Post's* article of Saturday, January 7, 1905, and James Connolly's *Book of the
Gloucester Fishermen*—as well as Joseph Altsheler's adventure novels.
"3rd letter on Georges, unwritten" allows Olson's persona to "come
across" from the dead letters of James Connolly, Bohlin, Sylvanus
Smith, and Marty Callaghan into the "projective" textuality of *Maximus.* The wind and water man of "Maximus, to himself" does the

world's businesses now in *Maximus* II through the mediation of a dialogic textuality. Through language, Olson renders the world's businesses, in Heraclitus's idiom, "familiar."

Such transaction with other writing typifies Olson's strategy throughout the later *Maximus*. He projects his wayward process poetics against the ideological closure of the modern verse epic. A hallmark of the epic genre, Bakhtin argues in "Epic and Novel," is its elevation over the social world. Epic is "memorial," distinguished by ideal traditions conceived *sub specie aeternitatis*.[26] Olson destroys such epic elitism as it underwrites the long poetry of high modernism. In particular, *Maximus* returns epic to its worldly foundations of nonliterary discourse. Pierced everywhere by literature's social text, the later *Maximus* dramatizes what in "Maximus, to himself" Olson calls his "undone business"—his poem's strategic failure to find "what will suffice." Olson's later work actively resists a unified stance, controlling ideological position, central myth, or authoritative voice— any aesthetic or political closure that would block poetry's projective kinesis. Moreover, his dense collage of textual citations, as a "rhapsodia," twists narrative meaning into verbal knots that thwart the coherent unraveling of a New Critical *explication de texte*. Instead, *Maximus* invites critical breaches that will further project its intertextual field. Such interpretive acts, however, founder inevitably on the sheer material presence of language itself throughout the later *Maximus*. To read Olson's long poem is both to trace and breach the poet's own passage through the text of "the familiar": the Heraclitean flux of linguistic landlessness.

In *Maximus* I the poet's cultural critique of American consumer society leads off-shore into the landlessness of discourse. Volume 2 makes a further leap into history's abyss. Olson's portulans of poetic "forwarding" is mapped out in "Maximus to Dogtown-II" (M, 179–181). In descending along the past's vertical axis—"right off the Orontes" (M, 171) back to pre-Homeric, Pleistocene culture— Olson recovers the equiprimordiality of space and time that he reads in Melville: "Time [for Melville] returned on itself. It had density, as space had, and events were objects accumulated within it, around which men could move as they moved in space" (CMI, 101–02). Reading Melville in this way, Olson probes history's field of discursive forces whose archival density is nevertheless open to his own poetic breachings and effractions. Trapped by the one-dimensional scene of commodification indicted in *Maximus* I, the poet seeks a deeper historicity now beneath the "surface underwater galaxy / time." Repeating the Orphic descents of Whitman and other American modernists such as Pound and Williams, Olson no longer pursues language's landlessness off-shore, but deeper "inland." There he enters a wholly other temporal order that approximates space in the patient flux of "carboniferous" coal—its prehistoric "Age / under / *Dogtown* / rills / Aquarian Time."

Such descents into American place sound the same fathomless depths that fascinated Melville: "In the deep," Olson says, "where Pip saw 'God's foot on the treadle of the loom,' Melville found Ahab's 'grim sire,' and the State-secret. Pip came to the surface mad, Melville possessed of his imagination. The Pacific gave him the right of primogeniture" (CMI, 115–16). The primogeniture of the word's vertical axis allows Melville as writer to survive Pip's delerium, immersed in the pelagic deep of history. Similarly, opening Gloucester to that prehistoric depth, Olson plumbs the abyss of past language. Thus, the "places most familiar" to the poet, such as Wingaersheek Beach at the mouth of Cape Ann's Annisquam River, are dispersed throughout the "migma"—literally "mixture"—of history's social text: "Wyngaershoek hoik Grape Vine HOYK the Dutch / & the Norse / and Algonquins." Just as Olson reads "Annisquam" as "Old Norse-Algonquin" for "Wannasquam," from *vanns-kvam* (river cove, or inlet), so "Wyngaersheek" is an etymological twist on a German, Low Dutch root *Wyngaerts Hoeck,* from *Wyngaerten* (Guide to Maximus, 548). Descending the textual "Ladder" of what he calls the "Vertical American Thing," Olson breaches the Norse-Algonquin myth of American place.

In *Maximus* II the poet's American identity is "decentered," or becomes, in the idiom of *The Special View of History*, "circumferential." The self's errant rhapsodia twists about the uroboric round of the Homeric past charted by Anaximander: "Homer's world was locked tight in River Ocean which circled it, in Anaximander's map, like a serpent with tail in mouth" (CMI, 118). Tracing the portulans of time's vertical axis to its most archaic cultural roots, Olson warps back onto the American present. His vision of language's eternal return flowers out of the discursive unfolding of the Black Chrysanthemum. Blossoming from the "other side of heaven," its "*under/* vault," "Carbon Ocean," "bituminous Heart," and "'mother' rock," Olson's "Black Gold Flower" blooms, finally, as a symbolic form. It embodies the poet's dictum that "language is the root and branch of content as well as it is patently the leaf that form is":[27]

up Dogtown hill on top one day the
Vertical American Thing will
surface underwater galaxy   show from heaven the Ladder
time: there is no sky
space or sea left   come down to the Earth
of Us All, the Many who
earth is interesting: know
ice is interesting   there is One!
stone is interesting   One Mother
One Son

flowers are
Carbon   One Daughter
Carbon is   and Each the Father
Carboniferous   of Him-Her-Self:
Pennsylvania
the Genetic
Age   is Ma the Morphic
under   is Pa the City is Mother:
Dogtown
the stone   Polis, the Child-Made-Man-Woman is

(Mary's Son
Elizabeth's

Man) MONOGENE:
in COLLAGEN
the monogene. /in KOLLAgen
TIME   LEAP onto
the LAND, the AQUARIAN
TIME
(M, 179–80)

This disorienting verbal "field" twists about the subtext of Olson's readings in Melville: "The beginning of man was salt sea, and the perpetual reverberation of that great ancient fact, constantly renewed in the unfolding of life in every human individual, is the important single fact about Melville. Pelagic." (CMI, 13). Man was salt sea, originally, for Olson, in the monogene, the single cell: the collagen or genetic matrix from which humanity unfolds. But monogene, in Olson's larger muthos, is also the Gnostic Son of God of whom the poet read in Jung's *Psychology and Alchemy:* "This same is he [Monogenes] who dwelleth in the Monad . . . This same [Monad] is the Mother-City of the Only begotten" (Guide to Maximus, 256). Fusing Gnosticism and genetics, Olson submits the Egyptian myth of Osiris to the projective textuality of *Maximus* II. Briefly, in *Maximus'* scheme of generation, Ma incarnates Isis, whose son Horus saves his father, Osiris, from drowning. Olson's source for this myth of drowning and resurrection is Henri Frankfort, author of *Kingship and the Gods,* who describes "Memphite Theology" in the figure of Ptah, the "Primeval Hill" or incarnation of "Gravelly Hill" god of the city (Guide to Maximus, 436). Through an act of individuation, Olson opens his personal identity as "Mary's son and Elizabeth's man" to incarnate the archetypal "Monad": "the City is Mother-/Polis, the Child-Made-Man-Woman is/(Mary's son/Elizabeth's/Man) MONOGENE:/in COLLAGEN."

In "Dogtown II," Olson embodies a kind of genetic metropolis that is, finally, a verbal space. If, as Olson believed, "FORM IS NEVER MORE THAN AN EXTENSION OF CONTENT" (SW, 16), then he projects this myth not so much as a literal belief as a textual "forwarding." The poet's linguistic troping, navigating, newing, and so on, traverse and twist mythic meaning according to the more wayward agency of the letter. Not incidentally, such verbal errancy undermines high modernism's mythic method—the strategy that lends an authoritative unity to the careers of Eliot, Yeats, and Pound. Throughout the latter two volumes of *Maximus,* Olson deconstructs his text's investment in standard archetypal narratives of transcendence. Unlike the archetypal tradition from which Bly writes, Olson's field poetics submits myth to the effracted textuality of muthos. Archetypes of mythic transcendence are systematically undermined and displaced by the differential play of language.

Fenris is Olson's mythic figure for the violence of the letter that rends apart the fabric of signified meaning. Resembling the "rough beast" of Yeats' "The Second Coming," *Maximus'* "God the dog" is a monstrous polyphony of Anubis, Cerberus, and Scylla—the "dog rocks" (M, 89) that both imperil and empower Maximus' first captains of the New World.[28] In "Stevens Song" Olson reads his family heritage and the record of Gloucester's traditional heroes through a dramatic struggle with Fenris. Olson names Stevens "the first Maximus" as early as "Letter 7" (M, 35). As "the chief ship builder / of England" (M, 399), he is also the ancient Phoenician carpenter, "Ousoos the / hunter" who was "the first man / to carve out / the trunk / of a tree / and go out / on the waters / from the shore" (M, 273).

By fashioning vessels, both Ousoos and Stevens migrate westward, thus becoming first men of their respective New Worlds. But more importantly, Stevens becomes "the first Maximus" through his self-imposed exile from Charles II. Such political strife looks ahead to the local struggle between Olson's father and Paddy Hehir, Worcester's foreman of letter carriers, and Blocky Sheehan, superintendent of mails. In "Stevens Song" Olson projects the battles of both these "first men" into a wider discursive field. Their political contests repeat the Norse war god Tyr's encounter with Fenris. Although Tyr becomes heroic by binding the "dog-god," in the bargain he suffers the loss of his hand: "when Tyr / put his hand / in Fenris / mouth /—it was not a test, / it was to *end* / that matter, Fenris / simply bit it / off" (M, 403). Similar metaphoric disfigurements send Stevens "away across Cut Bridge," Olson's father toward a serious involvement in local politics, and the poet more deeply into language.

Through Fenris, Olson ruminates on the word's violent disfigurement of the referential world: "Space and Time the saliva / in the mouth / your own living hand amputated living on / in the mouth / of the Dog" (M, 414). Later in *Maximus* III Olson repeats this textual echo of Keats' "This Living Hand," now in a direct quote: "This Living hand, now warm, now capable / of earnest grasping . . ." (M, 506). Olson's "hand" lives on as his handwriting, his inscription of "Space and Time" in the text of his long poem and those of his readers. The poet's amputated hand abides, albeit in the kind of life-in-death order that Yeats witnesses in "Byzantium." That sign of authorial survival, however, is not ideally present to itself; it is not whole. Nevertheless, the poet's hand/writing endures as a sacrifice of disfiguration "in the mouth/of the Dog."

Following Nietzsche, Derrida, and Thomas Altizer, Mark Taylor argues that sacrificing the logos as a transcendental signified engenders the (a)theology of the word's fruitful dissemination: "If, as Nietzsche anticipates, deconstruction is the hermeneutic of the death of God, then the death of God is the (a)theology of deconstruction. A death of God (a)theology, however, really is a *radical* Christology. . . . The death of God is the birth of the Word."[29] Like Olson and Norman O. Brown, Taylor depicts writing as a scene of dismemberment/incorporation—a feast where "sacrifice of Author through inscription in Word (or text) is self-negation which is self-realization" (p. 71). In *Maximus* III Olson likewise views writing as an Orphic ritual of the self's sacrifice to writing. "I've sacrificed everything," he admits in "Maximus of Gloucester," "to this attempt to acquire complete/concentration," which he says is "Only my written word" (M, 473). Not insignificantly, such linguistic concentration breaks through the closure of archetypal imagery that locks Bly's later work into the Jungian tradition.

Olson's use of archetypes throughout the later volumes, especially his fascination with transmigration in the "Dogtown" sequences, resembles the archetypal subjects of Bly's post–Vietnam poetry. Both poets choose deep psychic landscapes as alternative vistas to the wasteland of contemporary American culture. Confronted with the deep image's abyss, each seeks refuge from psychic vertigo in archetypes of transcendence. In particular, the Victorian stereotyping of Bly's archetypal "mother" poetry leads him unwittingly into a somewhat sexist poetics. Likewise, the archetypal "mother rock" of the "Dogtown" sequence's "throne of creation" threatens to ground Olson's process poetics in the same aesthetic closure. Olson more than Bly, however, sacrifices these enframing archetypal narratives to the more radical indeterminacy of language as such. Throughout the later *Maximus* he moves beyond the desire for emotive psychic presence typifying the deep image poetics of Wright, Bly, and Rich. He keeps his deep archetypal imagery in dialogic play with a greater field of textuality. Moving through the "pelagic" expanse of language itself, Olson's projective poetics leaves in its wake a textual field of deconstructive breachings. In *Maximus,* the word's violent landlessness disrupts the ideological ground of the high modernist aesthetic, causing it to tremble before the abyss of language. Writing in this way, he resists his precursors' penchant for cultural domination as they delimit the modern verse epic with narrative closure. Choosing instead the cartographer's play of textual breachings, Olson's verbal "forwarding" joins him both to the deconstructive lyricism of W. S. Merwin and to James Merrill's errant postmodernism.

4.

A Poetics of Errancy:
James Merrill's The Changing Light
at Sandover

W ITH THE very first lines of Merrill's magnum opus—"Admittedly I err by undertaking / This in its present form"—the whole vexed issue of generic form is at once underscored and taken into a ludic, self-parodic register.[1] Such an arch admission subverts the more doctrinaire stances of high modernism. But more importantly, it betrays a deeper unease with the modern verse epic's claim to cultural authority. In the prolegomenon to the trilogy that makes up *The Changing Light at Sandover* (1982)—*The Book of Ephraim* (1976), *Mirabell: Books of Number* (1978), and *Scripts for the Pageant* (1980)—Merrill features at once his own anxious sense of belatedness to past writing and the now unsettled status of traditional genres in the face of postmodern mass culture: today's mechanically reproduced and hyperreal fusion of film media, video, pop music, and advanced computer

graphics. By this point in his career the poet has grown impatient
with his earlier lyricism. Nor does he have much use for the "fancy
narrative concoctions" of the *nouveau roman,* deriding it as "an or-
phaned form" of modernism (CLS, 3–4). Ideally, he would com-
pose a transparent, original discourse—what Roland Barthes describes as a "zero-degree" writing.[2] But the poet's nostalgia for "the
kind of unseasoned telling found/In legends, fairy tales"—for a narrative at once "limpid" and "unfragmented" (CLS, 3–4)—is frus-
trated from the start by the larger failure of his cultural moment.
The Book of Ephraim finds Merrill casting about for a new verse mode,
one that would reclaim the mythic stature of traditional epic yet be
resilient to history.

Like Eliot, Pound, and Yeats, Merrill would celebrate "The incarnation and withdrawal of/A god" (CLS, 3). Yet he must heed
the Nietzschean dictum that "God is Dead"—that, as the Madman
of *The Gay Science* charges, we have killed him. The epic authority
of a Dante or Milton now seems anachronistic, and reviving it risks
a vulgar theology. If incarnation can at all take place, it must be "in
paraphrase," through a constituting fiction:

> But, after all, we bookish people live
> In bondage to those reigning narrative
> Conventions whereby the past two or three
> Hundred years have seen a superhuman
> All-shaping Father dwindle (as in Newman)
> To ghostly, disputable Essence or
> Some shaggy-browed, morality-play bore
> (as in the Prologue to Faust). Today the line
> Drawn is esthetic. One allows divine
> Discourse, if at all, in paraphrase.
>
> (CLS, 348)

Writing in a late cultural moment, the poet has to deal with the
entire linguistic baggage of the past: its set forms, textual protocols,
and verbal habits. Given that endless discourse prior to his own,
Merrill invokes his muse within "reigning narrative/Conventions"
that for several centuries have pushed divine "presence" little by little to the margins of things. His complaint repeats Olson's own angst

about poetry's discursive status in the postmodern era. But like Olson's sacrifice to the word, Merrill accepts the death of God as the (a)theology of deconstruction, as the birth of writing.

Although language is fallen, Merrill nonetheless employs its discursive resources in a powerful cultural critique of aesthetic and scientific formalisms. In *The Changing Light* he dethrones the privileged status of the high modern verse epic. Moreover, through dialogic satire, Merrill unmasks science as fictive narration. "I think science," he says, "is a visionary landscape in the twentieth century and was even in the nineteenth. . . . I suppose the point would be to show or to somehow open the possibility that classical myths and the scientific myths are really one and the same. They're talking about the same things in different ways."[3] At the very moment science would transcend narrative, aspiring to some wholly disinterested or "ideal" knowledge, it is always already a textual enterprise. By bringing literature and science into dialogue, the trilogy foregrounds the discursive language games underwriting their cultural power.

Incarnations and Withdrawals

DABBLING IN the occult—the poet's "Thousand and One Evenings Spent / With David Jackson at the Ouija Board" (CLS, 4)—has conjured an improbable yet successful "divine" fiction. Apparently the two mediums take dictation from their cast of familiars in the red dining room of Merrill's home in Stonington, Connecticut. The poet then edits the transcripts in an adjoining blue room, supplementing the uppercase text of the dead with his own lowercase commentary. The trilogy's format is based on the Ouija board. Each section of *Ephraim* follows a letter of the alphabet; similarly, the board's arabic numerals form the sections of *Mirabell,* while its words "yes" and "no" plus its ampersand shape the major sections of *Scripts.* According to David Jackson, Merrill's long-time companion and collaborator on the Ouija transcripts, the two made contact with Ephraim, their spiritual guide, in August of 1955. A parodic version of Dante's Virgil, "E" in Merrill's myth is a Greek Jew who was executed by Tiberius in the first century for seducing Caligula, the emperor's nephew. At first he serves as a kind of otherworldly Deep

Throat who leaks the cosmic system of the afterlife to the "rover boys." Later we learn that he is, in fact, an incarnation of Michael, the archangel of light who plays a guiding role in the lessons of *Scripts*.

Heaven, Ephraim reveals, is not unlike a modern Kafkaesque bureaucracy, embodying nine levels in an ascending hierarchy. Divine "patrons" at various stages oversee the spiritual progress of their human "representatives" through numerous incarnations. Merrill's own patron, for example, was formerly a nineteenth-century editor of the writings of Alexander Pope, which explains *The Changing Light*'s neoclassical nuances. While Eliot had little use for such parlor games—maligning them in "The Dry Salvages" as merely the "usual / Past times and drugs, and features of the press"[4]—the romantic tradition, especially Blake's Prophetic Books and Yeats' *A Vision*, offer powerful precedents for Merrill's occultism. Borrowing from Blake's "The Mental Traveller," Yeats held that "Solitary men in moments of contemplation receive . . . the creative impulse from the lowest of the Nine Hierarchies, and so make and unmake mankind, and even the world itself, for does not 'the eye altering alter all'?"[5] Less visionary than either Blake or Yeats, however, Merrill at once revives and lampoons their leanings toward the mythic imagination.

In negotiating what Robert Pinsky derides as "the romantic persistence," the poet eludes the rhetorical trap of confessional "talk" poetry.[6] He finesses the often deadpan, colloquial style of James Wright's and Robert Bly's emotive verse by drawing on the ludic resources of equivocation. Merrill's interviews sum up the triology's verbal strategy. Echoing the format of *Scripts,* Merrill evades the question of literal belief with a typical Janus-like response: "Yes and No. I simply couldn't say. . . . As Yeats said, when you are caught up in it you believe in it wholeheartedly; when you cool off you see it as a stylization of various things in your experience or in the world's experience" (JMH, 31, 30). Like every other playful gloss in the trilogy, such a casual allusion to Yeats seems so effortless that one might almost miss Merrill's tactic of framing his precursor as an object of camp consumption. Even the poet's most marginal commentary on *The Changing Light* reproduces in miniature the grand strategy of deflating what Yeats called "monuments of unaging intellect" to the camp status of, say, a Flash Gordon comic, a Busby Berkeley spectacle, or a Bellini opera.[7]

The camp aesthetic, as Susan Sontag defined it in the early 1960s, is the last refuge of aristocratic dandyism in mass culture. Beyond what is merely precious or kitsch, the truly camp aesthetic, she says in "Some Notes on Camp," possesses "the proper mixture of the exaggerated, the fantastic, the passionate, and the naive."[8] Camp valorizes the artificial, the decorative, and the theatrical over what is merely "natural." Meaning, literally "to posture boldly," it is the art of the *poseur*: parodying what is properly passé, old fashioned, démodé. Along with Jewish moral seriousness, Sontag praises camp as a "pioneering force" in modern life, particularly so in the gay community. Playfully ironic and elegantly off-beat, camp is highly congenial to what Robert K. Martin calls, for lack of a better term, the "gay sensibility."[9] As a Greek Jew, Merrill's Ephraim is, of course, a figure for just such a fusion of Hellenistic wit and Hebraic sobriety. Yet while Sontag limits camp to what is strictly "frivolous" and "disengaged, depoliticized—or at least apolitical" ("Some Notes on Camp," p. 107), Merrill employs the camp aesthetic in a more socially mediated performance. In *The Changing Light,* camp satire functions as a political critique of various brands of formalism: aesthetic, religious, and scientific.

Verbal wit, sarcasm, lampoon, burlesque, parody, and black humor have always served revolutionary ends—overturning hierarchies among literary genres and subverting the wider hegemony of cultural discourses. Bakhtin's study of carnival humor in Rabelais, for example, traces its origins back to the fool's witty disruptions of ecclesiastical authority in medieval fabliaux. Whether camp or carnivalesque, the comic masks writers adopt deploy the force of satire dialogically. "They grant the right," Bakhtin writes, "*not* to understand, the right to confuse, to tease, to hyperbolize life; the right to parody others while talking, the right to not be taken literally . . . the right to act life as comedy and to treat others as actors, the right to rip off masks."[10] Not just a frivolous game, camp satire permits Merrill to exploit the broader powers of critique offered by the epic form. At the same time, the camp style also gives Merrill a way of interrupting the epic's traditionally didactic impulse. Differing, for example, from the devoutly puritan John Milton, Merrill is not at all interested in justifying the ways of God to men. Such humanizing impulses, however consoling, are too ideologically loaded in the twentieth century and, as in Eliot's God of Thunder, simply foster master narratives of cultural domination. Like much poststructuralist writing, Merrill's ludic textuality is designed to baffle and disperse the windy platitudes of the Western humanist tradition.

Many of Merrill's readers, however attentive to the poem's allusive range, actually ignore the verbal texture of equivocation that hedges the poet's "divine" mythology. Arguably, such critical oversights are not entirely innocent. Seeking to anchor Merrill's trilogy in traditional canons of epic and elegiac literature, several critics privilege and thus reproduce the very history and status of the "literary" that Merrill sets out to debunk. These appeals to Merrill's literary heritage lend authority to his enterprise but are necessarily blind to his more playful unraveling of traditional forms. Peter Sacks, for example, grounds The Changing Light in the elegiac line of Osiris, Adonis, Dionysus, Orpheus, Persephone, Plato, Milton, and others. Yet Sacks' failure to reflect critically on Merrill's subversion of such literary touchstones leads him to misconstrue the poem as a literal ritual of "intellectual ascent, guaranteeing spiritual resurrection."[11] Willard Spiegelman similarly mystifies Merrill's long poem. Borrowing a romantic model from M. H. Abrams, Spiegelman misreads the trilogy as a circuitous journey toward transcendence.[12] This same desire to invest The Changing Light with a myth of unity leads David Lehman to view the Ouija transcripts as "invitations extended to the divine unknown."[13] Merrill's ludic errancy escapes these critics even as they try to prop up The Changing Light's divine myth. Uniformly, such readings legitimate the trilogy by claiming that it rests on universal and ideal foundations of belief.

But Merrill treds an ontological path quite different from the circuitous journey of German idealism.[14] In fact, his understanding of "truth" more closely parallels Heidegger's thinking in "On the Essence of Truth." Here Heidegger reconsiders truth in light of the historicity of the modern epoch. Breaking with Christian theology, Heidegger does not think of truth as the adequation of things or events to ideas preconceived in the mind of God. Nor is truth wholly propositional: it cannot be grasped through rational understanding (*veritas est adequatio intellectus et rei*). Rather, "the essence of truth," says Heidegger, "is freedom": a "letting be" that allows beings to come toward us (*An-wesen-lassen*). Such a phenomenological openness "lets beings be the beings they are." But in possessing truth as freedom, we are "possessed" by an otherness: "Man does not 'possess' freedom as a property. At best, the converse holds: freedom, ek-sistent, disclosive Da-sein possesses man."[15] Moreover, the disclosure of beings (*a-letheia*) also entails a forgetting (*lethe*) of beings. Truth and error ek-sist equiprimordially: even as we turn toward, we are turned back from the mystery of beings. Thus the essence of truth, for Heidegger, is necessarily errant.[16]

Significantly, Heidegger's notion of truth as "possession" and "errancy" sheds light on Merrill's occult poetics. As medium, Merrill is "possessed" by that open region where he notes both "The incarnation and withdrawal of / A god" (CLS, 3). The *via negativa* of divine withdrawal is as central to Merrill's aesthetic as Keats' negative capability is for Charles Olson's. Merrill writes a long poem that is, in Olson's idiom, "post-humanist": a work whose "truth" parts company with the Western humanist tradition. Not incidentally, language is the ground for their inscriptions of errancy's (a)theology. The trilogy's movement, Merrill says in *Scripts for the Pageant,* is from "Romance to Ritual" (CLS, 319). But its "truth" is immanent in its textual withdrawals. The strategy in *The Changing Light* is to resist and dismantle mystified representations of the divine through the poet's errant medley of choral passages.

The trilogy's vision of heaven, for example, is blurred by the differing accounts of Merrill's dramatis personae. Such a polyphony of voices both insists on and debunks the afterlife's transcendental aura. To the dreaming Maya Deren of section M, heaven appears as a radiant ballroom: "a blaze / Of chandeliers, white orchids, silver trays / Dense with bubbling glassfuls" (CLS, 44). Similarly, in *Scripts* an awed WHA describes Michael, the archangel of light, in the same splendor:

A GREAT ORIGINAL IDEA   A TALL
MELTING SHINING MOBILE PARIAN SHEER
CUMULUS MODELED BY SUN TO HUMAN LIKENESS
            .   .   .   .   .

O IT WAS A FACE MY DEARS OF CALM

INQUIRING FEATURE FACE OF THE IDEAL
PARENT CONFESSOR LOVER READER FRIEND
(CLS, 286)

Ephraim, however, keeps a sarcastic distance from these kinds of ecstatic witnessings, describing Maya's vision as "a low-budget / Remake—imagine—of the *Paradiso*" (CLS, 45). In *The Changing Light* grace itself, instead of bestowing an unmediated ecstasy, withdraws in a parody of Pope's neoclassical chain of being, described in "Essay on Man." The afterlife, according to Ephraim, is simply an officious corporate bureaucracy. Its moral order is "post-humanist," functioning through forces beyond good and evil. There, power "kicks upstairs those who possess it, / The good and bad alike" (CLS, 54). Moreover, in section C, Ephraim betrays a somewhat demonic penchant for playing practical jokes on the uninitiated. Because he is willing to "SLIP THE SOULS / LIKE CORRESPONDENCE INTO PIGEONHOLES" (CLS, 20), he exploits the "rover boys" as midwives to his "representative," Wendell Pincus, in section F. He flaunts at once his complicity as a patron in heaven's bureaucracy, described as Kafkaesque in section I, and his worldly savvy in finessing its Law.

Such sharply contested versions of life "beyond the grave" (CLS, 15) actively resist the New Critical desire to master textual difference through unifying schemes of irony, paradox, and ambiguity. Instead, the idea of the afterlife in *The Changing Light* is dispersed across an undecidable network of narrative contradictions. Nor does the trilogy restore a more humanizing vision of the self and its lyric optimism. *Ephraim* records the rover boys' declining relationship from 1955 to 1974 and their attempts to work through the deaths of several close friends, lovers, and immediate family members. DJ's parents, in particular, have rendered life "A death's head to be faced" (CLS, 41). Their retirement to section Y's "senior / Citizen desert ghetto" (CLS, 88) stands as an unsettling emblem of American consumer society. The days of their lives mime the sorry drama of pop soap operas: "Before talk show or moon walk, when at length / The detergent and the atrocity / Fight it out in silence" (CLS, 88). *Ephraim*'s bleak confessional surface is further tainted by America's tawdry cultural failures of the 1970s. Life, in section L, is reduced to a seamy tabloid of America's bankrupt political scene. In Merrill's metaphor, "Life like the periodical not yet/Defunct kept hitting the stands" (CLS, 40). The only respite Merrill finds in the 1970s from the demoralizing revelations of Watergate is communion with his familiar spirit: "Impeachment ripens round the furrowed stone/Face of a storyteller who has given/Fiction a bad name (I at least thank heaven/For my executive privilege vis-à-vis/Transcripts of certain private hours with E)" (CLS, 41).

As a familiar spirit, Ephraim compensates the lovers, offering a redemptive identity beyond the failures of both their personal and cultural lives: "Will figures of authority/Who lived like Mallarmé and Montezuma,/So far above their subjects as to fear/Them not at all, still welcome us inside/Their thought?" (CLS, 57). The couple's *folie à deux,* their desire for "figures of authority," is answered in the specular image of Ephraim:

> Despite our insights (Section *I*) we fall
> Back on the greater coziness of being
> Seen by him, and by that very seeing
> Forgiven for the spectacles we've made
> Of everything, ourselves, the world, the mud
> Gullies skipped over, rut on trickling rut,
> All in the name of life. *Life?* Shh. En route.
> (CLS, 38)

Ideally, Ephraim's visionary charisma should dispel the "spectacle" of the lovers' lives, leading them to invest in a more ideal role model. But section I's visit to Merrill's psychiatrist raises the spectre of the "Father Figure" who "shakes his rod/At sons who have not sired a child" (CLS, 30). Following Lacan's well-known revision of Freud, one could read Merrill's *folie à deux* as an oedipal drama, one that initiates the poet into language. That is, the father as an agent of language—his "rod" arguably stands for the phallus as signifier—compels Merrill to abandon the *imaginary* consolation Ephraim offers: "the coziness of being/Seen by him" and thus given a bounded, fixed identity. Moving beyond the specular unity of the imaginary, Merrill comes to view the self as in process—"En route"—and shaped by the agency of the letter, "the name of life." Jettisoning his imaginary investment in Ephraim, Merrill advances into a more *symbolic* register of linguistic transaction that the Ouija board bestows.[17]

Merrill's Textual Medium

SEVERAL OF Merrill's critics have discussed the Ouija board as an obvious symbol for language. But most humanize and normalize language's place in the poem.[18] Subordinating language to the imagination leads David Lehman to a somewhat mystified reading. "And what else," he asks, "is the Ouija board if not a clear though audacious metaphor for language as the source of death-defying poetry?"[19] Merrill's vision of language, however, is not always this ideal. Often he will overturn language's expressive and mimetic roles, allowing the word actively to shape self and world. As "scribe" to the Ouija board, Merrill's authorial role serves as a kind of medium for language—not the other way around. Like Merwin's lyric verse and Olson's long poetry, Merrill's trilogy undermines the emotive self as the privileged source of poetic expression. He renounces what Olson describes as "lyrical interference."[20] The author, instead of coming before and voicing the work, is more a function of sheer linguistic production in the trilogy: "We, all we knew, dreamed, felt and had forgotten, / Flesh made word, became through [Ephraim] a set of / Quasi-grammatical constructions which / Could utter some things clearly, forcibly, / Others not" (CLS, 31).

Textuality itself, as "flesh made word," unseats the author's mastery over writing. Not incidentally, Merrill's role as medium is mediated by the vast discursive network from which he writes. Staging literary tradition as camp spectacle, he prefaces *Scripts* with a cast of authorial personae and presents an expanded "guest list" of the distinguished dead in his "Coda: The Higher Keys." The poet's sources have already been noted at length: Auden, Blake, Congreve, Dante, Milton, Pope, Proust, Stevens, and Yeats, among others. But critical readings of *The Changing Light,* still largely limited to standard New Critical influence studies, have failed to grasp Merrill's more subversive textuality.[21] In the trilogy's choral polyphony of authorial voices and textual echoes, even the most intimate lyric utterance is never wholly personal but always already saturated by a broad linguistic economy of other writing.

Mirabell's scientific metaphor of "cloning" further parodies the poet's role as a textual medium. In Merrill's myth, literature, like all other cultural labor, serves the Heavenly V, whose "WORK MUST SING OUT/PAEANS TO THE GREENHOUSE" (CLS, 216) of God Biology. In the trilogy's fictional hierarchy, God Biology oversees the work of the Heavenly V. Throughout their many lifetimes, they guide the growth of religion, art, and science. Texts, as "V work," are engineered from a vast stock of verbal codes. Thus, we find in Book 6 that *The Waste Land* was a "greenhouse" hybrid, "cloned" from a linguistic hodgepodge gleaned from the discourse of Eliot, Pound, and Rimbaud. One's language, Merrill learns: "LIVES BY THESE FREQUENT CONTACTS WITH YR OWN & OTHERS' WORK" (CLS, 219). The composition of *The Changing Light* likewise assumes an unsettling autonomy as Mirabell informs Merrill that "I AM MERELY USING YR WORD BANKS" (CLS, 237). Such decenterings of the lyric self shape the poet's identity according to the radical agency of the letter.

Yet the fact that "THE REVEALD MONOTHEISM OF TO-DAY IS LANGUAGE" (CLS, 239) is not entirely consoling. As poet, Merrill finesses the theological impulse that would tie textuality to some transcendent ideal. Quite early in *Ephraim,* he resists Yeats' desire for the kind of "unity of being" that binds *A Vision* into a "maze of inner logic, dogma, dates" (CLS, 14). Instead, Merrill's mentor is Henry James, "that past master of clauses/whose finespun mind 'no idea violates'" (CLS, 14). Parodying Eliot's praise of James, Merrill's appeal to canonical authority is itself marked by camp deflation.[22] Because signified meaning is produced, not merely reflected, in discourse, it is susceptible to the poet's own linguistic unravelings. Similarly, for Merrill, thought itself, normally considered as originary or ideal, comes after language's ludic illuminations:

> Hadn't—from books, from living—
> The profusion dawned on us, of "languages"
> Any one of which, to who could read it,
> Lit up the system it conceived?—bird-flight,
> Hallucinogen, chorale and horoscope:
> Each its own world, hypnotic, many-sided
> Facet of the universal gem.
>
> (CLS, 31)

In *Mirabell,* the poet is reminded that language constitutes our cultural world. That dwelling of the word, moreover, is not ideal but wholly material: "MANS TERMITE PALACE BEEHIVE ANT-HILL PYRAMID JM," says 741, "IS LANGUAGE" (CLS, 118). Everything that illuminates *The Changing Light* with a charmed metaphysical aura—its myth of the afterlife, soul, consciousness, even poetic sensibility—follows from language's symbolic order.

Merrill's critics, despite his explicit leanings toward textuality, often try to contain and domesticate the political force of his writing within the more acceptable range of high modernist aesthetics. Helen Vendler, for example, normalizes the trilogy so as to blunt *Ephraim's* cultural critique: "Like Proust and Nabokov, two other sensibilities more attached to the Beautiful than to the Scientific, the Philosophical, the Ethical, or the Ideological, Merrill avoids being polemical or committed, in the ordinary sense of those words" (*Part of Nature, Part of Us,* p. 217). Throughout the trilogy, however, Merrill taps poetry's dialogic resources to undermine high modernism's aesthetic closure. The early careers of Eliot, Pound, and Yeats celebrated an emergent poetics—a literary vortex that would, in the idiom of Wyndham Lewis, "blast" away the literary malaise of *fin de siècle* English decadence and thus inaugurate a revolutionary modernist aesthetic. After World War I and throughout the 1920s, however, they fled from what Yeats indicted as the "blood-dimmed tide" of anarchy. Attempting to salvage the modern wasteland, each retreated finally into dubious schemes of cultural and political elitism. On the face of it, Merrill's crucial turn from the largely confessional focus of *Ephraim* to a wider cultural project seems to repeat their later politics. He seems to fall into a typically American pattern, that of, for example, Whitman's move beyond the existential immediacy of the 1855 and 1860 editions of *Leaves of Grass* toward the more cosmic revisions of 1891–1892. The forces of social change pressure American poets out of a poetics open to history's own emergent process, toward some more consoling mythology.

But Merrill's critical hindsight on the failure of modernism to transcend history cautions him against such epic conservatism. The epic, after all, is the genre *par excellence* of ideological narration, typically commemorating a people's founding moment, national myths, and heroic ideals. Merrill's trilogy, however, by virtue of its errant textuality, cuts across the grain of such foundational themes, thus opening epic to the more playful and camp discourse of contemporary pop culture. Unlike Yeats' vision of an all-embracing "unity of being," Merrill's project is to craft an antiepic: a long poem that undermines any ideal harmony among literature, science, and religion. The strategy is both to work within fixed forms and to "err" from past conventions. Although many of Merrill's critics would like to invest *The Changing Light* with canonical and, in some cases, even divine authority, the trilogy more radically dismantles the foundational status the epic normally enjoys. Merrill, it is true, does exploit epic as an arena in which to showcase his technical mastery of elite fixed forms. The trilogy incorporates, for example, syllabic verse (ten-syllable uppercase lines for the distinguished "dead," and fourteen for his spiritual mentors), blank verse, heroic couplets, terza rima, sonnet sequences, Spenserian stanzas, a ballade, a villanelle, and a canzone variation. Moreover, he fuses *Scripts'* closet drama, a high art form traditionally written against the lower forms of burlesque and melodrama, with comic opera.

Such masterful generic conflations are subverted, however, by Merrill's radically bizarre method of composition that he flaunts in the very structuring of *The Changing Light*. By inmixing epic with the more marginal discourses of science fiction, the occult, opera buffa, and so on, *The Changing Light* plays out the present struggle of discursive forces contending for cultural hegemony. Subverting the epic tradition in this way, Merrill checks the high modernist drift toward cultural domination. Yet surprisingly, the sense of relevance Helen Vendler finds in Merrill's work—that, as she says, he is "writing down your century, your generation, your language, your life" (*Part of Nature, Part of Us,* p. 205)—is often misunderstood by the poet's reviewers. Clara Claireborne, for example, praises the trilogy as an exemplary synthesis of "science and poetry, past and present, public and private, cosmic and domestic, the living and the dead."[23] This kind of reading, however attuned to Merrill's eclectic range of subjects, is nonetheless blind to his stylistic subversion of such a reconciling humanism.

In *The Changing Light,* "high art" goes out on the limb of pop theology, as in this complaint to the poet's avuncular familiar, W. H. Auden:

Dear Wystan, VERY BEAUTIFUL all this
Warmed-up Milton, Dante, Genesis?
This great tradition that has come to grief
In volumes by Blavatsky and Gurdjieff?
Von and Torro in their Star Trek capes,
Atlantis, UFOs, God's chosen apes—?
Nobody can transfigure junk like that
Without first turning down the rheostat
To Allegory, in whose gloom the whole
Horror of Popthink fastens on the soul,
Harder to scrape off than bubblegum.

. . . . .

        Some judgment has been passed
On our intelligence—why else be cast
Into this paper Hell out of Doré
Or Disney?

                                (CLS, 136)

The trilogy's pop theogony, cast here in heroic couplets, comprises an audacious blend of Milton, Dante, and Star Trek. Merrill's baroque parody of science fiction opens epic to the whole cultural spectacle that would enshrine UFOs, trance channellers, extraterrestials, Atlanteans, and the rest in a new contemporary mythology. In *Mirabell* Ephraim's role as a narrator and spiritual guide passes to an unlikely figure, literally a number: "741." Briefly, in Merrill's myth centaurlike creatures populated earth's "first" world, but were gradually supplanted by a race of intellectual beings of whom 741 is a surviving remnant. These entities created an angelic world moored to the earth by giant cables that over time fell into disrepair. Both races perished in the ensuing cataclysm, ushering in more elemental white and dark beings that dwell in conflict "WITHIN THE ATOM." According to 741, God Biology and "Queen Mum"—Mother Nature—shape at the atomic level the struggle between the forces of order and chaos, evolving matter and entropic antimatter. The "Heavenly Five," a group of lesser deities, oversee earth's evolution through their "V" work in God Biology's Research Lab. History's various geniuses and spiritual luminaries—Plato, Galileo, Blake, Einstein, and so on—are representatives of the same "Deathless 5."

The strategy in *Mirabell* is quite simply to expose the epic tradition to "the whole / Horror of Popthink." That mix of elite and mass culture is dictated, in part, by the poet's rhetorical situation. Merrill's textuality negotiates the pragmatic forces of what Auden in the trilogy describes as two conflicting audiences:

DANTE'S LUCK LAY IN HIS GULLIBLE
& HEAVENLY WORLD   WE MY BOY DRAW FROM 2
SORTS OF READER: ONE ON HIS KNEES TO ART
THE OTHER FACEDOWN OVER A COMIC BOOK.
OUR STYLISH HIJINKS WONT AMUSE THE LATTER
& THE FORMER WILL DISCOUNT OUR URGENT
    MATTER

(CLS, 147)

Clearly, Merrill is not entirely satisfied with his rhetorical options. While skeptical about the epic's contemporary relevance, he is as uneasy with writing a long poem mired in a public world of "Popthink." On the one hand, Merrill wants to return epic to a broad popular audience. On the other hand, he takes care to preserve those elite aesthetic forms that might serve to alienate readers from the ideological forces of American consumer society.

Under advanced capitalism, as Lucien Goldmann and Adorno argued, progressive art may well seem elitist to a mass audience largely conditioned to the rule of the commodity form and profit motive. Late in his career, Marcuse reached this same conclusion:

If "the people" are dominated by the prevailing system of needs then only the rupture with this system can make "the people" an ally against barbarism. Prior to this rupture there is "no place among the people" which the writer can simply take up and which awaits him. Writers must rather first create this place, and this is a process which may require them to stand against the people, which may prevent them from speaking their language. In this sense "elitism" today may well have a radical content . . . Revolutionary art may well become "The Enemy of the People."[24]

While Marcuse aids our understanding of how aesthetic "elitism" can muster revolutionary resistance to commodity culture, his tendency to privilege art as an autonomous zone, somehow above or outside more secular discursive modes, cannot adequately grasp Merrill's dialogic transactions with a complex network of discourses, each affiliated with particular social contexts. Split by the contemporary struggle of elite and secular cultures, Merrill is denied the traditional consolations of aesthetic decadence. He can no longer rely on art—as could Huysmans, Pater, or Wilde—to dispel or escape from the spreading "Popthink" and junk-space of consumer society. Rather than resolve those "readerly" tensions, his strategy is, in Roland Barthes', idiom more "writerly."[25] Merrill deftly negotiates the edge between high and pop art through the parodic stylistics of camp reference. Moving beyond the conservative aesthetics of high modernism and the Frankfurt School alike, Merrill at once passionately asserts and playfully deflates the poet's cultural authority.

"ALL GOOD DISCOURSE," the archangel Michael dictates in *Scripts,* "MUST, LIKE FORWARD MOTION, / KNOW RESISTANCE" (CLS, 414). Merrill has taken this maxim seriously, for the languages of *The Changing Light* describe a latticework of internal resistances. On the one hand, the logic of his cultural myth demands "The baldest prose / Reportage . . . that would reach / The widest public in the shortest time" (CLS, 3). On the other hand, the poet's lyric aestheticism denies that didactic charge. "Yet in these sunset years," Merrill informs us, he will "hardly propose / Mending my ways, breaking myself of rhyme / To speak to multitudes and make it matter" (CLS, 82).

Merrill finesses this rhetorical dilemma through a Derridean maneuver. *The Changing Light* inscribes a double mark, one that simultaneously overturns and transgresses the conventional difference between epic and pop art. By remaining both within and outside the textual norms he would dismantle, Merrill's strategy follows what Derrida describes as a "double science."[26] The tactic is to unmask the functional opposition between epic and popular literature while not necessarily valorizing one over the other. Epic maintains its center of cultural authority through a formal distance from the discourse of popular culture. Working within the epic tradition, however, Merrill submits this discursive opposition to his own playful sub-

version. He decenters the epic's generic privilege by rendering it susceptible to the rhetoric of "Popthink." Like *Maximus, The Changing
Light* negotiates an eclectic textuality through a poetics open to the
errancy of its own verbal process.

Science, Literature, and Other Linguistic Games

THE SAME strategy guides Merrill's critique of scientific idealism.
While somewhat put off by the "baldest prose/Reportage" of science's technical idiom, he responds to our moment's demand for
"POEMS OF SCIENCE" (CLS, 113). But instead of valorizing science as value-neutral inquiry, Merrill employs satire to unmask its
grounding in ideological narration. On the one hand, he is attracted
to the consolation of permanence, order, and certainty that science
seems to offer. On the other hand, he is skeptical about the modern
impulse to reduce history to the leveling norms of scientific "truth."
Ultimately Merrill reads scientific optimism as symptomatic of a
deeper repression of our moment's social and cultural failures. As a
result, he turns the cultural demand for "POEMS OF SCIENCE"
against itself. He unmasks science's desire to manage the anxious
record of postwar history. To begin with, Merrill's ambivalence toward science splits his sense of poetic vocation. As scribe to the
Heavenly "5," he is appointed to the heroic task of rescuing earth's
"greenhouse" with "THE LIFE RAFT LANGUAGE" (CLS, 119).
"THE SCRIBE'S JOB," he learns in *Mirabell*, "IS TO HELP SPEED
ACCEPTANCE / OF THE 5'S WORK" (CLS, 143). If language in
Merrill's myth has become "THE REVEALED MONOTHEISM
OF TODAY" (CLS, 239), then the poet is its chief hierophant. At
first, that vocation is a straightforward calling. But in *Mirabell* it
becomes unmanageably problematic. Given science's nuclear apoc-
alypse, the epic poet's didactic charge is so unsettling as to be futile.

Turning toward the atomic realm of God B, *Mirabell* takes as its
epigraph Laura Fermi's fateful account of her husband's pioneering
work in atomic fission. Merrill's opening supplants the epic's Homeric and Judeo-Christian pantheon with masters of modern science. The traditional hubris of the epic hero belongs in the twentieth
century to the atomic physicists, of whom Laura Fermi writes: "They

were the first men to see matter yield its inner energy, steadily, at their will" (CLS, 94). Merrill, however, cannot celebrate these technologic "first men." He is all too mindful of science's ideological and political ties that belie its claim to disinterested inquiry. Choosing the Manhattan Project as the site for his critique, Merrill probes science's ostensible aim of liberating humanity. Traditionally, science has sought legitimation through appeals to the life of the mind. The stated goal of scientific research, to foster the growth of knowledge into an ideal contemplative unity transparent to itself, ought to lead to the betterment of the human condition. But the hegemony of modern science, in our time, has brought us to the brink of extinction.

Fermi's willful appropriation of the atom's "inner energy" takes on a horrible irony from the hindsight of Hiroshima and Nagasaki. His science, instead of inaugurating a new age of progress, only revives an ancient spectre. J. Robert Oppenheimer's dreadful recognition of Shiva—"I am become Death, the destroyer of worlds"— echoes through Merrill's afterworld: "THE AIR/ABOVE LOS ALAMOS IS LIKE A BREATH/SUCKED IN HORROR TOD MORT MUERTE DEATH" (CLS, 33). Recalling the "vast image out of Spiritus Mundi" that Yeats envisions in "The Second Coming," the atomic mushroom cloud is a symbol of the same monstrous birth:

> Minutes nearer midnight. On which stroke
> Powers at the heart of matter, powers
> We shall have hacked through thorns to kiss awake,
> Will open baleful, sweeping eyes, draw breath
> And speak new formulae of megadeath.
> NO SOULS CAME FROM HIROSHIMA U KNOW
> EARTH WORE A STRANGE NEW ZONE OF ENERGY
> Caused by? SMASHED ATOMS OF THE DEAD MY DEARS
> News that brought into play our deepest fears.
>
> (CLS, 55)

Just as Yeats' "rough beast" possesses a "gaze blank and pitiless as the sun" (YVE, 402), so the brain-child of atomic physics regards the human with an awesome indifference. Beyond the sheer destructive power of nuclear weapons, the atom's "strange new zone of energy," for Merrill, is a demonic force. Hiroshima's "SMASHED ATOMS OF THE DEAD," he learns, are so traumatized as to be no longer viable for the soul's transmigrations.

While the legacy of Hiroshima haunts *Ephraim*, *Mirabell* and *Scripts* look forward to the future shock of genetic engineering. Already in Book F of *Ephraim*, Merrill considers how this new technology will unsettle the foundational assumptions of Western humanism. Witnessing genetic experiments with primates, he is introduced to *Ephraim's* "GREAT GENETIC GOD." Merrill's response to God Biology, however, is less reverent than critical. In fact, he deflates science's epic authority through camp parody. Here he playfully glosses *Paradise Lost* in staging the serpentine figure of DNA's double helix:

> Is DNA, that sinuous molecule,
> The serpent in your version of the myth?
>   Asking, I feel a cool
> Forked flickering, as from my very mouth.
> YES & NO THE ATOMS APPLE LEANS PERILOUSLY
>   CLOSE
> Drawn by an elation in the genes . . .
> THE ATOM GLIMPSED IS A NEARLY FATAL CONSUM-
>   MATION
>
> (CLS, 119)

In Merrill's ludic punning, nuclear science reaches fruition in the ATOMS APPLE—a metaphoric *pharmakon* that can both heal and poison. The poet plays with tropes of indeterminacy in the "forked" tongue of affirmation and denial. As Heisenberg has shown, merely observing matter's microcosmic fabric changes it. We can only gauge atomic forces through acts that alter the very processes we would measure. Our witnessing leaves a trail of material effects. Thus, "the atom glimpsed," for Merrill, is a fateful envisioning, because in simply reading DNA's "sinuous molecule" we recast the deep structures of the natural world.

Merrill playfully returns to this motif of the fall from natural grace in Lesson 9 of the "NO" section in *Scripts*. Here it is revealed that the libretto Auden and Kallman wrote for Igor Stravinsky's operatic version of *The Rake's Progress* in the 1950s is, in fact, an allegory for man's willful tampering with nuclear forces:

> NAT. NOW WHY DID I CHOOSE
> TO PLAY MOTHER GOOSE?
> FOR MAN MY HERO IS A RAKE!
> YES SENIOR POET, YOU SAW THAT & MORE:
> SAW NATURE AS HIS PASSION AND TOO OFT
> HIS WHORE.
> JM. Listen! That's where Shadow turns the clock
> Back for Tom—
> WHA. SO APT MY BOY THE BLACK
> OF TIME REVERSED & TOM OUR
> THREATENED ATOM
> JM. Don't tell me that's what you and Chester *meant?*
> WHY NOT! (Shushing all round) NO ACCIDENT
>   (CLS, 485)

Throughout Lesson 9, Merrill chooses the Spenserian stanza, a verse form traditionally employed to tie together key themes through three rhyming elements in the pattern *a b a b b c b c c*. Shelley in "The Revolt of Islam" and "Adonais" and Keats in "The Eve of St. Agnes" revived the form, utilizing its movement from iambic pentameter to the final alexandrine line for memorable, epigrammatic statements. Similarly, Merrill relies on the Spenserian stanza to depict the dialectic struggle between the forces of light, as embodied in the archangel Michael, and Gabriel's lessons in "ALL DEEP AND DIRE THINGS" (CLS, 410):

> *George* and *Wystan* diligently comply
> —To no avail. They look up. There's a glow
> Of vexed endeavor, too, in *Robert*'s eye:
> His script's been altered. Why does *Nature* so
> Frustrate us? Is Her mood both Yes and No?
> Or are there words of ours She will not say?
> Or is it that *Experience* must show

Up *Innocence?* that *Michael*'s airy way
With things will not quite wash on *Gabriel*'s holiday?

(CLS, 484)

Nature's "DEEP AND DIRE" truths in *Mirabell* pose fundamental challenges to the humanizing myths of bourgeois individualism. Standing before a model of DNA's molecular helix in the Boston Museum of Science, Merrill is struck by the sheer complexity of the universe we have so recently invaded:

22.vii. Boston Museum of Science
Studying a model (2.5
Cm. per anstrong) of the DNA
Molecule—a single turn blown up
Tall as a child
    .   .   .   .   .
        . . . the carbons
And nitrogens all interlinked on pins
But letter-perfect, purines, pyrimidines,
Mute intelligences that indwell
The chromosome and educate the cell . . .
Even grossly simplified, as here,
It's too much. Who by reference to this
3-D Metro map's infernal skeins
And lattices could hope to find his way?
Yet, strange to say, that's just what everyone
On Earth is promptly known for having done.

(CLS, 203)

Merrill's "infernal skeins" of DNA open onto a demonic scene: everywhere weaving the human order of things into a genetic latticework of otherness. The genetic codes which "indwell / The chromosome and educate the cell" deny any sense of personal identity. Loss of self in the "Metro map" of DNA's genetic metropolis is inescapable, for the soul is merely an "expendable force in meaning's growing molecule":

            . . . IF AS WE PRESUME GOD B'S
EYE PEERS DOWN THRU HIS MICROSCOPE AT THE
    SWIMMING PLANETS

U ON THE SLIDE CALLD EARTH MAY GUESS AT THE
SCALE OF YR LIVES:
LESS THAN THOSE LEAST PARTICLES THAT IN
ISOLATION DIE
EACH WITH ITS OWN STRANGENESS & COLOR &
CHARM A PRICELESS
IF EXPENDABLE FORCE IN MEANING'S GROWING
MOLECULE

(CLS, 210)

From the perspective of God B's "Research Lab," "What must at length be borne," Merrill realizes, "Is that the sacred bonds are chemical" (CLS, 209). Tracing out "his link with termite, bee, and ant" (CLS, 118), Merrill pursues the logic of genetic science to an inhuman conclusion. There, the scribe's hierophantic role is demonic.

The humanizing impulse that most of Merrill's critics bring to the trilogy domesticates his political assault on contemporary science. Such consoling readings are blind to the poet's bioethical critique of science's apocalyptic "RULE OF NUMBER": "THE NUMBERS OF/MAN IN PARADISE WILL BE DETERMINED BY THE LIMITS/HE SETS ON HIS OWN NUMBERS" (CLS, 247).[27] In Merrill's satire, vestiges of utilitarian thought lead to scientific ideologies of fascism: "Soul," JM learns, "falls into two/Broad categories" (CLS, 139). On the one hand is mass man—a genetic underclass made up of billions of "run of the mill souls." In Book 5, their lives are recycled as dross in the Research Lab's cosmic disposal. "The other soul," in contrast, "belongs to an elite:/At most two million relatively fleet/Achievers" (CLS, 139–40). Not surprisingly, the cultural supremacy of this "scientific" myth sanctions tyranny. In a telling lampoon of *Mirabell*'s neo-Malthusian myth, the poet is offered "the white man's burden" where "A MERE 2 MILLION CLONED SOULS LISTEN TO EACH OTHER WHILE/ OUTSIDE THEY HOWL & PRANCE SO RECENTLY OUT OF THE TREES" (CLS, 247). The same racist ideology espouses the regime of the gulag: "THE HITLERS THE PERONS & FRANCOS THE STALINS & THE/LITTLE BROTHER-LIKE AUTHORITIES ARE NEEDED EVEN/ALAS INEVITABLE IN A

SURVIVAL GREENHOUSE" (CLS, 188). Here Merrill launches a stinging satire against God B's "V" work as it leads to the same political hierarchy marking the high modernism of, say, Ezra Pound.

In such parodic passages, Merrill's role as epic scribe is double-edged. On the one hand, as medium he faithfully takes dictation from the reigning hegemonic discourse of our cultural moment. On the other hand, he systematically undermines the residual elitism that guides the new genetic technologies. On the one hand, he dutifully records that "SKINNER & THOMAS," as Mirabell informs him, ". . . ARE ALSO OURS" (CLS, 118). On the other hand, however, he unmasks the behavioral "utopia" of B. F. Skinner, and lampoons Lewis Thomas' *Lives of a Cell* as "One of a rash of nutty paperbacks" (CLS, 118). While admitting their power as key "representatives" of contemporary culture, Merrill shows how Skinner and Thomas project brave new worlds managed by bureaucratic technocrats. The strategy in *Mirabell* is to push God Biology's genetic scheme to its logical conclusion, in order to subvert its Spencerian argument.

Ideally, science should contribute to the life of the mind by offering certain disinterested and objective truths. Science asserts its validity through an appeal to verification grounded in empirical observation, rules of technical competency, and the formal manipulation of reality. The force of verification tends to invest science with an aura of authority that makes other forms of knowledge appear arbitrary and trivial compared with itself. But in the postmodern era, the conventional image of modern science as a stable, continuous, and valid body of knowledge has been called into crisis by, among other arguments, Thomas S. Kuhn's disruptive, revolutionary understanding of scientific paradigm shifts, by Paul Feyerabend's critique of scientific method, and by Jean-François is Lyotard's focus on scientific discourse as narrative performance.[28]

Lyotard, in particular, mounts a convincing critique of science's legitimation crisis in the postmodern age, arguing that scientific narration is simply one more field of "language games" among others. Reading science through Austin's performative linguistics, Wittgenstein's investigation of language games, and other cybernetic and communication theories, Lyotard exposes science's investment in power rather than truth. The strategy is to uncover the performative, social forces at work within scientific inquiry, shaping both its "pure" research and institutional practice. Science's recent disciplinary proliferation entails considerable performative pressure. The pragmatics of scientific research dictate that sheer agonistic, competitive innovation supplants the rule of "truth":

> To the extent that science is differential, its pragmatics provides the antimodel of a stable system. A statement is deemed worth retaining the moment it marks a difference from what is already known, and after an argument and proof in support of it has been found. Science is a model of an "open system," in which a statement becomes relevant if it "generates ideas," that is, if it generates other statements and other game rules. . . . Postmodern science—by concerning itself with such things as undecidables, the limits of precise control, conflicts characterized by incomplete information, *"fracta,"* catastrophes and pragmatic paradoxes—is theorizing its own evolution as discontinuous, catastrophic, non-rectifiable, and paradoxical. It is changing the meaning of the word *knowledge* while expressing how such a change can take place. It is producing not the known, but the unknown. And it suggests a model of legitimation that has nothing to do with maximized performance, but has as its basis difference understood as paralogy.[29]

The performative situation Lyotard describes here opens scientific idealism to its "other": the unknown, the catastrophic, the inexplicable. But equally important, Lyotard implicates scientific inquiry in the circulation of capital through a network of academic politics, grant institutions, corporate policies, and State bureaucracies. Given the pragmatic forces at play in this kind of support environment, science can hardly maintain its traditional legitimation through "disinterested" contributions to the life of the mind. On the contrary, its "knowledge" is always already involved in wider sociopolitical and cultural agendas.

Merrill, of course, is all too aware of science's complicity with power. He knows that science is as vulnerable to ideological manipulation as all other linguistic productions. Consequently, his textuality in *Mirabell* and *Scripts* unmasks science's rhetorical claim to ideal truth. As scribe, Merrill plays with the language games of science. Like Robert Bly's satiric assaults on bureaucratic neologisms and media jargon during the Vietnam War, Merrill's parodies function dialogically to subvert the discourse of contemporary science.

Some of Merrill's critics, however, misread his ludic satire as a kind of baroque self-indulgence, an effete version of *fin de siècle* art-for-art's-sake decadence. Although Merrill does possess a high camp sensibility, he seldom pursues humor as an end in itself. Nor do his trenchant witticisms resemble, for example, the solipsistic self-parodies of Prufrock's interior monologues. Rather, the trilogy's satiric edge probes the authority of our dominant cultural myths. Specifically, he mobilizes the force of his puns, burlesques, lampoons, and black humor in dialogic resistance to the bald reportage of contemporary scientific writing. Merrill's linguistic genius, however playful, presents a powerful subversion of the neologistic jargon that would reshape the world in the image of science's instrumental reason. "Opaque / Words like 'quarks' or 'mitochondria,'" he says, "Aren't *words* at all" (CLS, 110). His trilogy inhabits the rhetoric of scientific discourse in order to undermine and disrupt its narrative representations from within.

Mindful of his precursors' political entanglements in various hierarchic orders, Merrill lampoons science's technologic hegemony. He is skeptical, for example, of any utopian faith grounded either in genetic engineering or behavioral conditioning. He parodies that brave new world in "Lesson 1: Black Magic" of *Scripts:* "It's only a 'thinning process,' George? THE KEY / WORD IS ALPHA Yes, yes— 'Brave New World.' / MY BOY U GOT IT WHAT OF THE OMEGAS? / 3 BILLION OF EM UP IN SMOKE POOR BEGGARS? / Wystan, how *can* you?" (CLS, 442). Moreover, through the trilogy's several dramatis personae, Merrill satirizes the "instruction" he receives from W. H. Auden and Maria Mitsotaki in the new myths of science. Thus, the verbal punning of *Mirabell's* Book 3 lampoons the absurd cultural stereotypes that result from reading literary tradition in terms of biological determinism:

THE GREAT AGE OF FRENCH & ENGLISH PASTORAL
    POETRY
& FROM ITS ORIGIN ALL JAPANESE POETRY WAS
THE RESULT OF OUR EXPERIMENTS IN VEGETABLE

CLONING IT TOOK, & IS NOW A MAINSPRING OF
  THE JAP MIND
(HENCE THEIR PASSION FOR THE CAMERA:
  PHOTOSYNTHESIS)
YR CONFRERE TURNING BRUTALLY AGAINST HIS
  VEG NATURE
LOPPD OFF HIS OWN HEAD AS IF WITH A CANE
  AMONG TULIPS
  Mishima, yes . . . And Marvell was half tree?
  Sidney's *Arcadia* is really yours?

(CLS 151–52)

Merrill's hybrid discourse joins the technical idiom of photosynthesis to the pastoral worlds of Marvell, Sidney, and Mishima for bizarre comic effects. This verbal "cloning around" looks forward to Maria Mitsotaki's amusing lectures in the "&" section of *Scripts*. In "The Middle Lessons," she introduces *Scripts'* mythic, elemental characters—Michael (light) and Emmanuel (water)—in terms of science's "visionary landscape." Her "lesson" proves Merrill's point that "classical myths and the scientific myths are really one and the same": "THESE MYTHS THAT ANTECEDE ALL MYTH ARE COUCHED/IN DAUNTING GENERALITIES. FOR MICHAEL/SUN/READ: GENERATIVE FORCE. FOR GENERATIVE FORCE/READ: RADIATION TO THE BILLIONTH POWER/OF EXPLODING ATOMS. FOR EMMANUEL,/H $_2$ O" (CLS, 388). His satire deconstructs the rhetoric of science's "urgent matter." Robert Morse, for example, appears in Book 8 of *Mirabell* to offer this stylistic admonishment: "The real no-no/Is jargon, falling back on terms that smell/Just a touch fishy when the tide is low/'Molecular structures'—cup and hand—obey/'Electric waves'? Don't *dream* of saying so!" (CLS, 256). Clearly, Merrill's trilogy does not seek to recast science fiction as twenty-first-century theology. Rather, his satire would alert us to the danger of deifying contemporary science.

Dialogic satire is essentially a dramatic mode—one that opens a theatrical space in which to stage its critique of other genres and cultural discourses. Merrill's trilogy, likewise, leads to comic spectacle. Beginning with the private, elegiac encounters with death in

Ephraim, The Changing Light moves through the mythic theogony of science's "visionary landscape" in *Mirabell* toward *Scripts'* operatic pageant. Two of its major dramatis personae, W. H. Auden and Chester Kallman, as at once poets and librettists, provided Merrill with an important precedent for his own fusion of literature and comic opera. He was attracted to opera, he writes, for "the way it could heighten and stylize the emotions—a kind of absurdity dignified by the music, or transformed by the music" (JMH, 25). The various "lessons" of *Scripts* join the processional presentation of mythic themes, historical figures and their prologues to operatic modes: recitatives, lyric arias, duets, trios, and choral passages.

But this blend of two traditions, literature and music, is only one moment in *The Changing Light*'s wider traversal of generic and cultural boundaries. Jettisoning his earlier experiments with the *nouveau roman,* Merrill returns to verse but in an eclectic, virtuoso performance. He opens the aesthetic closure of the modern verse epic to his trilogy's postmodern pastiche. Like Charles Olson in *The Maximus Poems,* he conceives of the long poem as a textual zone that mobilizes shifting genre boundaries, leading into the social text of the contemporary American scene. *The Changing Light* deconstructs high art's hermetic insulation from popular culture. Broadening the trilogy's textual strategy, Merrill unmasks science as narrative performance. Finally, reading the discourse of science against its social text, he returns epic to the heart of contemporary cultural life.

PART III

The Social Text in Contemporary American Poetry

5.

From Silence to Subversion:
Robert Bly's Political Surrealism

Working within long, encyclopedic verse forms, Charles Olson and James Merrill at once depart from James Wright's lyric subjectivity and project Merwin's more discursive lyricism into extraliterary registers. Their dialogic negotiations with popular culture and other fields of writing on the one hand question the "literary" status of the American verse canon and, on the other hand, render social history susceptible to poetry's own linguistic powers of cultural critique. Thus, in Olson's and Merrill's textual practice, the contemporary verse epic functions more as a critical than an affective discourse. Similarly, in pursuit of America's social text, Robert Bly, Adrienne Rich, and Gwendolyn Brooks all exceed in different ways the emotive lyricism of the introspective subject. Each interrogates the bourgeois myth of the sovereign self to expose how the conventionally valorized doctrine of individual creativity actually interrupts and impedes poetry's verbal transactions with history. Each collapses the political and disciplinary boundaries dividing confessional verse from the public world as we know it. Experience itself in their writing is mediated by group praxis, while poetic expression emerges as a distinctively intersubjective, rather than solitary, act of the imagination.

In the 1950s, Robert Bly gained a popular following from his irreverent gibes that lampooned American New Criticism and the modernist agenda it espoused. Like Theodore Roethke, he waged a tireless campaign to promote his own literary fame. By the end of the decade, he regularly published fulminations against the Fugitives in his home-grown journal *The Fifties* (1958). "A Wrong Turning in American Poetry" (1963) summed up his quarrel with both the "generation of 1917"—Eliot, Pound, Moore, and Williams—and the later poets of 1947—Karl Shapiro, Robert Lowell, John Berryman, Randall Jarrell, and Howard Nemerov. In this essay Bly advertised his "subjective image" poetry as a corrective to modernism's "objective" and "scientific" milieu.[1] Collaborating with Wright in the late 1950s, he promoted a distinctively private and pastoral sensibility for American verse. His career's founding moment turned on a decisive break with America's urban present, dramatized in Bly's retreat from New York City to the family farm in rural Minnesota. His early "subjective" poetry not only takes this pastoral flight as its major theme but, more importantly, inscribes it as an immanent feature of its rhetorical forms and verbal style.

Not surprisingly, Bly's "subjective" polemic appealed to a whole generation of mainstream American critics who leaned toward an emotive poetics in a similar effort to unseat New Criticism.[2] Thus, Charles Altieri in *Enlarging the Temple* welcomed Bly's poetics of "radical presence" that "makes visible latent orders of being where nature and consciousness, existential facts and the metaphor or poetic image share the vital life."[3] But for the Frankfurt School theorists, the lyric desire for a consoling, natural presence before social experience was itself underwritten by deeper historical forces. For his part in "Lyric Poetry and Society," Adorno viewed the lyric's social reticence as a symptom of alienation:

> This demand, however, that of the untouched virgin word, is in itself social in nature. It implies a protest against a social condition

which every individual experiences as hostile, distant, cold, and oppressive. . . . The idiosyncrasy of poetic thought, opposing the overpowering force of material things, is a form of reaction against the reification of the world, against the rule of the wares of commerce over people which has been spreading since the beginning of the modern era—which, since the Industrial Revolution, has established itself as the ruling force in life.[4]

In reading lyric poetry as a socially mediated discourse, Adorno was careful to separate his approach from vulgar reductions to the poem's social viewpoint, its representation of social events or interests, or the author's biographical or psychic life. Instead, he called for an *immanent* critique of how verse inscribes the social in its linguistic content and poetic forms. In fact, he said, the more authentically a work embodies history, "the more the poem eschews the relation of self to society as an explicit theme and the more it allows this relation to crystallize involuntarily from within the poem" ("Lyric Poetry and Society," p. 61). In the postwar epoch, Bly's career offers a *prima facie* case for how the text of social history always already inhabits even the most intimate expressions of emotive verse. Thus, Bly's obsessive promotion of "subjective" images, now viewed from the vantage point of Adorno's critique, appears less as a visionary alternative to postwar history and more a symptom of resistance to it. Read in this way, the very mainstays of the deep image's pastoral surrealism, its authentic privacy and its psychic distance from everyday life, bespeak a profound unease with America's social milieu.

The Rhetoric of the Deep Image

THE DEEP image's repression of history is patent in much of Bly's verse, but particularly so in "Depression," published in Bly's first volume, *Silence in the Snowy Fields* (1962). The poem's political subtext is the dramatic spread of American agribusiness that, in the postwar decades, steadily supplanted the small family farmer with giant corporate growers. During the 1950s, the Eisenhower administration rolled back New Deal incentives to small rural farmers such as the health and social services offered through the Farm Security Administration and Rural Electrification Administration. Moreover, throughout the 1950s the American Farm Bureau Federation, and Soil Bank Program in particular, offered generous subsidies to large landowners. In addition, USDA research funds to major land-grant university research and extension programs fostered the growth of expensive high-tech machinery and new methods of capital-intensive farming. Burgeoning agribusiness also fed the chemical industry, which conceived a wide array of pesticides and herbicides, such as DDT, Malathion, Aldrin, Dieldrin, and Endrin, specifically targeted for the giant monoculture combines of the 1950s. It was not until Rachel Carson's devastating exposé *The Silent Spring* (1962) that Americans began to take the environmental impact of such methods seriously. During the 1950s, however, government and business interests waged a largely unchecked campaign to reify farming. The national mood was best summed up by former Secretary of Agriculture Earl Butz's terse dictum: "adapt or perish."[5]

Signs of Midwest agribusiness frequently mar Bly's pastoral landscapes, but "Depression" more radically inscribes industrial references on the body:

> I felt my heart beat like an engine high in the air,
> Like those scaffolding engines standing only on planks;
> My body hung about me like an old grain elevator,
> Useless, clogged, full of blackened wheat.
> My body was sour, my life dishonest, and I fell asleep.
>
> I dreamt that men came toward me, carrying thin wires;
> I felt the wires pass in, like fire; they were old Tibetans,
> Dressed in padded clothes, to keep out cold;
> Then three work gloves, lying fingers to fingers,
> In a circle, came toward me, and I awoke.
>
> Now I want to go back among the dark roots;
> Now I want to see the day pulling its long wing;
> I want to see nothing more than two feet high;
> I want to go down and rest in the black earth of silence.[6]

Divorced from nature, the poet wears the "dishonest" forms of alienated labor, embodied in stanza one's old grain elevator with its "scaffolding engines." Seeking to escape the "sour" and blighted harvest of agribusiness, Bly regresses back toward the deep psychic exotica of stanza two. But even in this dream world, the Old Tibetans of the mind are menaced and dispelled by "Three work gloves, lying fingers to fingers/In a circle." Bly, of course, desperately wants to escape the grim scene of Midwest agribusiness, and so represses it throughout the whole of the last stanza. Nonetheless, the poem's relation to history is "crystallized involuntarily," in Adorno's words, in what he would describe as an immanent feature of the poem's rhetorical makeup.

In "Depression," Bly's unrelenting assertion of the self compensates for the poem's failure to sustain the lyric myth of a world elsewhere. His anaphoric refrain—"I want to see nothing . . ./I want to go down"—is compulsive and, through its repetitive form, signals regression into what Freud theorizes in *Beyond the Pleasure Principle* as the "death instincts."[7] Significantly, no less than nine of the poem's fourteen lines open with "I" or "my." Wholly repressing America's contemporary scene, Bly can only possess visionary privacy finally in "the black earth of silence." These lines carry lyric autonomy to its logical end. The privacy of the subjective image can only be preserved, at last, through the mind's extinction. As "Depression" shows, the poet's early flight from modern middle-class values is profoundly blocked. Despite its lyric critique of America's commercial scene, the poem registers Bly's continuing investment in the mental habits and linguistic forms of bourgeois individualism.

This verbal shortcoming is something that Bly shares with much of American confessional and other brands of postwar "talk" poetry. The deep image's essentially conservative aesthetic, its transparent and seemingly unmediated verbal style, drains his writing in *Silence* of its discursive power. Like Wright, Bly banks on lyric authenticity. He wants to deploy the immediacy of voice, colloquial diction, subjective viewpoints, "natural" locales, and bucolic themes against American consumer culture of the 1950s. Ideally, his pastoral surrealism should blur the boundary separating psychic and political vision, thus freeing landscapes from the signs of reification. But like Wright's cloistral turn from the American present, Bly's pastoral blunts the incisive social critique otherwise registered in his verse. Frequently, the poet fails to craft rhetorical forms that resist advanced consumer capitalism. As "Depression" illustrates, his early work often stages merely a regressive flight from historical pressures.

Beyond disclosing the emotive plenitude of the deep image, Bly's portraits of the Midwest's sprawling agribusiness in poems such as "Depression," "Unrest," and "Awakening" escalated the political stakes of his writing. But more importantly, through translating Third World surrealists in the 1950s, he came to open his local project onto a broader, global critique of American multinational capitalism. Poems such as Pablo Neruda's "The United Fruit Company," for example, alerted Bly to the social injustice of corporate policies in Latin America. A growing critic of American foreign policy in the early 1950s, Bly fulminated against the policies of The United Fruit Company (now Standard Brands) in Guatemala. United Fruit, of course, was a fierce opponent of local minimum wage legislation and land reform throughout Central America. Responding to the 1953 nationalization of 234,000 acres of United Fruit land, the Eisenhower administration ordered a naval blockade of the Guatemalan coast. Moreover, then Secretary of State John Foster Dulles (a former member of the board of directors of United Fruit) and his brother Allen (CIA head and former president of the company) orchestrated a military coup installing pro–American Colonel Carlos Castillo Armas in 1954. The Armas regime, like those of Fulgenscio Batista in Cuba and Anastasio Somoza in Nicaragua, undermined land reform, voting privileges, and labor movements in an effort to foster a cheap pool of labor for American transnational business interests in the Third World.[8]

Silence shows the awakening to political consciousness that later guides Bly's writing in *The Light Around the Body* (1967) and *Sleepers Joining Hands* (1973). But *Silence*'s aesthetic distance from history drains the book of its political force. In "Poem Against the Rich," for example, he filters Third World imperialism through a mystified surrealism: "The rich man in his red hat/Cannot hear/The weeping in the pueblos of the lily,/Or the dark tears in the shacks of corn" (S, 27). Lines like these idealize poverty as a means to rarefied aesthetic vision. Here the poet evades the social abuses of advanced global capitalism by searching out "The tear inside the stone." Bly's failure to deal with political history in *Silence* became increasingly problematic as he faced the growing national crises of the mid-1960s. Little by little, he recognized that his subjective poetics was simply powerless to speak to the 1960s' political assassinations, urban race riots, and the Vietnam War. Responding to America's turbulent history, Bly fashioned a poetic discourse that moved the deep image into public registers. In his next book, *The Light Around the Body,* the poet renounced *Silence*'s solipsism and jettisoned its plain-spoken lyricism.

Cultural Poetics in the Vietnam Era

IN THE epigraph to *Silence* Bly featured Jacob Boehme's motto: "We are all asleep in the outward man." But in *The Light,* the poet's pastoral dream gives way to a commodified nightmare from which he struggles to awake. Consequently, Bly's next book underscores the constitutive role language plays in shaping political praxis. No longer pastoral, his surrealism adopts a subversive tone, often flouting the half truths and windy abstractions of bureaucratic propaganda. *The Light*'s opening epigraph, also from Boehme, modifies the struggle of inwardness with outwardness, now as a verbal clash: "For according to the outward man, we are in this world, and according to the inward man, we are in the inward world. . . . Since then we are generated out of both worlds, we speak in two languages, and we must be understood also by two languages" (L, 1). In his critical writings, Bly joins the discourse of outwardness to two ideological impulses: "These two strains—puritan fear of the unconscious and the business drive toward dealing in outer things—meet in our poetry to push out the unconscious" (WT, 40). Capitalism's business drive, in other words, reifies the deep image's lyric privacy within what is a public linguistic register.

In *The Light*'s second section, "The Various Arts of Poverty and Cruelty," Bly recognizes that his early pastoral rhetoric was already underwritten by the material culture it sought to transcend. As a result, he crafts the deep image now into a subversive discourse, one that would undermine what Boehme calls the "art and rationality" of outwardness. In "Come With Me," Bly moves beyond *Silence*'s "snowy field" into the junk-space of American consumer society.

There he finds the life of things everywhere driven by the reign of
the commodity form: "Come with me into those things that have
felt this despair for so long—/Those removed Chevrolet wheels that
howl with a terrible loneliness, . . ./Those shredded inner tubes
abandoned on the shoulders of thruways,/Black and collapsed bodies, that tried and burst,/And were left behind" (L, 13). Poems such
as "Come With Me" lament the leveling of the American scene by
planned obsolescence, the profit motive, spreading signs of consumerism, car culture, and the growing traffic between country life and
suburban sprawl.

Throughout the 1960s, Bly broadened this critique of reification,
thus resisting America's push for new economic frontiers in the Third
World and Southeast Asia. Faced with the apocalyptic scene of Vietnam, *Silence*'s pastoral aesthetic appeared increasingly bankrupt. By
the late 1960s, Bly was an outspoken critic of the war. Along with
David Ray, he organized American Writers Against the Vietnam War
in 1966. Orchestrating protest readings, demonstrations, and draft
card burnings, he assumed a viable public role in the antiwar movement. Moreover, he used his National Book Award acceptance speech
in 1968 to foster draft resistance. *The Light*'s antiwar poetry spearheaded this public commitment by probing the ideological forces
shaping American policy in Vietnam. In *The Light*'s third section,
"The Vietnam War," Bly's assault on the rhetoric of Third World
"pacification" was at once a local political action and a psychic critique of American manifest destiny.

To begin with, Bly's political project retrieves America's long-
standing desire to capitalize on virgin frontiers. In "Asian Peace Offers Rejected Without Publication," for example, he links military
escalation in Vietnam to a standard icon of westward expansion—
the railroad: "something inside us/Like a ghost train in the Rockies/
About to be buried in the snow!/Its long hoot/Making the owl in
the Douglas fir turn his head" (L, 30). This emblem of industrial
machinery recalls Thoreau's classic depiction of the steam engine's
predatory advance on the American wild: "The whistle of the lo-
comotive penetrates my woods summer and winter, sounding like
the scream of a hawk sailing over some farmer's yard, informing me
that many restless city merchants are arriving within the circle of the
town."[9] Following Thoreau, Bly depicts the railroad as shuttling be-

tween two worlds of experience. It operates as a line of metaphoric exchange between on the one hand the culture, politics, and economy of "restless city merchants," and on the other hand the wilderness of the American unconscious. Through metaphor, Bly fuses nature and culture into an imaginative spectacle. Like Hawthorne's schizophrenic dream of evil in "Young Goodman Brown," Bly's text elicits the scenic "otherness" of the American psyche. There, he witnesses what is anathema to the heritage of Western humanism:

> Tonight they burn the rice-supplies; tomorrow
> They lecture on Thoreau; tonight they move around the trees,
> Tomorrow they pick the twigs from their clothes;
> Tonight they throw the fire-bombs, tomorrow
> They read the Declaration of Independence; tomorrow they are
>   in church.
>
> (L, 5)

In such moments, the poet blurs the "natural" boundaries variously dividing forest and clearing, the night of the unconscious and the lecture hall's rational daylight, tonight's mayhem and tomorrow's justifying rhetoric. Through these uncanny fusions, he joins America's humanistic posturing to its more willful political praxis in the Third World.

Vietnam, of course, was the nation's first televised war, avidly promoted as a media spectacle by America's culture industry. Throughout the 1960s, the war's daily cruelties were instantly broadcast as a kind of grotesque national theatre. The atrocities appeared even more obscene in light of the weekly Pentagon reports of enemy body counts. Bly wrote "Counting Small-Boned Bodies," he says, "after hearing on radio and television, Pentagon 'counts' of North Vietnamese bodies found."[10] Bly's burlesque performance memorably registers the poet's outraged dissent from state propaganda:

> Let's count the bodies over again.
> If we could only make the bodies smaller,
> The size of skulls,
> We could make a whole plain white with skulls in the moonlight!

If we could only make the bodies smaller,
Maybe we could get
A whole year's kill in front of us on a desk!

If we could only make the bodies smaller,
We could fit
A body into a finger-ring, for a keepsake forever.

(L, 32)

In "Counting," black humor unmasks American consumer society, particularly its penchant for controlling data. Managerial efficiency, of course, is the hallmark of high technology under advanced capitalism. Bly's point is simply that today's sheer exchange of information is itself driven by the forces of reification. The poem's anaphoric refrain lampoons such communication management in a radically hyperbolic parody. The strategy is to estrange America's postwar "telecommunity" through the grim imagery of Vietnam body counts. The poet plays with the desire to tabulate a "whole year's kill" on a desktop or to view it neatly displayed, say, on your personal computer screen. Rereading Pentagon propaganda, Bly's strange persona offers a fateful "keepsake" that weds the war's dehumanizing scene to America's contemporary information economy.

In the early 1970s, Bly's long meditative poem, "The Teeth Mother Naked at Last" (1970), advanced his deep image dissent from Vietnam. Specifically, in it he deploys Jung's program of archetypal therapy as a political critique. Beyond working through the trauma of Vietnam, Bly more unflinchingly notes a personal investment in the sheer power of America's technologic will:

Massive engines lift beautifully from the deck.
Wings appear over the trees, wings with eight hundred rivets.

Engines burning a thousand gallons of gasoline a minute sweep
over the huts with dirt floors.

(SJH, 18)

In these lines, Bly joins America's war machinery to a deeper libidinal economy driven by the "Teeth Mother" archetype. Reminiscent of James Dickey's "Firebombing," such images describe the shocking knowledge of the Teeth Mother as ecstasy: as "the thrill that leads the President on to lie" (SJH, 21). The poem lays bare what Bly calls the "desire to take death inside" (SJH, 21). Significantly, in the preface to *Forty Poems Touching on Recent American History* (1970), he reflects on the psychic continuity of America's public and personal spheres: "It's clear that many of the events that create our foreign relations and our domestic relations come from more or less hidden impulses in the American psyche. . . . But if that is so, then the poet's main job is to penetrate that husk around the American psyche, and since that psyche is inside *him* too, the writing of political poetry is like the writing of personal poetry, a sudden drive by the poet inward."[11] Reading public history through the deep image, Bly views the racial upheavals of the late 1960s and Vietnam as symptoms of America's troubled political unconscious.

For many critics "Teeth Mother" is a controversial work whose high moral tone verges on the very propaganda it indicts. James F. Mersmann, for example, points out that some of Bly's assaults on the Johnson administration lapse into prosaic didacticism.[12] The poet's aim, however, is not just to mimic propaganda, but to set it in dialogue with the discourse of the deep image. Faithful to the text of Vietnam, Bly aims to unsettle the reader's unthinking complicity in administration propaganda.[13] "Like the Marxists with their notions of false consciousness," writes Charles Molesworth, "Bly posits a common awareness of mundane reality as something to be altered, and if necessary smashed, if we are to uncover the truth (and truth-revealing) relations that shape the polis and the psyche."[14] As Molesworth suggests, Bly deploys the spectacle of Vietnam so as to destroy official state myths of America's democratic mission in the Third World. More to the point, the poet stages his ideological critique through the linguistic resources of poetic discourse.

Ideologies as "world outlooks," according to Louis Althusser, represent "the imaginary relationship of individuals to their real conditions of existence."[15] Through language, ideologies solicit individuals as "subjects" for the material functioning of religious, corporate, and state institutions. Linguistic representation models the subject's attitudes, values, and self-image so as to mirror ideological "truth," now regarded as a "natural" given of everyday life. But by seizing on language as ideology's functional locus, Bly resists its power. His surrealism interrupts the verbal representations through which ideologies enlist subjects for political praxis. Deploying poetry as a linguistic force, Bly subverts the discursive work of America's oppressive domestic and foreign policies in the 1960s.

"Leaping" is the term Bly gives to surrealism's verbal fusions of conventionally unrelated things, images, and discourses.[16] Resting his verse on the depth psychology of Freud, Jung, and Neumann, Bly regards poetry as "something that penetrates for an instant into the unconscious." His surrealist tenet that "one thing is also another thing" (S, 30) enables his radical leaps of psychic association. But more importantly, Bly follows Spanish surrealism in employing such associative leaps in a political dialogue with the empty administration slogans that obscure a more willful praxis. The psychic resources of the deep image underscore the mendacities of bureaucratic rhetoric:

> "*From the political point of view, democratic institutions are being*
> *built in Vietnam, wouldn't you agree?*"
>
> A green parrot shudders under the fingernails.
> Blood jumps in the pocket.
> The scream lashes like a tail.
>
> "*Let us not be deterred from our task by the voices of dissent. . . .*"
>
> The whines of the jets
> pierce like a long needle.
> As soon as the President finishes his press conference, black
>   wings carry off the words,
> bits of flesh still clinging to them.
>
> (SJH, 20–21)

The "voices of dissent" could deter administrative policy only if they could be heard. The state, however, enforces its regime through verbal repression. Here Bly gauges the intent of bureaucratic language not in what it says but through its censored discourse. The strategy in "Teeth Mother" is both to mimic American propaganda and to voice what it cannot speak. Describing his political poetics in a 1976 interview, Bly says that "it would be wrong to use only part of our language, because in that way you'd be leaving out half of our world. So you have to try and enter that [bureaucratic] language as well as you can and bring it into the poem."[17] Talking back to administrative silences in the deep idiom of psychic association, Bly baffles and unmasks official state rhetoric. Such a dialogic fusion of the languages of our public and unconscious selves makes for a successful political poetics, one that speaks powerfully beyond the privacy of the lyric self.

Matriarchal Memory Within the Patriarchal Tradition

DURING THE Vietnam decades Bly's subjective aesthetic opened onto the social text of America's public scene. Offering the deep image as a counterstatement to bureaucratic rhetoric, he dissented from the republic's misadventure in Vietnam. Significantly, his political verse both eludes Wright's failed lyricism and takes Merwin's textuality into extraliterary domains. Less viable, however, are Bly's later attempts to elide history through a feminist poetics based in depth psychology. Working from the tradition of Johan Jacob Bachofen, Carl Jung, and Erich Neumann, Bly's feminist verse is contaminated by patriarchal representations that oppress even as they seek to celebrate feminine experience.

As Adrienne Rich has observed, Bly's nostalgia for a prepatriarchal *her*story actually distorts the historical experience of real women:

> This "feminine principle . . . " remains for such writers elusive and abstract and seems to have, for them, little connection with the rising expectations and consciousness of actual women. In fact, Marcuse and Bly might be likened to the Saint-Simonians and Shelley, who likewise insisted theoretically on the importance of the feminine, yet who betrayed much of the time their unconscious patriarchal parochialism.[18]

Such residual sexism, however consciously resisted, underlies Bly's reflections on matriarchy. At the root of this problem is the poet's reliance on Bachofen's *Mother Right* (1861). Briefly, Bachofen hypothesized three universal stages common to all cultures. The first is an oppressive period marked by male dominance and a lack of clearly defined systems of kinship, agriculture, and civil law. But with the rise of matriarchal rule, powerful women come to enjoy civil and religious authority. Bachofen, of course, identified the Golden Age of women's rule with monogamy, agriculture, the domestic arts, and the mysteries of maternal fertility and natural religion. In the final stage, women's "mother right" leads to what he thought of as the more culturally advanced rule of patriarchy. Lacking anthropological data, Bachofen's theory rests on his readings in Greek and Roman literature. Joan Bamberger, however, points out the historical flaws of Bachofen's myth, claiming that anthropology has found little evidence of any social matriarchies.[19] Similarly, in *The Second Sex* Simone de Beauvoir rejects Bachofen, stating that "society has always been male; political power has always been in the hands of men."[20] Not only does Bachofen's theory lack factual support, but his ideas, feminists charge, merely reflect the Victorian stereotypes of his time. Bachofen, of course, defined matriarchal consciousness as a "strange, aimless striving peculiar to women."[21] Compounding this bias, Bachofen's stress on matriarchy as the necessary step "to the education of mankind and particularly of men" relegated women to the position of nurturing patriarchal civilization.[22] Unhappily, Bly is heir to such dubious assumptions about women's domestic roles.

Not surprisingly, the Victorian sexism marking Bachofen's project also shaped other works of the same period. Henry Sumner Maine's *Ancient Law* (1861) sought the genesis of patriarchal rule in biblical scriptures as well as in Greek and Roman law. John F. McLennan's *Primitive Marriage* (1865) and Edward Westermarck's *The History of Human Marriage* (1891) analyzed the nuclear family in terms of women's historic submission to patriarchal authority. Also working within the Bachofen tradition, Henry Morgan was an important influence on Friedrich Engels' *The Origin of the Family, Private Property, and the State* (1884).[23] Bachofen's Victorian bias also persisted, through the influence of Freud, in Jung's thinking about women's psyche.[24] In "Women in Europe" he wrote: "Women's psychology is founded on the principle of Eros, the great binder and loosener, whereas from ancient times the ruling principle ascribed to man is

Logos."[25] Moreover, Erich Neumann, another of Bly's key sources, repeated Jung's subliminal sexism.[26] Predictably, Neumann's *The Origins and History of Consciousness* lumped men's and women's psyches into roughly the same stereotypes Bachofen set forth. Neumann also betrayed, at times, a Jungian bias toward projecting unconscious Eros onto woman, who, he says, is "out of her element in consciousness."[27]

Jung's and Neumann's archetypal readings of myth and folklore, as feminists have shown, often consign women to nature, the unconscious, and passive sexual roles.[28] For her part, de Beauvoir argues that such essentialist images cast the feminine as a deviant Other in relation to patriarchal rule. Pushed to the margins of male civil authority and state power, women, she says, have been associated historically with what is "outside" or "beyond": nature, the unconscious, and the mysteries of life and death.[29] Unfortunately, this is the very problematic that shapes Bly's feminism. Although lamenting sexual division, he ironically perpetuates it by falling into Bachofen's Victorian representations of women. Bly's thematic critique of patriarchy is blocked by the somewhat sexist stereotypes his writing projects. Like Marcuse, Bly associates patriarchal rule with the aggressive repression of erotic life instincts, what Freud and Jung define as Eros. Both Bly and Marcuse identify this century's increasing political totalitarianism, militarism, resource exploitation, and environmental pollution with the death instincts.[30] As a corrective to patriarchy, Bly features the more life-affirming ideals of matriarchy, derived largely from Bachofen's nurturing "mother right."

Working with Jungian theories of archetypal memory, Bly tries to talk back to patriarchy in the idiom of the deep image. But like Bachofen, Jung, and Neumann, he often projects feminine Eros in merely passive rather than empowering images of otherness. Although *Silence* does not foreground sexual division, it betrays an underlying tension between male and female roles. "A Man Writes to a Part of Himself" typifies Bly's early blindness to the feminine vision he would celebrate:

> What cave are you in, hiding, rained on?
> Like a wife, starving, without care,

> Water dripping from your head, bent
> Over ground corn . . .
>
>   You raise your face into the rain
> That drives over the valley—
> Forgive me, your husband,
> On the streets of a distant city, laughing,
> With many appointments,
> Though at night going also
> To a bare room, a room of poverty,
> To sleep among a bare pitcher and basin
> In a room with no heat—
>
>   Which of us two then is the worse off?
> And how did this separation come about?
>
>   (S, 36)

As his title suggests, in this domestic drama Bly as "a man" con-
descends to his anima, viewing her as "part of himself." The poem
confirms the anima's essentially passive role. Hiding within the cave's
wet enclosures, the poet's feminine other is primitive and endures
the poverty of earth, nature, and traditional staples. Her masculine
counterpart, however, dwells in the distant city, where he enjoys
the public sphere of his many appointments. In Bly's family romance, nightfall leads the husband back to a "room of poverty" that,
like its pitcher and basin—objects Bly would associate with the feminine—is comfortless and bare. Although questioned, the poet's anima is mute. However penitent, Bly's male persona has the last word,
while his anima remains a silent "other" on the margins of male
identity.

Beyond *Silence*, *The Light* calls this divorce from the feminine into
more urgent crisis. Bly's second volume revises *Silence*'s pastoral lyricism, which appears now as a feminine discourse opposed to patriarchy's public rhetoric. As in his Vietnam poetry, Bly's feminist
verse draws on satire, burlesque, and black humor to unmask capitalist patriarchy. This dialogue succeeds insofar as it lampoons the
reified icons of American consumer society. But because Bly lodges
his feminist critique within Bachofen's myth of mother right, he ste-

reotypes women in "natural" roles that are severed from political history:

> Not to the mother of solitude will I give myself
> Away, not to the mother of love, nor to the mother of conver-
>   sation,
> Nor to the mother of art, nor the mother
> Of tears, nor the mother of the ocean;
> Nor to the mother of sorrow, nor the mother
> Of the downcast face, nor the mother of the suffering of death;
> Not to the mother of the night full of crickets,
> Nor the mother of the open fields, nor the mother of Christ.
>
> But I will give myself to the father of righteousness, the father
> Of cheerfulness, who is also the father of rocks,
> Who is also the father of perfect gestures;
> From the Chase National Bank
> An arm of flame has come, and I am drawn
> To the desert, to the parched places, to the landscape of zeros;
> And I shall give myself away to the father of righteousness,
> The stones of cheerfulness, the steel of money, the father of rocks.
>
> (L, 4)

In "The Busy Man Speaks," Bly escalates the psychosexual conflict explored in "A Man Writes to a Part of Himself." "The Busy Man" renounces *Silence*'s pastoral life in a language that threatens its subjective aesthetic. As in "Counting," the strange persona's anaphoric hyperbole forcefully ridicules patriarchal values. Yet the poem fails to liberate women from the margins of patriarchy's civic power. Granted, the "father of cheerfulness" and "perfect gestures" is an empty figure as he moves through an abstract "landscape of zeros." But the "mother of sorrow" and the "suffering of death," who dwells in nature's dark oceans and open fields, seems equally shallow. Shaping Bly's mother/father division is Jung's Logos/Eros binarism. Although Bly offers his feminine imagery as a progressive alternative to the busy man's deluded pledge, his repetition of "not" and "nor" tends to oppress the mother in a negative otherness to the more aggressive will of the father—here featured in a misguided but still emphatic role. The poem's tone rather perversely registers Bly's un-conscious investment in the very patriarchal stances he consciously lampoons. Whether we can sense here some subliminal trace of what Rich describes as Bly's "patriarchal parochialism" ultimately de-pends on personal reading habits. But if Bly's satire displaces pa-triarchal representations, his mystification of Woman as nurturing Earth Mother provides actual women little access to public centers of social and political power.

Such sexual division locks him into the same dilemma time after time. In "The Teeth Mother Naked At Last," for example, he would critique patriarchal domination, but the title tends to saddle women with the poem's psychic burden. The repressed feminine, as Neumann's death mother, returns as the violent Other of male civil order. Bly, of course, tries to empower women's otherness in his well-known essay on matriarchy, "I Came Out of the Mother Na-ked," published in *Sleepers Joining Hands*. But its "feminine" argu-ment is flawed, investing in the very stereotypes that de Beauvoir locates on the passive margins of patriarchal power.[31] Even more troubling is the failure of Bly's feminism in his title piece, "Sleepers Joining Hands," a long Jungian meditation on matriarchy. Here he employs surrealism as a way of fusing the male and female psyches. But falling back on the father's phallic authority, Bly finds sexual difference unmanageable: "I love the Mother. / I am an enemy of the Mother, give me my sword" (SJH, 66). Naively endorsing Bacho-fen's version of women's "mother right," "Sleepers" lacks revision-ary force.[32]

Contrasted with Continental theorists of *écriture féminine,* Bly's relegation of women to hearth and home appears woefully lacking. Feminist authors such as Luce Irigaray, and Hélène Cixous pursue more "re-visionary" retrievals of women's experience. The writing of Irigaray, for example, subverts patriarchy's hierarchic oppositions in a multiple play of sexual difference:

> How can we speak to escape their enclosures, patterns, dis-tinctions and oppositions: virginal / deflowered, pure/impure, in-nocent/knowing? . . . How can we shake off the chains of these terms, free ourselves from their categories, divest ourselves of their names? . . . It's the total movement of our body. No surface holds:

no figures, lines, and points; no ground subsists. But there is no abyss. For us, depth does not mean a chasm. Where the earth has no solid crust, there can be no precipice. Our depth is the density of our body, in touch "all" over. There is no above/below, back/front, right side/wrong side, top/bottom in isolation, separate, out of touch. Our "all" intermingles. Without breaks or gaps.[33]

Although Bly embraces a poetics of the body, he neglects such a "gyn/ecology" of feminine sexuality. Failing to reflect critically on the sources of his depth psychology, Bly disfigures what Irigaray calls the "density" of the feminine body and unconscious. The rhetoric of the deep image succeeds when it moves beyond Wright's private lyricism into a public dialogue with America's bureaucratic discourse. Retrieving altered states of consciousness through archetypal reverie further serves to undermine patriarchal assumptions about women. But when Bly asserts nature, the unconscious, mother right, and the rest as intrinsic to the female psyche, rather than part of the cultural network of signs that the feminine disrupts and mobilizes in revolutionary ways, his writing is self-defeating.[34] Beyond the shortcomings of Bly's matriarchal poetry, Adrienne Rich's cultural feminism pursues a more sophisticated inscription of the feminine psyche, *her*story, and community.

6.

Feminism and Representation: Adrienne Rich's Wild Patience

B Y THE end of the Vietnam era, Herbert Marcuse no longer viewed advanced capitalism as the cultural monolith he had indicted in the mid-1960s. Moving beyond *One-Dimensional Man* (1964), he increasingly regarded postwar consumer society as traversed by shifting and contradictory impulses. Where he once saw only the same bleak scene of cultural reification, he began to describe more nuanced sites for progressive change. Works such as *An Essay on Liberation* (1969) and *Counterrevolution and Revolt* (1972) found Marcuse rummaging at the margins of the 1970s' commodity culture. What he was looking for were revolutionary bearers of social change. Late in his career, he espoused a mixed bag of countercultural praxes ranging from various Third World national liberation fronts to America's black power movement, the 1968 student uprisings, and new aesthetic trends as embodied in beat poetics, rock music, guerilla theatre, avant-garde film, and other emergent media. Marcuse promoted these emancipative struggles in his effort to undermine advanced capitalism's "surplus repression," diagnosed earlier in *Eros and Civilization* (1955).

Sigmund Freud's *Civilization and Its Discontents* (1930) had already theorized society as driven by aggressive death instincts, everywhere binding, like Blake's grim priests, erotic "joys and desires." But parting company with Freud, Marcuse did not regard cultural domination as an inevitable psychic law. Instead, he thought such repression was historically produced and in time could be shrugged off. But the liberation of Eros is unlikely under capitalism, he held, where every social advance is canceled by a surplus of repression. The "total mobilization of aggressiveness," Marcuse complained, "is only too familiar to us today: militarization, brutalization of the forces of law and order, fusion of sexuality and violence, direct attact on the life instincts in their drive to save the environment, attack on the legislation against pollution and so on."[1] Nor did he have any illusions about mainstream American labor fomenting revolutionary change. Rather, he solicited other more disenchanted and marginalized groups.

By the 1970s, he sought to join with those who were already pursuing social alternatives to American consumer society. Such utopian projects, he hoped, would foster liberating modes of "radical sensibility" that might lead to a "qualitative leap" into a properly social register of emancipatory needs, desires, and satisfactions. Increasingly, Marcuse looked to the women's liberation movement for such revolutionary cultural work. Social feminism, he thought, embodied "the *antithesis,* the definite negation of the aggressive and repressive needs and values of capitalism as a form of male-dominated culture" (Marxism/Feminism, 282). He valorized as distinctively feminine qualities "receptivity, sensitivity, non-violence, tenderness." "These characteristics," he said, "appear indeed as opposite of domination and exploitation. On the primary psychological level, they would pertain to the domain of Eros, they would express the energy of the life instincts, against the death instinct and destructive energy" (Marxism/Feminism, 283).

Although Marcuse was an ardent feminist, he has been criticized for giving short shrift to the concrete political linkages and institutional mediations that would bring an end to sexism. While granting Marcuse's importance as a theorist, Adrienne Rich charges that he never worked out a blueprint for women's emancipation from patriarchy. "Herbert Marcuse," she says, "sees the women's liberation movement as a 'radical force' and a 'free society' as a 'female society'; he hastens to add that this 'has nothing to do with matriarchy of any sort,' but with the 'femalization of the male' (to be achieved through what specifics he does not tell us)."[2] Although suspicious of the matriarchal images of the Bachofen tradition, Rich is not as willing as Marcuse to give up the ideal of a distinctively female community. Instead, she is careful to preserve women's own history and political goals within broader movements of social change. As a long-standing theoretician and activist in the women's liberation movement, Rich offers more cogent responses to the evolving issues under debate within feminism.

Her poetics shuttles through a fourfold narrative warp comprising women's spirituality, mother-daughter bonding, *écriture féminine*, and women's history. But far from binding her writing into a unity, these four discursive strands are often tangled in knots of verbal representation. Such a dialogic poetics, however, resists stereotyping women's experience. Rich's openness to change and her capacity to question images that are complicit with natural, romantic, or domestic sexisms have placed her in the vanguard of writers emerging from the women's movement. In the 1970s and 1980s, her poetry presents feminine desire as a discourse of "wild patience"—that is, through a poetics at once radically visionary and critically engaged.

From Formalism to Feminism

IN A 1956 journal entry reflecting on her second pregnancy in two years, Rich noted with deep dismay the failure of her creative powers—a sense of having reached a decisive impasse as a writer and as a person: "Whether it's the extreme lassitude of early pregnancy or something more fundamental, I don't know; but of late I've felt, toward poetry—both reading and writing it—nothing but boredom and indifference. . . . If there is going to be a real break in my

writing life, this is as good a time for it as any. I have been dissatisfied with myself, my work, for a long time" (OWB, 7). Rich's
alienation from her own writing in the 1950s arguably stemmed from
her filiation to a distinctively patriarchal literary milieu. Reflecting
back on these years in her well-known essay "When We Dead
Awaken: Writing as Re-vision," Rich theorizes concerning the limits
of women's writing within patriarchy. "No male writer," she says,
"has written primarily or even largely for women, or with the sense
of women's criticism as a consideration when he chooses his materials, his theme, his language. But to a lesser or greater extent,
every woman writer has written for men even when, like Virginia
Woolf, she was supposed to be addressing women" (LSS, 37–38).
By thus situating women's literature in the worldly realities of sexual
politics, Rich writes against the critical habit of excluding and repressing the historical and institutional contexts of literary production and reception, common to New Critical and poststructuralist
formalisms alike.

Like the early writing of Roethke, Wright, and Merwin, Rich's
first poems were shaped by New Critical formalism. In bestowing
the Yale Younger Poets Award on her *A Change of World* (1951),
W. H. Auden, the godfather of postwar American verse, confirmed
but also framed her early career within the "family tree" of Eliot,
Yeats, and Frost. Distinguishing her "genuine personal experience"
from a mere "parrot-like imitation" of modernism, Auden's back-
handed compliments to her craft's "proportion," quiet "modesty,"
and "respect for elders" displaced Rich even as they joined her to
the modernist aesthetic.[3] Such equivocation also marked Randall Jarrell's somewhat condescending praise for her next volume, *The Diamond Cutters* (1955): "she is also an endearing and delightful poet,
one who deserves Shakespeare's favorite adjective, *sweet*."[4] From the
hindsight of the 1980s, Auden's and Jarrell's need to keep Rich at
the margins of an all-male tradition betrays a telling sexism. Failing
to mention either her themes of women's experience or her likeness
to other American women poets such as Anne Bradstreet and Emily
Dickinson, they cast her as the dutiful daughter of the great modernist patriarchs. Like Virginia Woolf, however, Rich survived this
role, recognizing that "the dutiful daughter of the fathers in us is
only a hack" (LSS, 201). While her first poems imitated the crafts-

manship of high modernist and New Critical precursors, they asserted a nascent feminism that would move beyond formalism altogether in the 1960s.

Rich's identity as a woman writer stretches back to the very beginnings of her career. In "Aunt Jennifer's Tigers" the "massive" wedding band that "Sits heavily upon Aunt Jennifer's hand" (FD, 4) is a memorable symbol of women's oppression under capitalist patriarchy in the 1950s. Aunt Jennifer's careful needlepoint mirrors Rich's own poetic formalism. Both crafts serve to buffer the traumatic domestic lives they record. "In those years," Rich has said, "formalism was part of the strategy—like asbestos gloves, it allowed me to handle materials I couldn't pick up barehanded" (LSS, 40–41). Despite its aesthetic veneer, "Aunt Jennifer's Tigers" registers blunt, unswerving truths. Recalling the grim finality of Emily Dickinson, the poem climaxes in a fateful epiphany: "When Aunt is dead, her terrified hands will lie/Still ringed with ordeals she was mastered by" (FD, 4).

Typically, however, the aesthetic formalism of Rich's first two books serves to distance and repress her emerging feminist vision. Her mature free verse seems a surprising feat when viewed against her poetry of the 1950s. For example, "The Diamond Cutters" (1955), the title piece of her second volume, belittles the very ideals her recent work upholds. As in "Aunt Jennifer," the poem's closed form— here loosely rhymed stanzas of iambic trimeter—insulates the poet from the angst of history. But the aesthetic mastery espoused in "The Diamond Cutters" is less a defensive strategy than an obsession. Rich's investment in the diamond cutters' ethic seems absolute:

> However legendary,
> The stone is still a stone,
> Though it had once resisted
> The weight of Africa,
> The hammer-blows of time
> That wear to bits of rubble
> The mountain and the pebble—
> But not this coldest one.
>
> Now, you intelligence
> So late dredged up from dark

Upon whose smoky walls
Bison took fumbling form
Or flint was edged on flint—
Now, careful arriviste,
Delineate at will
Incisions in the ice.

Be serious, because
The stone may have contempt
For too-familiar hands,
And because all you do
Loses or gains by this:
Respect the adversary,
Meet it with tools refined,
And thereby set your price.

Be hard of heart, because
The stone must leave your hand.
Although you liberate
Pure and expensive fires
Fit to enamor Shebas,
Keep your desire apart.
Love only what you do,
And not what you have done.

Be proud, when you have set
The final spoke of flame
In that prismatic wheel,
And nothing's left this day
Except to see the sun
Shine on the false and the true,
And know that Africa
Will yield you more to do.
                    (FD, 20–21)

Predictably, the poem's themes and images are encoded by the same
high modernist and New Critical values of craftsmanship and im-
personal detachment for which Auden praises Rich's first volume:
"In a young poet, as T. S. Eliot has observed, the most promising
sign is craftsmanship for its evidence of a capacity for detachment

from the self and its emotions without which no art is possible" (Preface, 126). Following this modernist doctrine, Rich espouses the same values that in subsequent volumes she will indict as patriarchal. Praising an "intelligence/So late dredged up from dark/Upon whose smoky walls/Bison took fumbling form," the poem's evolutionary drift runs counter to Rich's later regressions to the "cratered night of female memory" in poems such as "Re-forming the Crystal" (1973) and "Turning the Wheel" (1981). Apprenticed to formalism's austere "intelligence," Rich assumes a cool detachment to "Delineate at will/Incisions in the ice." Such images of surgical mastery culminate in the third stanza with the poet's growing "contempt/For too-familiar hands." "Tools refined" stand in for the midwife's hands that in "Integrity" (1978) catch "the baby leaping/from between trembling legs" (FD, 274). Rich so insists on the diamond cutter's ethic that she thrusts it on her reader like a coach or boot camp sergeant. Cast into the role of green recruit, her reader is subjected to the usual slogans and pep-talk: "Be serious. . . . Respect the adversary. . . . Be hard of heart. . . . Keep your desire apart. . . . Be proud." But even more troubling, Rich's formalism leads her to reify Africa as a monolithic dark continent, wholly drained of social history. Confident that South African mines will supply the raw materials for art, Rich sums up the poem's formalist agenda: "And know that Africa/Will yield you more to do." Such glib assurances, however innocent, suffer from the same racism that taints Conrad's "emissaries of light." Reflecting back on this colonial metaphor, Rich admits to an aesthetic failure, that deserves to be quoted in full:

> Thirty years later I have trouble with the informing metaphor of this poem. I was trying, in my twenties, to write about the craft of poetry. But I was drawing, quite ignorantly, on the long tradition of domination, according to which the precious resource is yielded up into the hands of the dominator as if by a natural event. The enforced and exploited labor of actual Africans in actual diamond mines was invisible to me, and therefore invisible in the poem, which does not take responsibility for its own metaphor. I note this here because this kind of metaphor is still widely accepted, and I still have to struggle against it in my work. (FD, 329)

After three decades of social change, Rich sees clearly that her early formalism was woefully blind to history. Unlike many of today's poets, who still unthinkingly reproduce such cultural domination, Rich culls her writing, rejecting metaphors that fail to "take responsibility" for their politics.

"The Cratered Night of Female Memory"

THROUGHOUT THE 1950s, however, Rich buffers herself from such social reflexivity by repressing history. Like Wright, she often longs for an ahistorical pastoral life. But that form of "nostalgia," she comes to realize, "is only amnesia turned around" (FD, 306). Nostalgia offers its seductive regressions to *illo tempore*—a bucolic past "when knowledge still was pure, / not contradictory, pleasurable / as cutting out a paper doll" (FD, 31). But even by 1954, writing "From Morning-Glory to Petersburg," Rich knows "it's too late" for such radical innocence. "Now knowledge," she admits, "finds me out; in all its risible untidiness / it traces me to each address" (FD, 31). Her revisionary cultural feminism emerges little by little in response to the turbulent history of the early 1960s. "The fifties and early sixties," she has said, "were years of rapid revelations: the sit-ins and marches in the South, the Bay of Pigs, the early antiwar movement, raised large questions—questions for which the masculine world of the academy around me seemed to have expert and fluent answers. But I needed to think for myself—about pacifism and dissent and violence, about poetry and society, and about my own relationship to all these things" (LSS, 44).

Significantly, Rich's feminist critique came at a time of increasing national debate about women's issues. In 1961, newly elected President John F. Kennedy created the first Presidential Commission on the Status of Women, headed by the ailing Eleanor Roosevelt. The campaign for such a commission was largely spearheaded by Esther Peterson, head of the Women's Bureau and Assistant Secretary of Labor. The Commission played an important role in lobbying for federal support for day care and women's continuing education programs, equal pay legislation, and equal social security and unemployment benefits. It also took up the ideological representation of women in mainstream American culture, sponsoring such forums as "Images of Women in the Media."

One of the most outspoken participants in this forum, Betty Friedan, had recently completed an important poll of former classmates and alumni of Smith College, asking such questions as "What difficulties have you found in working out your role as a woman?" "What do you wish you had done differently?" and "How do you visualize your life after your children have grown?" Although Friedan had been a regular contributor to such magazines as *Cosmopolitan*, *McCall's* and *Mademoiselle*, so controversial were her new findings that *Ladies' Home Journal*, *McCall's*, and *Redbook* all refused to publish them.[5] Nonetheless, Friedan would find a national audience in her landmark study *The Feminine Mystique* (1963), published the same year as Rich's third volume, *Snapshots of a Daughter-in-Law*. Both writers fulminated against patriarchy's distorted "mystique" of women's place in postwar society: "The mistake, says the mystique, the root of women's troubles in the past is that women envied men, women tried to be like men, instead of accepting their own nature, which can find fulfillment only in sexual passivity, male domination, and nurturing maternal love."[6]

Like Friedan, Rich also undertakes a distinctively feminist critique in the title piece to *Snapshots of a Daughter-in-Law* (1963). Moving now into more open and colloquial forms, she challenges women's historic role as what Simone de Beauvoir called the "second sex" under patriarchy. Beyond confessing to the stifling routine of her own domestic life, Rich speaks more broadly to contemporary America's widespread sexism:

> Sigh no more, ladies.
>   Time is male
> and in his cups drinks to the fair.
> Bemused by gallantry, we hear
> our mediocrities over-praised,
> indolence read as abnegation,
> slattern thought styled intuition,
> every lapse forgiven, our crime
> only to cast too bold a shadow
> or smash the mold straight off.
>   (FD, 38)

"Snapshots" reflects back on the pervasively antifeminist attitudes of the 1950s that cast women in nurturing, intuitive, emotive, and self-effacing roles for men. Throughout the 1950s, popular women's magazines such as *Ladies' Home Journal, McCall's,* and *Redbook* fostered such passive images of women in articles entitled "It's a Man's World Maybe," "Have Babies While You're Young," "How to Snare a Male," "Should I Stop Work When We Marry?," "Are You Training Your Daughter to be a Wife?," "Careers at Home," "Do Women Have to Talk So Much?," "Why GI's Prefer Those German Girls," "What Women Can Learn from Mother Eve," "Really a Man's World, Politics," "How to Hold On to a Happy Marriage," "Don't Be Afraid to Marry Young," "The Doctor Talks About Breast-Feeding," "Our Baby was Born at Home," "Cooking to Me is Poetry," and "The Business of Running a Home."[7] Such attitudes, of course, are deep seated, as Rich's glosses from traditional literary figures make clear. Alluding to Campion, Diderot, Horace, Samuel Johnson, and other "great" authors, "Snapshots" interrupts the patriarchal stereotyping of women. Here Rich flouts images that stylize women as *Dulce ridens, dulce loquens*—sweetly laughing, sweetly speaking—or as symbols of *fertilisante douleur*—life-giving sorrow (FD, 36–37). Beyond its confessional themes, the poem's strategy is to invoke the "masterpieces" of a distinctively male canon in order to undermine and unmask them. In this way, "Snapshots" works through the legacy of Western chauvinism.

Beyond lodging a powerful feminist critique, Rich turned back to traditional feminist writers such as Emily Dickinson and Mary Wollstonecraft, retrieving a "re-visionary" poetics in the face of patriarchy. "Snapshots" concludes with a glimpse of the female messiah, patterned after Rich's reading in Simone de Beauvoir's *The Second Sex* (1953):

> Well,
> she's long about her coming, who must be
> more merciless to herself than history.
> Her mind full to the wind, I see her plunge
> breasted and glancing through the currents,
> taking the light upon her
> at least as beautiful as any boy

> or helicopter,
>   poised, still coming,
> her fine blades making the air wince
>
> but her cargo
> no promise then:
> delivered
> palpable
> ours
>
> (FD, 38–39)

However improbable, Rich's initiating *visio beatifica* breaks away from the Victorian stereotypes that would shape Bly's feminism a decade later. Instead, the feminine savior here emerges from a distinctively female heritage as portrayed in de Beauvoir: "She comes down from the remoteness of the ages, from Thebes, from Crete, from Chichén-Itzá; and she is also the totem set up deep in the African jungle, she is a helicopter and she is a bird; and there is this, the greatest wonder of all: under her tinted hair the forest murmur becomes a thought, and words issue from her breasts."[8] Bearing "her cargo" of a re-visionary cultural feminism, Rich's helicopter metaphor is an enduring symbol for women's spirituality in her next volume, *Necessities of Life* (1966). "More merciless to herself than history," "she" reverses Victorian representations of woman's angelic spirituality. Rich's writing inscribes the feminine as historically immanent, through a language that is "palpable" and "delivered" in the present.

Pursuing a more authentic selfhood in the mid-1960s, Rich's archetypal feminism negotiates the confessional surrealism of Bly, Roethke, and Wright. Like these deep image writers, Rich follows Roethke's regressive credo from the early 1950s: "Sometimes, of course, there is regression. I believe that the spiritual man must go back in order to go forward."[9] "Go back so far," Rich says, "there is another language / go back far enough the language / is no longer personal" (FD, 181). In the title piece to Rich's fourth volume, *Necessities of Life,* that other language of psychic individuation stems from what Kenneth Burke described as the "vegetal radicalism" of Roethke's celebrated greenhouse poems.[10] Resembling Roethke's organic poetics, Rich's self-explorations come through an openness to nature's subhuman beings: "I'll / dare inhabit the world / "trenchant in motion as an eel, solid / as a cabbage head" (FD, 56). Such communions with the subhuman repeat Roethke's and Bly's surrender to the small, regressive forms of the deep image:

> I learned to make myself
> unappetizing. Scaly as a dry bulb
> thrown into a cellar.
>
> Nothing would sleep in that cellar, dank as a ditch,
> Bulbs broke out of boxes hunting for chinks in the dark,
> Shoots dangled and drooped
>
> There is a joyful night in which we lose
> Everything and drift
> Like a radish.

Reading these passages blind, it would be difficult to say based on style alone whether they belong to Rich, Roethke, or Bly. In the first excerpt above, from "Necessities," Rich's descent into nature's simple lives is encoded by the same organic rhetoric that Roethke employs in "Root Cellar" or Bly in "When the Dumb Speak."[11] Stylistically, such vegetal tropes are, as Rich says, "no longer personal" but part of the common verbal economy of deep image poetics. Similarly, the archetypal feminism of Rich's middle career is rooted in the depth psychology of the "subjective" image writers. Her pilgrimages to the American Southwest—where she finds the "cratered night of female memory" in "Re-forming the Crystal" (1973) or the "female core of a continent" in "Turning the Wheel" (1981)— recall Roethke's western passages in "Journey to the Interior." Possessed by the vast and primordial vistas of the American West, both poets journey into the domain of the archetypal unconscious.

But whether traveling through the "cratered night of female memory" or diving into the "wreck" of personal disaster, such regressions often betray a blindness to the historicity of women's past. As in the Midwest pastorals of Bly and Wright, Rich's bucolic images of women's Golden Age are drained of political history. "The clouds and the stars didn't wage this war / the brooks gave no information/. . . the raindrop faintly swaying under the leaf/had no political opinions" (FD, 313). Such pastoral nostalgia, however life-affirming, simply elides the minefield of Western patriarchy, lapsing into clichéd representations of women's grounding in nature.[12] Clearly, though, Rich is dissatisfied with the nostalgic flight into nature's Golden Age before patriarchy. Even her "deep" scenes of primordial memory are fraught with sexual politics:

> If I am dream like a wire with fire
> throbbing along it
>
> if I am death to man
> I have to know it
>
> His mind is too simple, I cannot go on
> sharing his nightmares
>
> My own are becoming clearer, they open
> into prehistory
>
> which looks like a village lit with blood
> where all of the fathers are crying: *My son is mine!*
>   (FD, 178)

To "dream" feminism intensely, Rich says in "Husband-Right and Father-Right" (1977), is to face the intimacy of our private lives as traversed by patriarchy's political unconscious. The ancient village of the mind is also a public world swept by social forces. However turned away from America's patriarchal milieu in the 1960s, Rich still finds that "Father-right" persists as at once a deeply rooted social and psychic problem.[13] Beyond the utopian dream of "re-visionary" gender roles, Rich sees the necessity for a concrete feminist critique. But in fending off patriarchy's psychic aggression, Rich, at times, lapses into her own sexist mythology.

Conjuring "the terrible mothers we long and dread to be" (FD, 231), Rich casts women into stereotyped roles that, however unsettling, are powerless. Instead of transforming anger, her personae often merely embody it. Such representations share the shortcomings of Bly's ahistorical "teeth mother" stereotype. Poems such as "The

Phenomenology of Anger" (1972) or "Hunger" (1975) short-circuit the currents of rage they otherwise muster. In "For Julia in Nebraska" (1981), Rich's figure of the Amazonian warrior presents similar problems in representation. The figure she addresses there as a kind of Wagnerian Valkyrie—"bearing your double axe and shield / painfully honed and polished" (FD, 281)—mirrors the martial images of patriarchal aggression that Rich had rejected twenty years earlier in "The Knight" (1957): "Who will unhorse this rider / and free him from between / the walls of iron, the emblems / crushing his chest with their weight?" (FD, 33). Such images, as stylized and often clichéd presentations of women's anger, differ hardly at all from the very stances Rich indicts as patriarchal. But rage can serve as a resource when it conceives a poetics of revolutionary cultural change.

Eleusis: The Mother-Daughter Cathexis

RICH'S TIRADES against patriarchy succeed politically when they lead to revisionary myths beyond patriarchy's "crumbling form" (LSS, 217). Her mythic meditations on the Kore/Demeter narrative of the Eleusinian mysteries is a case in point. Like other female authors such as Margaret Atwood, Rachel Blau DuPlessis, Kate Ellis, and Tillie Olsen, Rich turns to Eleusis in what Alicia Ostriker describes as "revisionist mythmaking."[4] Dating from between 1400 and 1100 B.C., Eleusis, Rich says, is the "keystone to human spiritual survival" (OWB, 240). Eleusinian mysteries deal with the seasonal return of agriculture and the soul's resurrection out of the underworld. But more importantly, at the heart of Eleusis lies the mythic primacy of the mother-daughter bond that Rich retrieves as a model for feminist solidarity. She reads the mythic abduction of Kore by Hades as man's historical intervention in the mysteries of birth and death, originally the domain of the grain goddess Demeter. Although rivaling the family tragedies of Western culture—Lear (father-daughter), Hamlet (son-mother), and Oedipus (son-mother)—Rich notes that the Demeter-Kore myth has been actively devalued. "The loss of the daughter to the mother, the mother to the daughter," she says, "is the essential female tragedy" (OWB, 240).

Rich's quest for Eleusis leads into the mythic domain of moth-

ering and its birth rites. Like Anne Sexton in her poem "In Celebration of My Uterus," Rich depicts feminine identity as an intuitive
and organic community of conceived selves. "Sometimes I feel," she
writes, "it is myself that kicks inside me" (FD, 250). But to embody
a new identity is hard labor, involving the poignant expiration of
past lives: "They say a pregnant woman dreams her own death. But
life and death / take one another's hands" (FD, 250). Margaret Atwood values Rich's work because it "forces you to decide not just
what you think about it, but what you think about yourself."[15] In
"The Mirror in Which Two Are Seen as One," Rich's intimate direct address beckons her reader to birth's primordial scene that is
bound in time to

> the graveyard where you sit on the graves
> of women who died in childbirth
> and women who died at birth
> Dreams of your sister's birth
> your mother dying in childbirth over and over
> not knowing how to stop
> bearing you over and over
>
> your mother dead and you unborn
> your two hands grasping your head
> drawing it down against the blade of life
> your nerves the nerves of a midwife
> learning her trade
>
> (FD, 161)

This ouroboric image of feminine apprenticeship as self-delivery appears in 1971, five years before the embryonic images of *The Dream
of a Common Language*. Unlike the deep image poets, Rich in the
early 1970s is writing a distinctively feminine mythology—one that
speaks to the lived experience of women. Critics often point to Rich's
fusion with her masculine "animus," claiming she espouses an androgynous identity.[16] But in "Mirror," her primary identification
with mothers, daughters, and sisters eludes the deep terrain of Jungian psychology.

In poems such as "Sibling Mysteries" from *Dream* or "The Images" (1978) from *Wild Patience,* Rich joins this re-birthing of the feminine to mythic and Eleusinian scenes:

> When I saw hér face, she of the several faces
> staring   indrawn   in judgment   laughing for joy
> her serpents twisting   her arms raised
>   her breasts gazing
> when I looked into hér world
> I wished to cry loose my soul
>   into her, to become
>   free of speech   at last.
>
> (WP, 5)

Yet Rich's mystified reveries, however visionary, are often blind to women's actual lived history. "To become/free of speech at last" is also a potential handicap. Mythic communion with "hér world," here at least, seems so wholly "indrawn" as to be autistic. Such "pure annunciations to the eye" (FD, 236) are merely nostalgic unless brought to bear on history. In "Cartographies of Silence," Rich more successfully resists the seductions of visionary idealism, turning instead to the more material powers of language:

> if from time to time I long to turn
>
> like the Eleusinian hierophant
> holding up a simple ear of grain
>
> for return to the concrete and everlasting world
> what in fact I keep choosing
>
> are these words, these whispers, conversations
> from which time after time the truth breaks moist and green.
>
> (FD, 236)

Rich's mythic passage through "hér world" does not come to a dead end, as does Bly's, in archetypal mystification. Quite the contrary, Rich's "re-visionary" mythmaking leads to a trenchant critique of traditional gender roles.

Rich's turn in the 1970s to a lesbian poetics based in the mother-daughter bond comes after a period of both personal and public crises in sexual politics. Not unlike Bly, in his fusion of the private and national psyches, Rich holds that "To try to understand what has been labeled the 'personal' as part of a greater political reality has been a critical process for feminism" (LSS, 215). Questioning "natural" assumptions about gender, she rethinks her own experience in light of recent American history. Rich's psychic emergency in her private relationships with men is exacerbated by the stark brutality of patriarchy's political scene in the late 1960s. In "Trying to Talk to a Man" (1971), she employs the metaphor of nuclear "testing" to probe unconscious reserves of sexual division: "we talk of people caring for each other / in emergencies—laceration, thirst—/ but you look at me like an emergency /. . . talking of the danger / as if it were not ourselves / as if we were testing anything else" (FD, 150).

Two years later, the same public scenes of American violence escalate the psychic danger of Rich's negotiations with patriarchy. "Dien Bien Phu" (1973) transcodes her metaphor for America's social "emergency" from Los Alamos to the battlefields of Vietnam. In nightmarish landscapes, the poem renders the minefield of heterosexual relations even more horrible: "A nurse on the battlefield / wounded herself, but working / dreams / that each man she touches / is a human grenade / an anti-personnel weapon / that can explode in her arms" (FD, 200–01). Such a radical blending of public and private histories leads Rich to question heterosexuality and the nuclear family.[17] Interrogating the domestic sphere of "the home, the hearth, the family" (LSS, 215), she becomes convinced that "only when women recognize and name as force and bondage what has been misnamed love or partnership, can we begin to love and nurture out of strength and purpose rather than out of self-annihilation and the protection of a crumbling form or fiction" (LSS, 216–17). Rethinking gender beyond patriarchy's crumbling form, she sets ancient myth into dialogue with psychoanalytic theory.

"The cathexis," Rich asserts, "between mother and daughter—essential, distorted, misused—is the great unwritten story" (OWB, 226). In "Sibling Mysteries" she explores the distinctively feminine cathexis at the heart of matriarchy. "The daughters were to begin with," she says, "brides of each other / under a different law" (DCL, 52). Partly discovering and at times inventing that "other" law, Rich joins myth to recent psychoanalytic accounts of mother-daughter bonding. Primary identification with the mother —a key theme in her recent poetry—follows a psychoanalytic model that parts company with patriarchal assumptions about women's sexuality.[18] Nancy Chodorow, in particular, presents a cogent argument for the social—rather than biological—organization of gender. Clinical evidence suggests, Chodorow argues, that daughters retain preoedipal attachments to the mother while they develop heterosexually. The daughter, she finds, invests in the father, and men in general, in a three-way bond with her lasting attraction to the mother.[19] Thus, while men become erotic objects for women, many women seek primary emotional satisfaction from each other.

Similarly, in "Transcendental Etude" (1977) Rich reclaims women's "mother right" as a "birth right" and "re-membering" of the preoedipal lesbian body. Here she recalls the "acute joy" of maternal sensuality, its primordial rhythms and deep somatic bonding: "to be / lifted breathtaken on her breast, to rock within her / —even if beaten back, stranded against, to apprehend / in a sudden brine-clear thought / trembling like the tiny, orbed endangered / egg-sac of a new world" (FD, 267–68). Such "re-memberings" flout the anonymous remove of patriarchal law, for "the element they have called most dangerous" is the sensuous fusion of mind and body in "sudden brine-clear thought."[20] Poems such as "Transcendental Etude" or the passionate *Twenty-One Love Poems* (1976) celebrate Rich's awakening to lesbian eroticism. But it would be a mistake to tie Rich's feminine bonding only to sexuality. On the contrary, the lesbian cathexis supports broader platforms of social, cultural, and political change. The term "lesbian" itself, she says, needs to be liberated to denote the "self-chosen" woman, the "primary intensity" among women, and the woman who denies patriarchal authority.[21] "The lesbian/feminist," she writes, "lives in a complex, demanding realm of linguistic and relational distinctions. . . . For us, the process of naming and defining is not an intellectual game, but a grasping of our experience and a key to action" (LSS, 202). Thus Rich, as a lesbian writer, actively reinscribes the biological, psychological, cultural, and linguistic representations that historically have mediated women's experience.

Language's Semiotic Body

BEYOND HER own lyric celebration of the lesbian cathexis, Rich labors to liberate others from patriarchal oppression. Her poetic discourse more broadly serves as a critique of the cultural representation of the feminine body. "The woman's body, with its potential for gestating, bringing forth and nourishing new life, has been through the ages a field of contradictions: a space invested with power, and an acute vulnerability; a numinous figure and the incarnation of evil; a hoard of ambivalences, most of which have worked to disqualify women from the collective act of defining culture" (OWB, 90). In Rich's political metaphor, "patriarchal culture . . . has literally colonized the bodies of women" (LSS, 225). In challenging patriarchy's "colonizing" of the feminine body, she forges new discourses of sexuality that reclaim women's power to reshape our psychic, cultural, and social lives.[22]

All too aware that "the woman's body is the terrain on which patriarchy is erected" (OWB, 38), Rich sets out to empower it both as subject and *semiotic* force in her poetry. And to this extent, her poetics parallels the *écriture féminine* of French theorists Hélène Cixous and Julia Kristeva. "Though masculine sexuality gravitates around the penis," Cixous writes, "engendering that centralized body (in political anatomy) under the dictatorship of its parts, woman does not bring about the same regionalization which serves the couple head/genitals and which is inscribed only within boundaries. Her libido is cosmic, just as her unconscious is worldwide."[23] Cixous' dispersal of women's "cosmic" desire dethrones the tyranny of masculine sexuality, centered in the phallus and encoding the body through the dictatorship of its "political anatomy." Likewise, Rich's "Reforming the Crystal" (1973) stages the same diffusion of erotic desire. Here she indicts a male lover as a figure addicted to phallocentric sexuality:

> I am trying to imagine
> how it feels to you
> to want a woman
>
> trying to hallucinate
> desire

centered in a cock
focused like a burning-glass

desire without discrimination:
to want a woman like a fix
(FD, 205)

The target of Rich's feminist critique in "Crystal" is the "centered" cock of what Cixous defines as a masculine "political economy." Overturning the patriarchal image of women's passivity, Rich celebrates the same worldwide libidinal forces that Cixous espouses: "Walking through the airport blazing with energy and joy. But knowing all along that you were not the source of that energy and joy; you were a man, a stranger, a name, a voice on the telephone, a friend; this desire was mine, this energy my energy; it could be used a hundred ways, and going to meet you could be one of them" (FD, 206–07). Such a "re-visionary" poetic discourse liberates powers of female energy and joy from the passive representations of patriarchy.

Like Kristeva, Rich links poetry's verbal play to the body's instinctual drives, libidinal energies, and somatic rhythms. In *Desire in Language,* Kristeva joins the *semiotic (le semiotique)*—her term for the unconscious forces mobilized in poetic language—to the preoedipal, presymbolic domain of the infant's bond to the mother.[24] In contrast to the semiotic, she defines the *symbolic*—language's nominative, predicative, communicative function—as a repression of the signifier's libidinal play. For example, she notes that much of scientific language is allied to the symbolic. Significantly, Kristeva employs this psycholinguistic theory as the base for a broader social critique, one that aims to unseat the (symbolic) "constraints of a civilization dominated by transcendental rationality": "This means that if poetic economy has always borne witness to crises and impossibilities of transcendental symbolics, in our time it is coupled with crises of social institutions (state, family, religion), and more profoundly, a turning point in the relationship of man to meaning" (Desire, 140).[25] Kristeva's theoretical nexus—her retrieval of the maternal body within semiosis as a political critique—looks forward to Adrienne Rich's cultural feminism in the 1970s and 1980s.[26]

"To love," writes Kristeva, "is to survive paternal meaning" (Desire, 150). One only has to glimpse Rich's first poems to see all that she has survived. In sharp contrast to the libidinal "pulsations" of her mature open-form verse, Rich's early formalism is policed by the repressive "transparent rationality" of the symbolic. Auden and Jarrell point out, albeit through a male bias, the Victorian modesty of her early style, as in "An Unsaid Word" (1951):

> She who has power to call her man
> From that estranged intensity
> Where his mind forages alone,
> Yet keeps her peace and leaves him free,
> And when his thoughts to her return
> Stands where he left her, still his own,
> Knows this the hardest thing to learn.
>
> (FD, 5)

"An Unsaid Word" typifies Rich's early verse written in service to patriarchal values. In this little lyric, woman's place as "angel of the house" is wholly sacrificial. Any genuine intensity of mind belongs to the husband, while the wife's passivity affirms his distance and authority. Like the rest of his property, she "Stands where he left her, still his own." The only power she possesses is patience, but it is belied by a false peace—"the hardest thing to learn." The poem's title, however, is even more revealing than its persona's self-effacing ethic. The silence of the poem's "unsaid word" is deeper and more forcefully repressed than its speaker knows. Nonetheless, rage is voiced here, however distorted, as an immanent feature of Rich's poetic style. The poem's formal rhyme scheme and iambic tetrameter measure register a suspicious "peace." Its tightly controlled and abstract diction is a further index of how the libidinal force of the semiotic has been effectively censored at the level of the symbolic as "An Unsaid Word."

Throughout the 1960s, Rich repudiates such formalist repression, at times choosing the persona of Emily Dickinson to indict it as "Perjury"— "buzzing with spoiled language" (FD, 71). In "I Am in Danger—Sir" (1964) Dickinson's word is no longer "unsaid" but emerges as "a condition of being" (FD, 71). But Rich speaks the poetry of being through an ongoing dialogue with its other: the "language of the oppressor." Even as late as 1975, Rich still searches for ways of liberating the "unsaid word" from the symbolic's formal network of lies: "The syllables uttering / the old script over and over / The loneliness of the liar / living in the formal network of the lie / twisting the dials to drown the terror beneath the unsaid word" (FD, 233). In her struggle to name the unsaid word, Rich unleashes language's libidinal forces. Like Kristeva, she disrupts patriarchy's symbolic "rationality" with semiotic verbal displays.

In the 1970s, Rich seeks to liberate language's semiotic body as in "Waking in the Dark" (1971), where she inscribes the body as an alienated text of stigmata, a "list of wounds" (FD, 99):

> Sometimes every
> aperture of my body
> leaks blood. I don't know whether
> to pretend that this is natural.
> Is there a law about this, a law of nature?
> You worship the blood
> you call it hysterical bleeding
> you want to drink it like milk
> you dip your finger into it and write
> (FD, 153)

Patriarchy, of course, would like to censor Rich's "re-membering" of the word's sensual body, labeling it as hysteria and madness. But like other women writers in the postwar period—Atwood, Lessing, Plath, or Sexton—Rich wants to be possessed by "The freedom of the wholly mad / to smear & play with her madness / write with her fingers dipped in it" (FD, 165). The discourse of madness, for Rich, has a certain strategic power when the body's semiotic breaching of patriarchal silence opens sites for uttering not only what is normally "unspoken" but more radically "unspeakable." In "It Is the Lesbian in Us . . . " (1976), Rich writes that "whatever is buried in the memory by the collapse of meaning under an inadequate or lying language—this will become, not merely unspoken, but *unspeakable*" (LSS, 199). To dispel such silence, she says, "I need a language to hear myself with / to see myself in / a language like pigment released on the board / blood-black, sexual green, reds / veined with

contradictions / bursting under pressure from the tube" (FD, 199).[27]
Like Kristeva, Rich invokes the word's somatic body, the libidinal
force of the semiotic normally repressed from the symbolic economy
of language. Her writing serves as a translation, or transcoding, of
somatic pulsations into poetic images, as in "Planetarium" (1968):
"I am an instrument in the shape / of a woman trying to translate
pulsations / into images for the relief of the body / and the reconstruction of the mind" (FD, 116). By translating the semiotic force
of the feminine body into the symbolic, Rich enters the discursive
war of representations mediating women's history.

The Feminine Subject on Trial

LIKE WRIGHT'S lyric subversions of America's public rhetoric or
Bly's parodies of government neologisms, Rich's assault on patriarchal discourse is politically charged. Her cultural poetics is at once
personal and social, realigning her own past commitments even as
it undermines patriarchy's "crumbling form." During the late 1960s
and early 1970s, poems such as "The Burning of Paper Instead of
Children" (1968), "Shooting Script" (1970), and "Meditations for a
Savage Child" (1972) are valuable exhaustions of her desire to transcend language.[28] "Burning" 's epigraph—a quote from Daniel Ber-
rigan at his Baltimore trial, "I was in danger of verbalizing my moral
impulses out of existence"—provides her with the license to "burn
the texts" (FD, 119), in Artaud's famous motto. Language's power
to shape culture, in these works, largely belongs to men. "This is
the oppressor's language," she admits, "yet I need it to talk to you"
(FD, 117). Two years later, Rich feels trapped by patriarchal speaking: "They come to you with their descriptions of your soul. / . . .
They believe your future has a history and that it is themselves"
(FD, 142–43).

Similarly, "Meditations for a Savage Child" joins "their" manifest destiny to the history of Western humanism. "Meditations" tells
the story of J. M. Itard's attempts to "civilize" the wild boy of Av-
eyron, a child found wandering in the forest in 1799. Itard would
like to re-educate the wild boy to the humanizing ideal of eigh-
teenth-century rationalism. The goal, she says, was "to teach you

names / for things / you did not need / . . . to teach you language: / the thread their lives / were strung on" (FD, 179–80). "Meditation" thus repeats the body's struggle with the power of discursive representation. It stages the semiotic's repression by what Kristeva terms the symbolic's "transcendental rationality."

But Rich's indictment of "their" language is even more trenchant as a self-reflexive critique. This more vulnerable probing of her own language calls into crisis the difference between "their" speaking and her own. Throughout the 1970s, key words that might have released the poet from the linguistic fetters of patriarchal discourse have just as often locked her into its "formal network of lies." Rich's use of the word "androgyny" surely is a *prima facie* case. In "The Stranger" of 1972, she writes "I am the androgyne / I am the living mind you fail to describe / in your dead language" (DW, 19). Rich's projection of "dead language" onto the poem's "other" joins its addressee to the "they" world of patriarchy indicted in "Burning," "Meditations," "Shooting," and other works of this period. She, in contrast, enjoys the "living mind" as an androgyne. "The letters of my name," she asserts, "are written under the lids / of the new born child" (DW, 17). But, in fact, the androgyne's name is inscribed elsewhere and in terms that betray the blindness of Rich's romantic image. Only five years later the poet notes the sexist etymology of the very word she valorizes in "The Stranger": "Finally, the very structure of the word replicates the sexual dichotomy and the priority of *andros* (male) over *gyne* (female)" (OWB, 62). And in another five years, writing in *Dream,* she altogether recants her earlier fondness for "androgyny": "There are words I cannot choose again: / *humanism androgyny* / Such words have no shame in them, no diffidence / before the raging stoic grandmothers" (FD, 262). Rich's openness to history leads her to negotiate such verbal realignments. One of Rich's strengths is her continual and unflinching scrutiny of the feminine self on trial.

Change, as in Rich's middle career, is welcomed as a joyful liberation because it is self-willed. Yet there is less occasion for celebrating when the self becomes the site rather than the source of historical transformation. "Bent on restoring meaning to / our lesbian names," a feminist, she writes, must become a "brave linguist" (FD, 281). But however valiant, a poet can never expect to win the war

of meaning. The language we would impress for ideal self-knowl-
edge arrives dialogically, already invested in other narratives that resist or betray our imaginary needs and desires. At best, one can only
possess the word's "verbal privilege" (FD, 325) momentarily in a
jostling gang of other authors, each intent on linguistic mastery. The
logos is not only fallen but, like property, tainted with the violence
of willful appropriation. Writers live on, but as antiheroes "in a
country / where words are stolen out of mouths / as bread is stolen
out of mouths" (FD, 326). As poet, Rich accepts her authorial displacement as a given. Moreover, she dares us as readers to face the
difficult knowledge that, as she says, "Everything we write / will be
used against us / or against those we love. / These are the terms, /
take them or leave them" (FD, 324).[29] Like Derrida, Rich knows
that language's systematic "iterability" underwrites one's personal
word. Because all language is repeatable, and indeed already a repetition, one's discourse is always subject to an endless contextual
"grafting" from one speech act or text to another.[30]

If Rich's feminist polemic at times borders on utopian propaganda, and if her nostalgia for a mythic preoedipal lesbian sexuality
seems somewhat mystified, her recent politics are refined by the kind
of skeptical unease Dickinson describes as "Internal Difference / where
the meanings are."[31] Rich's self-questioning turns on whether any
of her versions of feminism can survive patriarchy's residual cultural
forces. Her skepticism is radically insistent. She aims to destroy her
reader's facile investments in ahistorical or utopian vision. "Will any
of this comfort you," she asks us: "and how," she further challenges, "should this comfort you?" (FD, 323). "Explicitly or im-
plicitly," writes Alicia Ostriker, "since *Snapshots* Rich's position has
depended on the idea of an enemy."[32] Ostriker argues that Rich's
poetry is weighed down by a state of "unrelieved crisis." A more
radical reading, however, would welcome crisis as the precondition
for revolutionary social change. In fact, Julia Kristeva argues that
women's otherness can be forceful only through such powers of negation: "If women have a role to play in this on-going process, it
is only in assuming a *negative* function: reject everything finite, definite, structured, loaded with meaning, in the existing state of society. Such an attitude places women on the side of the explosion
of social codes: with revolutionary moments."[33] In the 1980s, Rich

turns her adversarial, deconstructive gaze on the "notable women" of women's past.

Rich's doubts about the ultimate fate of postwar cultural feminism color her recent portraits of exceptional women, as in "Power" (1974), "Heroines" (1980), "Turning the Wheel" (1981), and "Education of a Novelist" (1983). Departing from her earlier depictions of heroines—such as Emily Dickinson, Mary Wollstonecraft, Natalya Gorbaneuskaya, Caroline Herschel, Elvira Shatayev, Paula Becker, and Clara Westhoff—Rich now presents her "remarkable" women in problematic, contradictory, and internally riven roles. Fame for many of these women leads to tragedy. "She died a famous woman," Rich writes of Marie Curie, "denying / her wounds / denying her wounds came from the same source as her power" (FD, 225).

The empowering wound that destroys Marie Curie also disfigures Mary Jane Colter in Rich's epistolary poem "Turning the Wheel." An architect, Colter oversaw the design of a chain of hotels and restaurants west of Chicago owned by the Fred Harvey Company. But Colter's art, which supports her mother and younger sister, is the source at once of self-esteem and shame. As Rich presents her in "Turning the Wheel," Colter thought of her designs as blending with Hopi and Navaho culture: "I want this glory. / I want to place my own conception / and that of the Indians whose land this was / at the edge of this incommensurable thing" (FD, 309). But her goal is at odds with history. Erected on the edge of the Grand Canyon, her designs come to deface "the female core / of a continent" (FD, 310). As Rich's note makes clear, "Her life-work—remarkable for a woman architect—was framed by the contradiction that made it inseparable from the violation and expropriation by white entrepreneurs of the original cultures she respected and loved" (FD, 334). The failure of Colter's aesthetic, no matter how well-intentioned, looks forward to Rich's own anxious brooding on poetry's impotence before history.

Rich's growing sense that "it was not enough to name ourselves anew" (FD, 298) echoes as a fateful judgment throughout her poetry of the mid-1980s. For example, in "Education of a Novelist," her dialogue with Ellen Glasgow's autobiography *The Woman Within* rejects Glasgow's art for its sentimental oppression of her southern mammy Lizzie Jones. The authentic Lizzy Jones "vanishes" (FD, 316) beneath Glasgow's "verbal privilege."[34] But Glasgow's guilt is Rich's own, which she admits in an unflinching confession: "It's not enough / using your words to damn you, Ellen: / they could have been my own: / this criss-cross / map of kept and broken promises / *I was always the one*" (FD, 317). Rich's portrait of Ellen Glasgow as notable woman probes how the cultural labor of feminist heroines is routinely incorporated by Western patriarchy. "The history of notable women," writes Gerda Lerner, "is the history of exceptional, even deviant women, and does not describe the experience and history of the mass of women."[35]

Heroic "deviancy" is the central dilemma that possesses Rich as a feminist intellectual and poet in the 1980s. Ironically, the very professional and commercial success that now makes her a notable poet threatens to sever her writing from its political base.[36] Like the nineteenth-century personae she presents in "Heroines," Rich is fated to "speak / in the shattered language / of a partial vision":

> You draw your long skirts
> > > deviant
> > > > across the nineteenth century
> registering injustice
> > > failing to make it whole
> How can I fail to love
> > > your clarity and fury
> how can I give you
> > > all your due
> > > > take courage from your courage
> honor your exact
> > > legacy as it is
> recognizing
> > as well
> > > that it is not enough?   (FD, 295)

It is not enough. However "notable," Rich's heroines are "deviant" precisely because they lack the political base to effect broad social change. In the 1980s, Rich is anxious lest she repeat such deviant careers. Indeed, her poetry's politics have been called into question by several feminists, who charge that her writing is blind to the diverse ethnic, racial, and class experiences of Afro-American, Chicana, and other subaltern women.[37] Throughout the 1980s in works such as *Blood, Bread and Poetry, Selected Prose 1979–85* (1986) and *Your Native Land, Your Life* (1986), Rich's openness to world history leads her constantly to negotiate crises in past commitments that are at once intimate and public. "Poetry," she comes to realize in "North American Time" (1983), "never stood a chance / of standing outside history" (FD, 325). Significantly, in a 1984 keynote address to the Conference on Women, Feminist Identity, and Society in the 1980s, Rich questions her more parochial feminism of the 1970s: "It's hard to look back," she says,

> on the limits of my understanding a year, five years ago—how did I look without seeing, hear without listening? . . . In my white North American world they have tried to tell me that . . . only certain kinds of people make theory, that white minds are capable of formulating everything, that white feminism can know for "all women," that only when a white mind formulates is the formulation to be taken seriously. It seems to me that these opinions can only isolate those who hold them, from the great movements for bread and justice within and against which women define ourselves.[38]

Her awakening to world feminist revolution has sent Rich back to history's apocalyptic record in "North American Time": "No use protesting *I wrote that / before Kollontai was exiled / Rosa Luxembourg, Malcolm, / Anna Mae Aquash, murdered, / before Treblinka, Birkenau, / Hiroshima, before Sharpeville, / Biafra, Bangla Desh, Boston, / Atlanta, Soweto, Beirut, Assam*" (FD, 326). Such a dark vision of history is the occasion at once for her despair and dedication to social justice:

> The almost-full moon rises
> timelessly speaking of change
> out of the Bronx, the Harlem River
> the drowned towns of the Quabbin
> the pilfered burial mounds
> the toxic swamps, the testing-grounds
>
> and I start to speak again
> (FD, 328)

Rich's feminist agenda leads finally to broader "testing-grounds" of political change. Having jettisoned modernism's formalist aesthetic, and worked through archetypal feminism, the mother-daughter cathexis, a poetics of *écriture féminine,* and women's history, Rich's "wild patience" continues. In the mid-1980s, her writing seeks alignment with other ethnic, racial, and Third World movements of social liberation from patriarchy's "crumbling form." This political agenda will no doubt demand further "re-visions" of her poetic discourse in response to America's evolving social text. Meanwhile, other writers have empowered women's experience with poetic languages of liberation. In particular, the career of Gwendolyn Brooks offers a distinctively woman-centered poetics rooted in the social text of Afro-American emancipation.

7.

The Word from "Warpland": Gwendolyn Brooks' Afro-American Aesthetic

ALTHOUGH RICH'S career ranges all the way from formalism to feminism, she finds herself in the 1980s just beginning to undertake the real work of social emancipation. A similar poetic journey shapes the career of Gwendolyn Brooks over the last four decades: "I—who have 'gone the gamut,'" she says, "from an almost angry rejection of my dark skin by some of my brainwashed brothers and sisters to a surprised queenhood in the new black sun—am qualified to enter at least the kindergarten of new consciousness now."[1] Significantly, Brooks pioneered the political resources of black vernacular expression, which Marcuse welcomed as a rhetoric of critical resistance. The Afro-American idiom, he held, "is largely the language of the oppressed, and as such it has a natural affinity to protest and refusal."[2] Few of today's poets better prove Raymond Williams' claim that "to write in different ways is to live in different ways."[3] Writing from the lived history of race, class, and gender oppression, Brooks goes to the heart of the black experience in America. Yet even though she is the first Afro-American author ever to have received a Pulitzer Prize for poetry, surprisingly few mainstream American critics have had much to say about her verse.

Beyond her central status in the black community of the 1940s and 1950s, Brooks received nothing like the mainline academic support that, say, Robert Lowell enjoyed from American New Criticism.[4] In fact, some set her verse to one side simply because it was rooted in black experience. The most notorious instance of such reception is Louis Simpson's denial of racial themes as "important" subjects for poetry. In reviewing Brooks' verse for the now defunct *New York Herald Tribune Book Week,* Simpson bluntly dismissed not only Brooks' project in particular but the whole enterprise of contemporary Afro-American aesthetics: "I am not sure it is possible for a Negro to write well without making us aware he is a Negro; on the other hand, if being a Negro is the only subject, the writing is not important."[5] Such resistance to black experience was not uncongenial to the Southern Agrarian agenda of the Fugitives. In a 1952 forum, "The Social Role of Art and Philosophy," for example, John Crowe Ransom praised black author Richard Gibson for rejecting "the race problem in America" as his prime literary concern.[6] Beyond Brooks' cool critical reception in the 1950s, her poetry also fell through the cracks of academic, black, and feminist criticism during the next two decades.

Most major studies of contemporary and modern poetry, even in the 1980s, have failed to devote full chapters to Brooks' writing and many have even neglected to mention her at all.[7] Typically, when Brooks has been discussed, her early formalism has been pigeonholed as merely a transitional style, linking the Harlem Renaissance to more populist Afro-American and black feminist aesthetics of the 1960s and 1970s.[8] Thus, Haki Madhubuti (Don L. Lee) credited *Annie Allen* (1949) with breaking the racial barrier surrounding America's literary establishment. But he concluded that it "seems to have been written for whites."[9] Similarly, feminist criticism has tended to see Brooks as somehow "on the way" to American feminism proper in the work of Adrienne Rich and to the black feminism of, say, Lucille

Clifton, Nikki Giovanni, or Audre Lorde. Suzanne Juhasz's criticism typifies how Brooks' remarkably woman-centered verse is often excluded nevertheless from the postwar canon of valorized feminist poets. "Over the years," argues Juhasz, "Brooks has developed a black consciousness. . . . But she has not developed at the same time a feminist consciousness."[10]

Such readings have shortchanged Brooks' social vision. Dismissing her writing as merely transitional, critics have largely ignored her foundational importance for contemporary feminist and Afro-American poetics. Brooks' first poems, however neglected, forcefully challenged New Criticism's severing of poetry from the discourse of social experience. Writing from within the formalist tradition, Brooks nonetheless lodged a powerful critique of race, gender, and class oppression in postwar America. In her more recent work, she rests her poetic language on the populist rhetorical forms of the Afro-American community. But this is not to say that her writing offers some realistic or naturalistic mirroring of historical reference. Quite the contrary, she employs her poetry, whether in fixed or open forms, as a discursive medium for cultural critique. The strong poem, she holds, does not merely reflect but actively produces political change in the social field.

Radical Formalism

BROOKS FIRST read the poetry of Eliot, Pound, and Yeats in a 1941 Southside poetry workshop sponsored by Gold Coast socialite Inez Cunningham Stark. By the end of the decade, she had carved out a lasting place for Afro-American aesthetics *within* the modernist canon.[11] Publishing with Harper and Row, she quickly won a host of major awards: Midwestern Writer's Conference poetry award (1943), *Mademoiselle* Merit Award (1945), American Academy of Letters Award (1946), two Guggenheim Fellowships (1946, 1947), *Poetry's* prestigious Eunice Tietjens Memorial Award (1949), and the Pulitzer Prize (1950). In addition, at this time she was a regular reviewer for local Chicago publications such as the *Chicago Daily News, Chicago Sun Times, Chicago Tribune,* and *Negro Digest,* as well as East Coast dailies such as the *New York Herald Tribune* and the *New York*

Times. Moreover, she enjoyed immediate recognition from black writers such as Claude McKay, Countee Cullen, Langston Hughes, and James Weldon Johnson.

Following these Afro-American precursors, Brooks concerned herself, from the very beginning, with the struggle for racial identity. Throughout her career, she has paid close attention to the textures of urban black experience. "Her special métier," writes Nathan A. Scott, Jr., "would seem to be that of the ordinary, day-by-day scene of black American life—which is for her not an object of research but something felt along the pulses, in the veins."[12] Brooks' use of South Chicago's everyday people as poetic material stemmed from Langston Hughes: "I read Langston Hughes's *Weary Blues,* for example, and got very excited about what he was doing. I realized that writing about the ordinary aspects of Black life was important" (R, 170). Brooks' Afro-American identity, however, did not come easy. Initially, her journey toward black pride had to work through, as she says, "an almost angry rejection of my dark skin" (R, 86).

Race alienation, as Houston A. Baker, Jr., Addison Gayle, Jr., and numerous others have pointed out, is perpetuated by long-standing stereotypes of black life. As Henry Louis Gates, Jr. has argued, many of the foremost writers of the Western humanist tradition have actually denigrated black culture.[13] In fact, the great white canon has not only functioned to exclude and expunge the literary history of people of color, but has served to reproduce denigrating stereotypes of black experience. Thus, the challenge for Afro-American writers concurs with the task of feminism, of retrieving women's past behind the back of patriarchy's demeaning representations of gender.[14] Making matters worse for Brooks, postwar sexism within the Afro-American community consigned black women to even more marginal roles. As Mary Helen Washington has shown, leading black periodicals of the cold war decades such as *Ebony, Negro Digest,* and *Crisis* featured black women "as idealized, childlike creatures and assumed that their basic role was to satisfy the male imagination."[15]

Brooks' poetry, her autobiographical novel *Maud Martha* (1953), and her nonfiction prose all testify to her struggle with America's hierarchic color standard, ranging from white at the top downward through all the various hues of tan, yellow, brown, to black at the bottom. From the very beginning, she was led to emulate white culture. "A truly horrible thing," she admits, "was that I grew up to womanhood and went through womanhood believing that the gleaming white family life on the motion picture screens *should be* my model" (R, 213).[16] Her chapter "low yellow" from *Maud Martha* records how traditionally within the black community a light skin has been an invaluable status symbol. Moreover, Brooks' 1951 *Holiday* tableau of South Chicago's Bronzeville offers a frank exposé of that urban enclave's own racial caste system. Describing the affluent black neighborhoods of Woodlawn, Brooks shows how Bronzeville's elite deals with dark pigmentation:

> The children of these people, the puzzled Stranger may hear, are very light, or maybe apricot, a sort of sunburst brown. If, unhappily, the children are dark, just plain out-and-out dark that nothing can be done about, that not even Golden Peacock or Black and White Bleach can "help," then their parents have to spend money on clothes, have to force music or art through those black unfortunate fingers, have to maneuver those black bodies into the right social situations, have to "scheme."[17]

Brooks learned this lesson at an early age, remarking in her autobiography, *Report from Part One* (1972), that as a girl she was shy "AND DARK. The boys did not mind telling me that *this* was the failing of failings" (P. 57). Not surprisingly, she depicts blackness as a social stigma in such early poems as "The Ballad of Chocolate Mabbie" and "The Anniad."

Visionary anger, as Rich describes it, is one defense against such assaults to self-esteem. Brooks' first lyrics, for all their indebtedness to traditional fixed forms, rage against American racism. Her World War II "Negro Hero," from *A Street in Bronzeville* (1945), breaks America's segregative "law" in order, ironically, to save a drowning democracy. "I had to kick their law into their teeth," the hero says, "in order to save them. / However I have heard that sometimes you have to deal / Devilishly with drowning men in order to swim them to shore" (B, 48).

"Negro Hero" commemorates Dorie Miller, a black ship's steward, who during the Japanese assault on Pearl Harbor helped rescue the wounded captain of the U.S.S. *West Virginia*. Although he lacked formal training in weaponry, Miller manned a machine gun and in the pitch of the battle dispatched four enemy aircraft. Miller was the first black to be awarded the prestigious Navy Cross; incredibly, however, he was only promoted to mess attendant first class. In 1941, almost all blacks were constrained, like Miller, to service positions as chefs, stewards, and mess men. Following a policy of strictly limiting and segregating black officers, the Navy had commissioned only 12 black ensigns in 1944. By the end of the war, the number had increased to a mere 52 black officers, compared to over 70,000 white officers.[18] Responding to this bleak social reality, "Negro Hero" concludes with "this possible horror: thay they might prefer the / Preservation of their law in all its sick dignity and their knives / To the continuation of their creed / And their lives" (B, 50). In the 1960s a new generation of black activists would subscribe to a more radical model of heroism, embodied in the "Shine Swam On" toast that Larry Neal touts as "part of the private mythology of Black America."[19]

The tone of bitter irony that "Negro Hero" registers mounts in Brooks' next volume, *Annie Allen* (1949). Less willing here to go along with the compromised ethic of the "Negro Hero," Brooks is quite candid about white racial privilege. "Beverly Hills Chicago," for example, presents a black family's drive through an affluent white neighborhood. Although struck by the telling contrasts between its luxury and Bronzeville's poverty, Brooks' persona tries to repress her natural resentment: "Nobody is furious. Nobody hates these people. / At least nobody driving by in this car" (B, 129). But by the end of the outing, the family has lost its cool: "When we speak to each other, our voices are a little gruff" (B, 129).

Deepening her critique of segregation, "The Ballad of Rudolph Reed" from *The Bean Eaters* (1960) offers a disturbing indictment of white class privilege. Reed "hungers" to escape urban tenement life— to live "Where at night a man in bed / May never hear the plaster / Stir as if in pain. / May never hear the roaches / Falling like fat rain" (B, 376). Buying a house in a "pleasant" Caucasian neighborhood, however, he violates its unspoken taboo against integration. After three nights of racial harassment, Read responds in kind to the violent assaults on his family:

He ran like a mad thing into the night.
And the words in his mouth were stinking.
By the time he had hurt his first white man
He was no longer thinking.

By the time he had hurt his fourth white man
Rudolph Reed was dead.
His neighbors gathered and kicked his corpse.
"Nigger—" his neighbors said.

(B, 378)

Breaking down the racial barriers dividing Bronzeville from lily-white neighborhoods like Beverly Hills, Reed is martyred to the struggle for black equality. His violent end demythologizes segregation's tranquil facade, uncovering its underlying barbarism.

Beyond such works as "Negro Hero," "Beverly Hills Chicago," and "The Ballad of Rudolph Reed," Brooks indicts racism from a distinctively feminist vantage point.[20] Anticipating Rich's feminist poetry by more than two decades, Brooks looks forward to Rich's themes of mother-daughter bonding. Rereading Brooks' first poems from the hindsight of Alice Walker's "In Search of Our Mothers' Gardens" (1974), one is struck by their cogent portraits of black women's generational lives. For example, "The Mother," from *A Street in Bronzeville* (1945), dwells on a woman's lived experience of abortion:[21]

Abortions will not let you forget.
You remember the children you got that you did not get,
The damp small pulps with a little or with no hair,
The singers and workers that never handled the air.

(B, 21)

The haunting persistence of the unborn in memory—"I have heard in the voices of the wind the voices of my dim killed children" (B, 21)—is made even more poignant through the mother's pledge that "Believe me, I knew you, though faintly, and I loved, I loved you / All" (B, 22). Brooks has described the mother as one "who decides that *she,* rather than her World, will kill her children. The

decision is not nice, not simple, and the emotional consequences are
neither nice nor simple" (R, 184).

The poet's early canon reveals all too clearly that, however desperate, this mother's choice is not unusual. Mindful of the daughter's
fate, another of Brooks' mother figures asks, in "The Womanhood,"
"What shall I give my children? who are poor / Who are adjudged
the leastwise of the land" (B, 116). Similarly, "Jessie Mitchell's
Mother" from *The Bean Eaters* further illuminates the bleak prospects of low-income black mothers. Waiting for yet another labor
to come on, Jessie Mitchell's mother envisions her own poverty repeated as her daughter's likely future:

> The stretched yellow rag that was Jessie Mitchell's mother
> Reviewed her. Young, and so thin, and so straight.
> So straight! as if nothing could ever bend her.
> But poor men would bend her, and doing things with poor
> men,
> Being much in bed, and babies would bend her over,
> And the rest of things in life that were for poor women,
> Coming to them grinning and pretty with intent to bend and to
> kill.
>
> (B, 344)

Such matrifocal poems as "The Mother," "The Womanhood," and
"Jessie Mitchell's Mother" inscribe the grim urban fate of black
households in the postwar decades. A generation earlier, during the
so-called Great Migration of 1916–1919, rural blacks poured into the
industrial centers of Chicago, Cleveland, Detroit, Manhattan, Pitts-
burg, and other cities. In Chicago alone, from 1910 to 1920 the black
population swelled 148 percent. Brooks' own family was part of this
growth, moving from Topeka, Kansas to Hyde Park, Illinois in 1917,
the year of her birth.

The exodus of rural blacks to Northern ghettos, however, had
decidedly unsettling effects on the Afro-American community. To
begin with, family hardships created by high black unemployment,
particularly in the postwar years, was exacerbated by federal and
state welfare regulations that refused payments to indigent women
and children when the husband was present. Such policies hastened

the degradation of the black family. By the 1960s, for example, 30 percent of the 690,000 women annually applying for Aid to Dependent Children were single heads of households.[22] The number of black single mothers increased steadily from 843,000 in 1960 to 1,940,000 in 1975, fully 44 percent of all black households in 1985.[23] Moreover, urban centers that had once been open to blacks increasingly adopted discriminatory policies in housing. Mounting economic pressures, restricted covenants and other Jim Crow legislation, as well as actual physical violence, were all forces that fed residential segregation in American cities through the mid-twentieth century. It was not until the 1960s that the National Association of Real Estate Boards reversed its long-standing policies of fostering such segregation. Under the Kennedy administration, federally funded housing was desegregated, but not until 1968 did Congress pass the Fair Housing Act barring discrimination in residential real estate transactions.[24]

Typically, even though in the ghetto the costs of rent, consumer goods, and services were routinely inflated, the median income for all black families was only half that of white households. Such urban exploitation fueled crime and violence.[25] In the postwar decades the frequency of black homicides swelled to seven times that of whites. By 1980, half of all American homicides involved murders between black males.[26] Similarly, impoverished health care led Afro-American mothers to perish from birth complications at a rate six times that of white women,[27] while throughout the postwar era black infant mortality percentages during the first year of birth have remained twice that of whites, exceeding the mortality rates in Jamaica and Cuba.[28]

Faced with such dire threats, Brooks often presents sheer survival as the city's brute law. "First fight. Then fiddle," she advises, "Carry hate/In front of you and harmony behind" (B, 118). Even more pessimistic, Brooks at times dwells on the mother's anxiety that her attempts to succor the next generation are in vain. Brooks' image of the mother's bandage, for example, is a frequent symbol that both heals and blinds: "sew up belief/If that should tear: turn, singularly calm/At forehead and at fingers rather wise,/Holding the bandage ready for your eyes" (B, 117). Similarly, "The Ballad of Rudolph Reed" ends with a poignant image of a mother's futile attempt to assuage the physical and psychic wounds of her widowed daughter: "Small Mabel whimpered all night long, / For calling herself the cause. / Her oak-eyed mother did no thing / But change the bloody gauze" (B, 378). "Today," Brooks writes in *Report from Part One,* "the general black decision would be that bandages are not enough" (p. 186).

The same tone of quiet rage is registered throughout Brooks' early feminist poetry. "The Crazy Woman," for example, laments in a gray dirge: "I shall not sing a May song. / A May song should be gay. / I'll wait until November / And sing a song of gray" (B, 360). "The Crazy Woman," Brooks says, represents the many women who "do not bloom in the flowery light, but actually cry up to November darkness. The 'reverse' ones. The deflected ones" (R, 185). Resembling James Wright's "social outsiders," Brooks' "deflected" women seem crazy because, like Yeats' Crazy Jane, they have few illusions about their social fate. Harassed by race, sex, and class oppression, they somehow survive in isolation, lacking the support of either the feminist or black community. "A Sunset of the City" depicts another of Brooks' " 'reverse' ones"—a mother at midlife who also accepts the despair of "The Crazy Woman" 's November season: "It is real chill out. The fall crisp comes. / I am aware there is winter to heed. / . . . I am a woman, and dusty, standing among new affairs. / I am a woman who hurries through her prayers" (B, 353–54). Having coped with the same trauma that Brooks' other feminine personae face, "the crazy woman" endures her life, the poet says, as some "monstrous joke": "She hurries through her prayers because she feels they are no longer of use: there will be no answers" (R, 184).

Moving beyond the isolated portraits of black lives in *Bronzeville* and *Annie Allen,* Brooks' third book, *The Bean Eaters* (1960), responded to the key events that rocked America's institutional racism in the postwar epoch. This pivotal volume both reflected back on the birth of the civil rights movement in the late 1950s and forged new, politically engaged subject positions that blacks would adopt throughout the turbulent racial history of the 1960s. Like Rich, Brooks turned at this time toward a radical critique of postwar American history. For example, "A Bronzeville Mother Loiters In Mississippi, Meanwhile a Mississippi Mother Burns Bacon" probes the notorious

1955 lynching of Emmet Till, a Chicago youth who was murdered while visiting with relatives in the South. After allegedly whistling at a white woman in Money, Mississippi, Till was kidnapped and lynched. Particularly scandalous was the fact that an all-white jury refused to convict Till's alleged murderers for any crimes. Widely publicized in such progressive Northern papers as *The Chicago Defender,* Till's murder symbolized the persistence of Southern taboos against interracial sex. Throughout the nineteenth and twentieth centuries, as Ralph Ginzburg and others have shown, the lynching of black men on trumped-up charges of having forced sex with white women was one of the most brutal forms of Southern racism.[29] Over a thousand blacks were lynched on allegations of rape between 1882 and 1936.[30] Even now, America's record of racial lynchings, Gwendolyn Brooks maintains, haunts the unconscious of Afro-American writers: "a black poet may be involved in a concern for trees, if only because when he looks at one he thinks of how his ancestors have been lynched thereon" (R, 166).

Significantly, Southern lynching, as Hazel V. Carby has shown, also served to tyrannize not only Afro-American males but also Southern women, whether black or white. Throughout the nineteenth century, Afro-American and feminist activists like Frances E. W. Harper, Anna Julia Cooper, and Ida Wells-Barnett fulminated against fraudulent charges of rape that oppressed women. As Carby points out, Barnett's *Southern Horrors: Lynch Law in All Its Phases* (1892) argued cogently "that white men used their ownership of the body of the white female as a terrain on which to lynch the black male."[31] Similarly, Brooks' political critique in "A Bronzeville Mother" links Southern patriarchy's harassment of black men to its sexual "ownership" of women. Her strategy is to present the psychic effects of racial violence on the poem's other victim: the Mississippi woman Till innocently admired. Shaken by the murder, the Mississippi mother anxiously tries to shore up her image as the chaste but alluring Angel of the House:

> Then, before calling Him, she hurried
> To the mirror with her comb and lipstick. It was necessary
> To be more beautiful than ever.
> The beautiful wife.

> For sometimes she fancied he looked at her as though
> Measuring her. As if he considered, Had she been worth It?
> . . . . .
>
> Whatever she might feel or half-feel, the lipstick necessity
>   was something apart. He must never conclude
> That she had not been worth It.
>
> (B, 335–336)

Carefully inscribed with the "lipstick necessity" of what Mary Wollstonecraft would call women's "corporeal accomplishment," the Mississippi mother must make herself even more beautiful for men. But once achieved, this seductive facade only thinly disguises her real dilemma. Now complicit in Till's murder, she unwittingly becomes her husband's chattel as "the beautiful wife" and is thus inescapably joined to patriarchy's other victims:

> She looked at her shoulders, still
> Gripped in the claim of his hands. She tried, but could not resist
>   the idea
> That a red ooze was seeping, spreading darkly, thickly, slowly,
> Over her white shoulders, her own shoulders,
> And over all of Earth and Mars
> . . . . .
>
> Gripped in the claim of his hands. She tried, but could not resist
> She did not scream.
> She stood there.
> But a hatred for him burst into glorious flower,
> And its perfume enclasped them—big,
> Bigger than all magnolias.
>
> (B, 399)

Gripped in the fierce embrace of male ownership, the Mississippi mother awakens to her own visionary anger, imaged here as at once a glorious and ghastly blossoming.[32]

Broadening Brooks' public assault on institutional racism, "The Chicago Defender Sends a Man to Little Rock" probes the South's repressive tolerance of racial tensions. Brooks published several of her first works in the *Chicago Defender,* a progressive Bronzeville newspaper founded in 1905 by Robert C. Abbot. In the poem, the reporter's persona serves as the vehicle for a stinging social critique of Southern living. Little Rock, of course, was the site of the first major federal and state clash over school desegregation emerging from the Warren Court's 1954 landmark ruling in *Brown v. Board of Education of Topeka*. During the fall of 1957 Arkansas Governor Orval E. Faubus ordered state National Guardsmen to prevent nine Negro students from attending Little Rock's Central High School. In response, President Eisenhower mobilized federal troops to enforce integration of Central High. Brooks' poem, however, does not overtly take up Little Rock's segregative stance as its subject. Nor is its tone marked by the racial tensions rampant in the fall of 1957. Instead, she focuses on how Little Rock simply ignored the civil rights struggle through its humdrum status quo:

> In Little Rock the people bear
> Babes, and comb and part their hair
> And watch the want ads, put repair
> To roof and latch. While wheat toast burns
> A woman waters multiferns.
>
> (B, 346)

As a social microcosm of provincial America, Little Rock is symptomatic of the unconscious functioning of institutional racism. The reporter for the *Chicago Defender* is understandably astonished to find little change in the Deep South's domestic routine. The poem's rhyming tercets mimic the facade of harmony that is Little Rock's means of "normalizing" racial tensions:

> In Little Rock the people sing
> Sunday hymns like anything,
> Through Sunday pomp and polishing.
>
> And after testament and tunes,
> Some soften Sunday afternoons
> With lemon tea and Lorna Doones.
>
> (B, 346)

Such small town rituals subtly smooth over any wrinkles in the social fabric of American segregation. Moreover, Little Rock's resources of tolerance repress black insubordination. The community envisioned here is one wholly incapable of critical reflection. Little Rock simply incorporates dissent within its own one-dimensional organization of social life.

The reporter admits that the expected "media event" is visible here: "And true, they are hurling spittle, rock, / Garbage and fruit in Little Rock. / And I saw coiling storm a-writhe / On bright madonnas. And a scythe / Of men harassing brownish girls" (B, 348). But what is so unsettling about Little Rock is not the momentary interest it holds for sensationalist journalism. More troubling, the correspondent fatefully recognizes that the spectacle of Little Rock's racist scene is only a local symptom of America's broader political unconscious: "The biggest News I do not dare / Telegraph to the Editor's chair: / 'They are like people everywhere' " (B, 348). In such moments, Brooks looks forward to Stokely Carmichael's mid-1960s critique of segregation as a pervasive social institution in the United States.[33] So widespread and unyielding is segregation in America, said Carmichael, that it is taken for granted as "natural": "This fact cannot be too strongly emphasized—that racist assumptions of white superiority have been so deeply ingrained in the structure of the society that it infuses its entire functioning, and is so much a part of the national subconscious that it is . . . frequently not even recognized" ("Toward Black Liberation," p. 123). But before Carmichael and others had theorized concerning America's racial unconscious, Brooks' poetry had already depicted it.

In the late 1950s Brooks' writing was taking her little by little beyond the integrationist stance of her first two volumes. Early poems such as "Negro Hero," "Beverly Hills Chicago" and her woman-centered verse are marked by what W. E. B. Du Bois defined as black Americans' "double-consciousness": "So one ever feels his twoness—an American, a Negro—two souls, two thoughts, two unreconciled strivings; two warring ideals in one dark body, whose dogged strength alone keeps it from being torn asunder."[34] Although mindful of black oppression, Brooks up until the 1960s was riven by such double consciousness. Endorsing the ideal of integration, she aimed to save whites from the misguided "law" and "creed" of segregation by awakening them to their own unconscious racism. But from the hindsight of active white resistance to 1950s civil rights legislation, Brooks renounced her earlier compassion for Caucasian America. Throughout the coming decade, her poetry would increasingly inscribe revolutionary subject positions that an emergent generation of Afro-American leadership would occupy in the political struggle for black power.

"The Language of the Unheard"

THE EARLY 1960s, of course, were years of turmoil and tragedy for black and white Americans. The 1960 lunch-counter sit-ins of Greensboro and Atlanta, the 1961 Freedom Rides throughout the Deep South, and James Meredith's campaign to register at the University of Mississippi in 1962 all exposed just how deep-seated was Southern resistance to integration. These and other actions, organized by the Congress of Racial Equality (CORE), the Southern Christian Leadership Conference (SCLC), and the Student Non-Violent Coordinating Committee (SNCC), culminated in the successful 1963 march on Washington for racial and economic justice. But these actions also spurred a barbarous white backlash leading to the assassination of Mississippi NAACP leader Medgar Evans and the deaths of four black children in the bombing of a Birmingham church that same year. The notorious media images of police brutality—as for example in the violent arrest of 959 youngsters during the 1963 children's march in Birmingham—became indelible symbols of America's institutional racism. In such a volatile social milieu of police clubbings, firehosings, and dog attacks, Brooks wrote her twelve-part poem "Riders to the Blood-Red Wrath," included in the "New Poems" section of her 1963 collection *Selected Poems*. Celebrating the various political actions of the civil rights campaign, the poem takes as its heroes, Brooks writes, "the Freedom Riders, and their fellows the sit-ins, the wade-ins, read-ins, pray-ins, vote-ins, and all related strugglers for what is reliably right" (R, 187).

Organized by CORE and SNCC, the Freedom Riders tested the 1960 Supreme Court ruling in *Boynton v. Virginia* that banned segregation on all interstate buses and trains, and in terminals. Traveling from Washington, D.C. to Jackson, Mississippi, the Freedom Riders were beaten, and even burned, by angry white mobs, espe-

cially in Anniston and Montgomery, Alabama. Finally escorted by
National Guard troops to Jackson, the twenty-seven survivors were
promptly arrested for sitting in the "white only" section of the city
bus depot. Inspired by their heroism, Brooks passionately espoused
such acts of black liberation. In the central metaphor of "Riders," a
dark "mare"—her symbol for the outward dumbshow of submission to white authority—masks the "charger" of Afro-American
"revolution":

> Did they detect my parleys and replies?
> My revolution pushed his twin the mare,
> The she-thing with the soft eyes that conspire
> To lull off men, before him everywhere.
> Perhaps they could not see what wheedling bent
> Her various heart in mottles of submission
> And sent her into a firm skirmish which
> Has tickled out the enemy's sedition.
>
> They do not see how deftly I endure.
> Deep down the whirlwind of good rage I store
> Commemorations in an utter thrall.
> Although I need not eat them anymore.
>   (B, 390)

In "Riders" Brooks launches her revolt beneath "mottles of submission." Such traditional ruses serve strategically as a kind of necessary aesthetic covering, as she makes clear in *Report*: "These traditions were a sort of art—(they were certainly *not* the manifestations
of *nature*)—developed; molded; decorated" (R, 187).

Increasingly, Brooks viewed her own formalist style as just such
an aesthetic mask. The poem adopts a traditional form—alternately
rhymed lines of iambic pentameter—to undermine from within formalism's remove from history. Ultimately, "Riders" breaks through
such poetic artifice to a distinctively African heritage: "I remember
my right to roughly run and roar. / My right to raid the sun, consult
the moon, / Nod to my princesses or split them open, / To flay my
lions, eat blood with a spoon" (B, 391). Like Adrienne Rich's "re-
memberings" of women's past, Brooks' quest for her African roots

is mediated by the legacy of patriarchal domination: "I recollect the latter lease and lash / And labor that defiled the bone, that thinned / My blood and blood-line" (B, 391). Not incidentally, Brooks borrows certain coded words from the social text of the civil rights movement, like "whirlwind," to celebrate her own push for democratic change. For example, in Martin Luther King's celebrated 1963 "I Have a Dream" speech, he wrote, "The Whirlwinds of revolt will continue to shake the foundations of our nation until the bright day of justice emerges."[35] More militant works, such as Brooks' "After Mecca" sequence and her *Riot* volume of the late 1960s, again summoned up a "whirlwind of good rage." Throughout the 1960s, Brooks increasingly brought her poetic discourse into closer alignment with the theory and rhetoric of black cultural nationalism.

While Brooks was waging black revolution in the aesthetic dimension, Afro-American theorists such as Amiri Baraka, James Boggs, Stokely Carmichael, Harold Cruse, Stephen Henderson, and Julian Mayfield were describing black America as a colonized enclave within the United States.[36] Drawn together initially by their common racial and economic oppression, black leaders such as Malcolm X of the Organization of Afro-American Unity (OAAU); Stokely Carmichael, chairman of SNCC; Ron Karenga, founder of the US organization, and others pointed out how both Martin Luther King's nonviolent campaigns and postwar civil rights legislation had failed to protect the Afro-American masses against white racism. In 1964, the year King received a Nobel Peace Prize and Congress created the Equal Employment Opportunity Commission under the Civil Rights Act, Lemuel Penn was shot by members of the Ku Klux Klan in Georgia. Moreover, three voting rights advocates—James Chaney, Michael Schwerner, and Andrew Goodman—were arrested in Neshoba County, Mississippi and later found buried in a makeshift dam.

Responding to such atrocities in the mid-1960s, the black power, black cultural nationalism, and the black aesthetic movements came into being. The OAAU's position statement, entitled "Basic Unity Program," summed up the emergent *Zeitgeist* of the black nationalist agenda. Malcolm X was scheduled to deliver the OAAU document as part of its February 21, 1965 program. During the course of the contentious session, however, he was assassinated before he could read it:

> We, Afro-Americans—enslaved, oppressed and denied by a society that proclaims itself the citadel of democracy, are determined to rediscover our history, promote the talents that are suppressed by our racist enslavers, renew the culture that was crushed by a slave government and thereby—to again become a free people.[37]

By the summer of 1966 Stokely Carmichael was espousing a similar concept of "black power" that would become the rallying cry that fall for the newly formed Black Panther Party in Oakland, California.

Closing ranks with these political movements, black artists, writers, and intellectuals adopted Malcolm X's agenda for the self-determination of Afro-American culture. By 1964 the influential editor of *Negro Digest,* Hoyt Fuller, had moved his journal increasingly toward an anti-integrationist stance. Deriding the European-existential leanings of Ralph Ellison, Fuller vigorously supported Imamu Amiri Baraka's controversial Black Arts Repertory Theatre and other militant black authors including Ossie Davis, Jr., John Killens, and Larry Neal, among others. Shaping the agenda of the black aesthetic movement, Fuller sponsored a national poll of influential black and white intellectuals in 1965. Three years later, he repeated the poll but dropped all whites from his sample. Fuller's *Negro Digest* was an important arena for fostering black cultural nationalism in the 1960s. Summing up the journal's ideological shift during this decade, the *Negro Digest's* name was changed to *Black World* in 1970.[38]

Besides editors such as Fuller and Dudley Randall—publisher of Broadside Press—two author-theorists crucial to the black aesthetic movement during the 1960s were Imamu Amiri Baraka and Larry Neal. Influenced at first by Charles Olson's "projectivism" and the Beat Generation, Baraka edited *Yugen* magazine with his first wife, Hettie Cohen, from 1958 to 1963. In the mid-1960s, however, he divorced Cohen and left the Lower East Side for Harlem, where he espoused the black cultural nationalism of Malcolm X and Ron Karenga. Beyond his provocative plays such as *Dutchman* (1964), *The Slave* (1964), *The Toilet* (1964), *A Black Mass* (1966), and *Slave Ship* (1969), Baraka produced key manifestoes of black cultural nationalism in *Home: Social Essays* (1966) and *Black Fire* (1968), an anthology of Afro-American writing he co-edited with Larry Neal. As arts editor for the black journal *Liberator,* Neal, like Fuller, gave early support to Baraka's Harlem Repertory Theatre in essays such as "Development of LeRoi Jones." *Black Fire* anthologized their efforts to foster the black aesthetic movement in journals such as *Liberator, Black Dialogue, Negro Digest,* and *Journal of Black Poetry.*

Other smaller journals of this period *(Anistand, Umbra, Soul-Book),* black presses (Free Black Press and Third World Press, Chicago; Journal of Black Poetry Press and Broadside Press, Detroit; Black Dialogue Press, New York; Jihad Press, Newark), and newly formed black organizations and conferences worldwide made up the cultural background against which Gwendolyn Brooks conceived her Afro-American poetics during the late 1960s. In the half-decade between *Selected Poems* (1963) and *In the Mecca* (1968), she became a pioneer in the emergent black aesthetic movement. Brooks dates her turn to a distinctively black identity from the 1967 Black Writer's Conference organized by John Killens at Fisk University. Impressed by such figures as Amiri Baraka, Hoyt Fuller, John Killens, David Llorens, and Ron Milner, she was struck by the special élan of the conference's new generation of black writers: "First, I was aware of a general energy, an electricity, in look, walk, speech, *gesture* of the young blackness I saw all about me. . . . I had never been, before, in the general presence of such insouciance, such live firmness, such confident vigor, such determination to mold or carve something DEFINITE" (R, 85).

Back home in Chicago following her Nashville initiation, Brooks attended Oscar Brown, Jr.'s production of *Opportunity, Please Knock.* Featured in the cast were several of Chicago's Blackstone Rangers with whom Brooks would deepen her local commitment to black culture. Allied with the youth organizer and writer Walter Bradford and poet Haki Madhubuti, she spent that year coaching the Rangers in a poetry workshop. Largely influenced by Madhubuti during this time, she read works such as Frantz Fanon's *The Wretched of the Earth,* Ferdinand Lundbert's *The Rich and the Super Rich,* Dubois' *The Souls of Black Folk,* and the novels of Zora Neale Hurston. Along with Madhubuti and other young Chicago-based black poets—such as Carolyn Rodgers, Etheridge Knight, Sharon Scott, and Mike Cook—Brooks gave public readings in black bars, prisons, churches, housing projects, and street festivals. These activities culminated in her inclusion on the Wall of Respect mural painted on a Chicago tenement on 43rd Street and Langley.

Such populist influences significantly changed Brooks' understanding of poetic discourse—its resources, status, and function:

> 1966. 1967. 1968. Years of explosion. In those years a young black
> with pen in hand responded not to pretty sunsets and the lapping
> of lake water but to the speech of physical riot and spiritual re-
> bellion. . . . The initial trend was away from decoration, away
> from dalliance. There was impatience with idle embroidery, with
> what was considered avoidance, avoidance of the gut issue, the
> blood fact. Literary rhythms altered! Sometimes the literature seemed
> to issue from pens dipped in, *stabbed* in, writhing blood. Music
> was very important. It influenced the new pens. There were veer-
> ings from Glenn Miller and Benny Goodman to Coltrane, Ornette
> Coleman, Charlie Mingus, Charles Earland—from "I'll Be Seeing
> You" to "Soulful Strut."[39]

Adopting a poetics based in local black vernacular and its folk idioms, she set out to recover the social text of Afro-American culture.
Her poetry began to employ black references from Afro-American
music, sermon, and popular discourses. Asserting that "ESSEN-
TIAL black literature is the distillation of black life" (Capsule, 3),
she espoused an aesthetic rooted in, but also stylizing, the rhythms
of black conversation—its intonations, verbal gestures, and situa-
tional nuances.

Brooks' turn to a black rhetoric emerged from her Chicago poetry workshops with figures such as Madhubuti and Carolyn Rodgers.
Both of these 1960s poets promoted black vernacular as the base for
a distinctively Afro-American language community. In defining black
discourse, Rodgers laid out ten varieties and twenty-three subdivi-
sions of black expression, including "signifying, teachin/rappin, covers
off, spaced, bein, love, shoutin, jazz, du-wah, and pyramid." "These
poets," she writes, "hip you to something, pull the covers off of
something, or run it down to you, or ask you to just dig it—your
coat is being pulled."[40] Madhubuti offered a more conventional
statement on black poetics, stressing:

1. polyrhythmic, uneven, short, and explosive lines
2. intensity; depth, yet simplicity; spirituality, yet flexibility

3. irony; humor; signifying
4. sarcasm—a new comedy
5. direction; positive movement; teaching, nation-building
6. subject matter—concrete; reflects a collective and personal life-style
7. music: the unique use of vowels and consonants with the developed rap demands that the poetry be real, and read out loud[41]

Brooks' mature poetry adopted these broad criteria, thus satisfying Madhubuti's "rap demand" for a poetry of oral performance. "We Real Cool," from the *The Bean Eaters,* is a prototype of the ironic, jazz-rappin, covers off poetics that, so to speak, pulls the reader's coat:

> The Pool Players.
> Seven at the Golden Shovel.

We real cool. We
Left school. We

Lurk late. We
Strike straight. We

Sing sin. We
thin gin. We

Jazz June. We
Die soon.

(B, 331)

In this compressed lyric, Brooks masterfully "runs down" the fate of urban gang members of the late 1950s. Even in her fixed forms, Brooks' improvisational sound sense and jazzy syntax invokes the linguistic nuances of black urban culture.

Turning toward the social text of the black community, Brooks moved beyond her lyric formalism, branching out to write a distinctively Afro-American long poem: "In The Mecca" (1968). Her goal was a "book-length poem, two thousand lines or more, based on life in Chicago's old Mecca Building" (R, 189). She chose the Mecca as her subject for, like its namesake in the Islamic world, it stood at the center of its cultural milieu. An emblem of Chicago's black heritage, it housed both its failures and funky vitality. Originally built in 1891, the Mecca began as an elegant white apartment building. It was home, during the Great Migration in 1912, to Chicago's black professional elite. By 1950, as John Barlow Martin suggested in a *Harper's Magazine* exposé, it embodied the kind of tenement life Brooks depicted in "The Lovers of the Poor": "The dirt courtyard is littered with newspapers and tin cans, milk cartons and broken glass. Pigeons roost on a car on blocks. A skinny white dog huddles in a doorway. . . . It has become one of the most remarkable Negro slum exhibits in the world."[42] Significantly, throughout the 1940s, the Mecca community successfully fended off attempts by the building's owner, the Illinois Institute of Technology, to tear it down. Thus, it stood as a symbol for inner city resistance to the kind of urban "renewal" that was gutting the local neighborhoods in East Harlem, Boston's North End, and other racial and ethnic enclaves.

Partly autobiographical, Brooks' poem depicts those whom she would have intimately known in the 1940s from her work for one of the Mecca's eccentrics, a savvy spiritual adviser. But unlike many of the confessional long poems of the 1960s, Brooks offers a panoramic view of the black urban spectacle, staging "a large variety of personalities against a mosaic of daily affairs" (R, 189). Following Eliot's use of Tiresias as "spectator" to *The Waste Land*'s unfolding action, Brooks employs a poet-speaker, Alfred, as a central interpreter of the poem's narrative. Brooks, however, resists the modernists' leanings toward cultural unity.[43] Moreover, she abandons the kind of historical sense Eliot finds, for example, in Joyce's *Ulysses*.[44] Embodying both "subtle wit" and "social width," her black epic takes up Whitman's dictum, as Brooks paraphrases it, to "vivify the contemporary fact."[45] "In the Mecca," she writes, "were murders, loves, lonelinesses, hates, jealousies. Hope occurred, and charity, sainthood, glory, shame, despair, fear, altruism. Theft, material and moral. 'Mental cruelty'" (R, 190). To stage such a turbulent world, Brooks parts company with her early formalism in favor of expansive and colloquial forms, employing "random rhyme, off rhyme, a long-swinging free verse, blank verse, prose verse" (R, 190).

The poem's narrative vehicle—Mrs. Sallie's search for her missing child Pepita—stages the Mecca's contingent and violent social world. Here we meet the poem's eccentric personae who are nonetheless familiar types of the black community. Each of Mrs. Sallie's eight children, for example, embodies familiar themes from Brooks' earlier work. Briggs pledges himself to the punk gang life that spells early doom for the delinquents of "We Real Cool." Similarly, the same dreamy romanticism that shapes Brooks' Chocolate Mabbie and Annie Allen also defines Yvonne. Among the Mecca's bathetic figures are Great-great Gram, a vestige of antebellum slavery; Loam Norton, who is haunted by memories of the Holocaust; John Tom, one of the city's dupes; Hyena, a funky "debutante"; Prophet Williams, the Mecca's mystical entrepreneur; Wezlyn, Mecca's late-night "wandering woman"; the janitor, "who is a Political Person" (B, 429); and old Mr. Kelly, "who begs / subtly from door to door" (B, 429). Beyond these portraits, the poem offers wry tableaux of radical militants that herald the coming black power movement.

Amos, the poem's crusty parody of the Old Testament prophet, invokes Judaism's patriarchal imagery of atonement to purge America of its racist history. Drawing on the traditional icon of Israel as the defiled virgin, Amos' prayer for America would "Bathe her in her beautiful blood. / A long blood bath will wash her pure" (B, 424). The other bizarre spokesman of revolution is the poem's urban survivalist, Way-out Morgan: "Way-out Morgan is collecting guns / in a tiny fourth-floor room. / . . . Way-out Morgan / predicts the Day of Debt-pay shall begin, / the Day of Demon-diamond, / of blood in mouths and body mouths, / of flesh-rip in the Forum of Justice at last!" (B, 431). Beyond such figures, Brooks offers a cameo portrait of the black cultural nationalist Don L. Lee (Haki Madhubuti). Lee envisions a utopian alternative to the Mecca's scenic despair:

> Don Lee wants
> not a various America.
> Don Lee wants
> a new nation
> under nothing;
> a physical light that waxes; he does not want to
> be exorcised, adjoining and revered;

> he does not like a local garniture
> nor any impish onus in the vogue;
> is not candlelit
> but stands out in the auspices of fire
> and rock and jungle-flail;
> wants
> new art and anthem; will
> want a new music screaming in the sun.
>
> (B, 424)

As a proponent of the 1960s' black aesthetic movement, Lee eschews the traditional careerism of contemporary poets: "he does not like a local garniture / nor any impish onus in the vogue." Instead, he is committed to a populist, revolutionary aesthetic.

Lee's utopian imagination balances the pessimism of Alfred, the Mecca's other visionary poet.[46] Like Lee, Alfred longs for a communal ground of Afro-American solidarity. He also pines for an African heritage, searching out the black roots of authentic belief: "When there were all those gods / administering to panthers, / jumping over mountains, / and lighting stars and comets and a moon, / what was their one Belief? / what was their joining thing?" (B, 409–10). But split by DuBois' "double consciousness," Alfred fails to grasp the elusive "joining thing" of primordial Africa. Trapped in the Mecca's urban present, he can only achieve "unity of being" through the *dérèglement de tous les sens*. Each night, he "drinks until the Everything / is vaguely a part of One thing and the One thing / delightfully anonymous and undiscoverable. So he is weak, / is weak, is no good. Never mind. / It is a decent enough no-goodness" (B, 209). Alfred's "no-goodness" is "decent enough," as it provides the necessary negative capability for fathoming the Mecca's obscure labyrinth:

> But he (who might have been an architect)
> can speak of Mecca: firm arms surround
> disorders, bruising ruses and small hells,
> small semiheavens: hug barbarous rhetoric
> built of buzz, coma and petite pell-mells.
>
> (B, 421–22)

Alfred's double vision of the Mecca's elegant destitution reaches after "an essential sanity, black and electric /. . . A hot estrangement. / A material collapse / that is Construction" (B, 433). His pessimistic vision of urban poverty tempers Lee's utopian aesthetic.

Ultimately, Brooks' black verse epic sides less with Lee's optimism and more with the poem's embittered extremists. The substanceless unity Alfred seeks out in the Mecca is even more radically negative than he can ferret out. As poet, however, Brooks makes the dark pilgrimage into the Mecca's inner recesses of despair. The poem's climax, the discovery of Pepita Smith's raped corpse under Jamaican Edward's shabby cot, betokens the fall of Afro-America. The "hot estrangement" of the Mecca's urban violence is symptomatic of America's institutional racism. Beyond City Hall's official bureaucratic line that "South State St. is Postulate," she says, "you discover / the paper dolls are terrible. You touch. / You look and touch. / The paper dolls are terrible and cold" (B, 421). Through such a negative epiphany Brooks would compel her readers to confirm the poem's epigraph, quoted from Russ Meek: "There comes a time when what has been can never be again."[47]

Blooming in the Whirlwind

THE MECCA'S bleak urban milieu bears out Stephen Henderson's claim that "this country has been built upon violence, physical, mental, and spiritual—by the virtual extermination of the Indian, by the enslavement of the African, and the systematic degradation of his progeny in America."[48] As Henderson says, racism's systematic violence is installed across the total social fabric of the contemporary American scene. Indeed, it is reproduced in such settings as Chicago's South Side, Los Angeles's Watts section, New York's Harlem, South Philadelphia, Detroit, Newark, and numerous other inner city wards throughout both the industrial North and the Southern black belt. Responding to the political fate of black America in the late 1960s, Brooks began to align herself with the kind of revolutionary cultural agenda espoused by Ron Karenga. "Black art," he insisted, "must expose the enemy, praise the people and support the revolution."[49] Brooks actually took a quote from Karenga as her epigraph to "The Sermon on the Warpland": "The fact that we are black is our ultimate reality." The Warpland series—"The Sermon on the Warpland" and "The Second Sermon on the Warpland" from the *Mecca* volume, and "The Third Sermon on the Warpland" from *Riot*—welcomed a black aesthetic revolution. In promoting the idea of black national culture, Brooks revamped her poetic discourse to fit the social context of an emerging black readership.[50] Borrowing from W. E. B. DuBois's belief that black folk are the "very warp of this nation,"[51] she pushed for a distinctively Afro-American political base.

In the poet's metaphor, the black aesthetic blossoms from a "doublepod." That is, it not only has to deal with racism but, more importantly, must imagine utopian possibilities for social emancipation:

> Say that our Something in doublepod contains
> seeds for the coming hell and health together.
> Prepare to meet
> (sisters, brothers) the brash and terrible weather;
> the pains;
> the bruising; the collapse of bestials, idols.
> But then oh then!—the stuffing of the hulls!
> the seasoning of the perilously sweet!
> the health! the heralding of the clear obscure!
>
> (B, 451)

Poetry inaugurates "the heralding of the clear obscure" as it plants the seeds of aesthetic liberation. It must find durable discursive forms and conceive revolutionary subject positions that are organically rooted in the "brash and terrible weather" of social change. "Blooming in the noise of the whirlwind" (B, 453), poetry has to go beyond formalism to celebrate revolutionary black America, whose "time / cracks into furious flower" (B, 456). "Not the pet bird of poets, that sweetest sonnet," she concludes, "shall straddle the whirlwind" (B, 454). Echoing the "whirlwinds of revolt" that King had invoked in 1963, Brooks asserted in a 1977 interview that "the social world is a whirlwind."[52] Her benedictal closing to "The Second Sermon on Warpland" looks forward to *Riot* (1969) in espousing political militancy

for the flowering of Afro-American culture. "Conduct your blooming," she advises, "in the noise and whip of the whirlwind" (B,
456).

Significantly, with her 1969 volume *Riot,* Brooks shifted to an
Afro-American publisher, Dudley Randall's Broadside Press, leaving
Harper and Row, which would only publish one more of her volumes, *The World of Gwendolyn Brooks* (1971). Like her Warpland series, Brooks' title piece heralds the "coming hell" of political militancy. In "Riot" she adopts the persona of John Cabot, a white dandy
who is supremely unconscious of the black ghetto's everyday people. An effete connoisseur of advanced consumer capitalism, Cabot
apes European *haut monde,* savoring "the sculpture at the Richard
Gray / and Distelheim; the kidney pie at Maxim's, / the Grenadine
de Boeuf at Maison Henri" (TD, 5). "Riot" exposes Cabot, however, to the other side of advanced capitalism's racial and class privilege, thus dramatizing Walter Benjamin's point that "there has never
been a document of culture which was not at one and the same time
a document of barbarism."[53] Beyond recording the 1960s' urban unrest, "Riot" marks the liberation of blacks from the cultural domination of consumer capitalism. Cabot's investment in the American
Dream is suddenly shattered,

Because the "Negroes" were coming down the street.

Because the Poor were sweaty and unpretty
(not like Two Dainty Negroes in Winnetka)
and they were coming toward him in rough ranks.
In seas. In windsweep. They were black and loud.
And not detainable. And not discreet.

(TD, 5)

Out of the "whirlwind" of such violent scenes, Brooks gleans the
seeds of a utopian social vision that she cultivates in the aesthetic
dimension. Quoting Martin Luther King, Jr., Brooks' epigraph asserts that "A riot is the language of the unheard" (TD, 5). As symptoms of long-standing social injustice, America's urban riots of the
late 1960s heralded what Brooks hoped would be the flowering of
a revolutionary black national culture. In the 1970s, Brooks listens

for the "unheard" languages of cultural change, nurturing them in her own poetic discourse.

In her next two volumes, *Family Pictures* (1971) and *Beckonings* (1975), Brooks' sensitivity to poetry's verbal resources maintains a tension of difference from a later generation of black poets. Her aim, as she says in a 1983 interview, is to preserve the careful verbal craft of her early period even as she adopts the more lyric intensity of the black aesthetic: "I don't want to say these poems have to be simple, but I want to *clarify* my language. . . . I want them to be direct without sacrificing the kinds of music, the picturemaking I've always been interested in. I'm not afraid of having a few remaining subtleties."[54] Consistently, Brooks has held that art "is refining and evocative translation of the materials of the world!" (Capsule, 11). She values poetic discourse, in part, for its worldly estrangements of the "natural" givens of the public status quo. Aesthetic alienation is the subject of such works as "The Chicago Picasso," where she asks: "Does man love Art? Man visits Art, but squirms. / Art Hurts. Art urges voyages" (B, 442). Moreover, Brooks' metaphoric "subtleties" temper black street language in "The Wall": "No child has defiled / the Heroes of this Wall this serious Appointment / this still Wing / this Scald this Flute this heavy Light this Hinge" (B, 445). Writing in this way, Brooks preserves the nuances of the black urban rap, refining its "serious appointments" with history into more sophisticated and critical aesthetic registers.

Throughout her poetry of the 1980s, Brooks' leanings toward Pan-African solidarity face up to the historical failure of the black aesthetic as a broad populist movement. The decline and final collapse of black cultural nationalism began shortly after the largest black political convention in American history, held in Gary, Indiana in 1972. Throughout the 1970s, both external threats and internal pressures fragmented the consensus of the National Black Political Assembly forged at Gary. In the late 1970s, the Afro-American community split up into several divisive splinter groups. Some, like the Black Panther Party, were harassed by the FBI's Counter-Intelligence Program (COINTELPRO). Others, such as the African Liberation Support Committee and the Congress of African People, were torn by bitter debates over the status of Marxism within the Pan-African movement. Moreover, at this time the gap separating the elite black bourgeoisie from the mass of working-class and unemployed blacks steadily widened. Although Southern Jim Crow had been largely wiped out, the gains of the 1960s' social programs—federal support for black colleges and universities, neighborhood self-help and planning assistance programs, school lunch programs, Aid to Families with Dependent Children, food stamp programs, Guaranteed Student Loan programs and so on—were unrelentingly cut back under the Nixon, Ford, and Reagan administrations. In addition, black religious life was rocked by struggles over the teachings of the Nation of Islam waged by such figures as Wallace Muhammed and Louis Farrakhan. Desperate for community support, many blacks flocked to evangelical movements such as Jim Jones' notorious People's Temple, whose in-house paper, the *People's Forum,* claimed a readership of 600,000 largely black parishioners.

Given such signs of the times, Brooks sought through poetry's aesthetic dimension both to preserve an African cultural heritage and to advance her trenchant critique of racism.[55] In the 1980s, she negotiates the tension between a utopian and negative poetics. On the one hand, she celebrates the birth of hope when, as in "A Welcome Song for Laini Nzinga," she adopts the role as spiritual midwife to a new generation of Afro-Americans. Language functions here as a kind of life-support medium for black solidarity:

Hello, little Sister.
Coming through the rim of the world.
We are here! to meet you and to mold and to maintain you.
With excited eyes we see you.
With welcoming ears we hear the
clean sound of new language.
The language of Laini Nzinga.
We love and we receive you as our own.

(TD, 43)

This joyous image of birth happens through the "clean sound of new language" that poetry nurtures and preserves.

Such symbols of Pan-Africanism, however, are balanced by Brooks' poems about disturbing failures to sustain the black community. "The Boy Died in My Alley," for example, probes a personal, lyric knowledge of black urban tragedy. Here Brooks witnesses the killing of one of the urban black boys she had dramatized with more aesthetic distance two decades earlier in "We Real Cool." In answer to a police investigator's questions, she says: "The Shot that killed him yes I heard / as I heard the Thousand shots before; / careening tinnily down the nights / across my years and arteries" (TD, 50). Questioned more closely, Brooks admits to a certain complicity in the boy's death: "I have closed my heart-ears late and early. / And I have killed him ever" (TD, 53). The same will not to know, for which Carmichael indicts white America, returns now as the poet's own personal moral failure: "I joined the Wild and killed him / with knowledgeable unknowing" (TD, 54). This negative epiphany expands "for a long / stretch-strain of Moment," climaxing in the loss of black community:

> He cried not only "Father!"
> but "Mother!
> Sister!
> Brother."
> The cry climbed up the alley.
> It went up to the wind.
> It hung upon the heaven
> for a long
> stretch-strain of Moment.
>
> The red floor of my alley
> is a special speech to me.
> (TD, 55)

Brooks' radical assertion that black poets must write with pens dipped in "writhing blood" (Capsule, 4) should not be dismissed as simple melodrama. On the contrary, the "special speech" of the ghetto's literal "red floor" testifies to the real threats to black survival in the 1980s. Ultimately, Brooks views her aesthetic commitment to the black community as an ethical obligation, one that satisfies Addison Gayle, Jr.'s criterion for a poetics of social justice. The black critic, he says, "calls upon the Negro writer to dedicate himself to the proposition that literature is a moral force for change as well as an aesthetic creation."[56]

The force of social change has led Brooks throughout her career to reassess the poet's craft. Like Robert Bly and Adrienne Rich, she conceives new poetic discourses critical of America's social milieu in the postwar era, at once reflecting and shaping its historical context. Having undermined from within the "apolitical" formalism of American poetry in the 1940s and 1950s, Brooks' early work anticipated later feminist retrievals of women's experience beginning in the mid-1960s. But more than Rich, Brooks offers a broader rapprochement between women's writing and black vernacular and folk traditions, without being limited to any of these idioms.

Just as Afro-American criticism has pointed to the failure of the black aesthetic to deliver a lasting black national culture, so Brooks also has undertaken her own "reconstruction of instruction."[57] In poems such as "A Hymn to Chicago" and "Mayor Harold Washington," her cultural critique of the 1980s dwells on the radical negativity of black urban life: "Need I italicize our truth / that this city / is imperfect," she asks, "that many citizens are / ragged and ragged-eyed?" (MHW, 7). Yet she also envisions utopian social alternatives. In taking stock of Chicago's "ragged weather," Brooks nonetheless continues to dedicate herself to working for an "Age of Alliance" that promises to be, she says, "our senior adventure" (MHW, 3).

Notes

PREFACE

1. John Crowe Ransom, *The World's Body* (New York: Scribner's, 1938), p. 29.

2. Theodor W. Adorno, "On the Fetish Character in Music and the Regression of Listening," in Andrew Arato and Eike Gebhardt, eds., *The Essential Frankfurt School Reader* (New York: Continuum 1985), p. 279.

3. Theodor W. Adorno, "Commitment," in Arato and Gebhardt, eds., *The Essential Frankfurt School Reader,* p. 318.

4. "The work of art," Marcuse wrote, "speaks the liberating language, invokes the liberating images of the subordination of death and destruction to the will to live. This is the emancipatory element in aesthetic affirmation." Herbert Marcuse, *The Aesthetic Dimension: Toward a Critique of Marxist Aesthetics* (Boston: Beacon Press, 1978), pp. 62–63.

5. Theodor W. Adorno, *Negative Dialectics,* E. B. Ashton, tr. (New York: Seabury Press, 1973), p. 320.

6. See James William Johnson, "Lyric," in Alex Preminger et al., eds., *The Princeton Encyclopedia of Poetry and Poetics* (Princeton: Princeton University Press, 1974), p. 461.

7. C. Hugh Holman, *A Handbook to Literature,* 4th ed. (Indianapolis: Bobbs-Merrill, 1980), p. 252.

8. For example, Marjorie Perloff's reading of encyclopedic verse in *The Dance of the Intellect,* however elegant, is symptomatic of the way formalist criticism ignores the ideological implications and effects of poetic form. This impasse is particularly acute in Perloff's rather pedestrian account of the oppositional aesthetics of the so-called L=A=N=G=U=A=G=E poets. See *The Dance of the Intellect: Studies in the Poetry of the Pound Tradition* (New York and Cambridge: Cambridge University Press, 1985), pp. 232–37.

9. Jacques Derrida, *Margins of Philosophy,* Alan Bass, tr. (Chicago: University of Chicago Press, 1976), p. 7.

10. V. N. Vološinov, *Marxism and the Philosophy of Language,* Ladislav Matejka and I. R. Titunik, trs. (New York: Seminar Press, 1973), p. 11.

11. See Vološinov, *Marxism,* pp. 45–64.

12. Theodor W. Adorno, "Lyric Poetry and Society," Bruce Mayo, tr., *Telos* (1974), 20: 58, 65.

13. For a powerful application of this theory, see Edward Said's critique of how the West's "disciplinary communications apparatus" distorts the narrative of Palestinian history in "Permission to Narrate," *London Review of Books,* February 16–29, 1984, pp. 13–17.

14. "Where there is power, there is resistance, and yet, or rather consequently, this resistance is never in a position of exteriority in relation to power. . . . These points of resistance are present everywhere in the power network. . . . It is in this sphere of force relations that we must try to analyze the mechanisms of power." Michel Foucault, *The History of Sexuality,* vol. 1, Robert Hurley, tr. (New York: Vintage/Random House, 1980), pp. 95, 97.

15. John Brenkman, "Deconstruction and the Social Text," *Social Text* (1979), 1:187.

16. See Raya Dunayevskaya, *Women's Liberation and the Dialectics of Revolution Reaching for the Future* (Atlantic Highlands, N.J.: Humanities Press, 1985).

17. For a discussion of how narrative subjectivity can be considered as dispersed through discursive sites exterior to the author's introspective life, see Foucault: "Thus conceived, discourse is not the majestically unfolding manifestation of a thinking, knowing, speaking subject, but, on the con-

trary, a totality, in which the dispersion of the subject and his discontinuity with himself may be determined. It is a space of exteriority in which a network of distinct sites is deployed." Michel Foucault, *The Archaeology of Knowledge,* A. M. Sheridan Smith, tr. (New York: Harper and Row, 1972), p. 55.

CHAPTER I

1. See Karl Malkoff, *Crowell's Handbook of Contemporary American Poetry* (New York: Thomas Y. Crowell Company, 1973), p. 1.

2. Cleanth Brooks and Robert Penn Warren, *Understanding Poetry,* 3d ed. (New York: Holt, Rinehart and Winston, 1960), p. 21.

3. William K. Wimsatt, *The Verbal Icon: Studies in the Meaning of Poetry* (New York: Farrar, Straus and Giroux, 1958), p. xvii.

4. Cleanth Brooks, "The Heresy of Paraphrase," in *The Well-Wrought Urn: Studies in the Structure of Poetry* (New York: Harcourt, Brace and World, 1947), p. 194.

5. Donald M. Allen, *The New American Poetry* (New York: Grove Press, 1960), p. xi.

6. Eisenhower's fateful warning against a burgeoning "military industrial establishment" was less a prophecy than a reaction to a fact. In response to the Soviet launch of its first intercontinental ballistic missile and Sputnik satellite in 1957, the United States deployed intermediate range ballistic missiles, Thor, Jupiter, and the Atlas ICBM, in 1958; the Titan ICBM in 1961; and the Minute Man ICBM in 1962. Moreover, in the early 1960s the United States and the Soviet Union both engaged in an alarming series of aboveground large megaton nuclear tests—over two dozen in the Soviet Union alone in 1961. See Arthur S. Link, *American Epoch* (New York: Knopf, 1963), pp. 794–95.

7. Quoted in Peter N. Carroll, *It Seemed Like Nothing Happened* (New York: Holt, Rinehart and Winston, 1982), p. 14.

8. See Jean Baudrillard, "The Masses: The Implosion of the Social in the Media," *New Literary History* (Spring 1985), 16:577–89; Theodor W. Adorno, "Television and the Patterns of Mass Culture," in Bernard Rosenberg and David Manning White, eds., *Mass Culture* (New York: Free Press, 1957), pp. 474–89; Kate Moody, *Growing Up on Television* (New York: McGraw Hill, 1980); and Donald Lazere, "Literary and Mass Media: The Political Implications," *New Literary History* (Winter 1987), 18:237–56.

9. Charles Olson, "Projective Verse," in *Selected Writings of Charles Olson,*

Robert Creely, ed. (New York: New Directions, 1966), p. 24. Hereafter cited in the text as SW.

10. "Feeling secure only when dealing with personally tested facts," writes Steven Stepanchev, contemporary poets "render the loneliness and terror of contemporary life with the terseness and immediacy of a diary record. They permit no veil of 'objective correlatives' to hang between them and their readers; they distrust the 'aesthetic distance' and 'anonymity' that were once prized by poets and critics"; *American Poetry Since 1945: A Critical Survey* (New York: Harper and Row, 1965), pp. 4–5.

11. David Ossman, *The Sullen Art* (New York: Corinth, 1963), p. 8.

12. Anthony Ostroff, *The Contemporary Poet as Artist and Critic* (Boston: Little, Brown, 1964), pp. vii–viii.

13. M. L. Rosenthal, *The New Poets: American and British Poetry Since World War II* (New York: Oxford University Press, 1967), p. 13.

14. Paul Carroll, *The Poem in Its Skin* (Chicago: Follet, 1968), p. v.

15. Ralph J. Mills, Jr., *Cry of the Human: Essays on Contemporary American Poetry* (Urbana: University of Illinois Press, 1975), p. 8.

16. Robert B. Shaw, ed., *American Poetry Since 1960: Some Critical Perspectives* (Chester Springs, Pa.: Dufour, 1974), pp. 11–12.

17. David Kalstone, *Five Temperaments: Elizabeth Bishop, Robert Lowell, James Merrill, Adrienne Rich, John Ashbery* (New York: Oxford University Press, 1977), p. 10.

18. Alan Williamson, *Introspection and Contemporary Poetry* (Cambridge: Harvard University Press, 1984), p. 1.

19. Jonathan Holden, *Style and Authenticity in Postmodern Poetry* (Columbia: University of Missouri Press, 1986), p. 32.

20. Mark Strand, *The Contemporary American Poets: American Poetry Since 1940* (New York: Meridian Books, 1969), p. xiii.

21. A. Poulin, Jr., *Contemporary American Poetry*, 4th ed. (Boston: Houghton Mifflin, 1985), p. 686.

22. Stuart Friebert and David Young, eds., *The Longman Anthology of Contemporary American Poetry, 1950–1980* (New York: Longman, 1983), p. xxix.

23. Dave Smith and David Bottoms, eds., *The Morrow Anthology of Younger American Poets* (New York: Morrow, 1985), p. 19.

24. Robert Lowell, quoted in Ostroff, *The Contemporary Poet,* p. 107.

25. This is William V. Spanos' phrase, from his introduction to existentialist literature, "Abraham, Sisyphus, and the Furies: Some Introductory Notes on Existentialism," in William V. Spanos, ed., *A Casebook on Existentialism* (New York: Thomas Y. Crowell, 1966), p. 7.

26. Richard Howard, *Alone with America: Essays on the Art of Poetry in the United States Since 1950* (New York: Atheneum, 1969), p. xiii.

27. Charles Molesworth, *The Fierce Embrace: A Study of Contemporary American Poetry* (Columbia: University of Missouri Press, 1979), p. ix.

28. Anthony Libby's introduction to *Mythologies of Nothing: Mystical Death in American Poetry, 1940–1970* (Urbana: University of Illinois Press, 1984) presents the clever argument that standard criticisms of the postwar era all strain to elude the dubious rubric of "mysticism" in their readings of contemporary poetry. In contrast, Libby sets out to provide a comprehensive definition of an American secular mysticism.

29. Jarrell's influence on contemporary poetry is taken up in detail in Jerome Mazzaro's *Postmodern American Poetry* (Urbana: University of Illinois Press, 1980); see, in particular, chapters 1 and 2: "The Genesis of Postmodernism: W. H. Auden (1907–73)" (pp. 1–31) and "Between Two Worlds: Randall Jarrell (1914–65)" (pp. 32–58).

30. See Jacques Derrida, "Structure, Sign, and Play in the Discourse of the Human Sciences," in *Writing and Difference,* Alan Bass, tr. (Chicago: University of Chicago Press, 1978), pp. 278–93, and "Différance," in *Margins of Philosophy,* Alan Bass, tr. (Chicago: University of Chicago Press, 1976), pp. 1–27. "The most basic and most violent acts of differentiation," writes Robert Scholes, "are those that divide a field into two opposed units. This sort of 'binary opposition,' as the structuralists call it, is fundamental to the phonemic structure of speech and is deeply embedded in all Western thought, whether logical or mythical. . . . Above all, the deconstructive critics have sought to mount critiques of those binary oppositions used to organize fields or systems of value in traditional kinds of writing. These critiques take the form of bringing the oppositions to light, showing how power and privilege are often surreptitiously mapped onto apparently neutral oppositions, and finally dismantling or deconstructing oppositions by showing how each term shares certain attributes with its opposite, or presenting cases that the opposition cannot assimilate." Robert Scholes, *Textual Power* (New Haven: Yale University Press, 1985), pp. 112, 113–14.

31. Isidor Schneider, "Proletarian Poetry," in Henry Hart, ed., *American Writers' Congress* (New York: International Publishers, 1935), pp. 116, 117.

32. For a discussion of "strategies of containment," see Fredric Jameson, *The Political Unconscious* (Ithaca: Cornell University Press, 1981), pp. 53–54, 210–19, 266–70.

33. John Crowe Ransom, *The World's Body* (New York: Scribner's, 1938), p. 42; T. S. Eliot, preface to *For Lancelot Andrewes: Essays on Style and Order* (Garden City, N.Y.: Doubleday Doran, 1929), p. vii.

34. The award panel, made up of fourteen Library of Congress Fellows in American Literature, included T. S. Eliot, W. H. Auden, Allen Tate, Robert Penn Warren, and Robert Lowell, among others. Its controversial award sparked a fierce debate in the *Partisan Review* and *Saturday Review*

among Irving Howe, George Orwell, W. H. Auden, and Allen Tate. Editors Harrison Smith and Norman Cousins commissioned Pulitzer Prize winners Robert Hillyer and Peter Vierek to comment on the panel's decision. These critiques drew equally heated responses from Hayden Carruth, editor of *Poetry*, and from Malcolm Cowley in *The New Republic*. By the end of that year, John Berryman published in *The Nation* a letter signed by eighty-four prominent writers and critics protesting Hillyer's articles. For a detailed analysis of the awarding of the first Bollingen Prize, see Robert A. Corrigan, "Ezra Pound and the Bollingen Prize Controversy," in Warren French, ed., *The Forties: Fiction, Poetry, and Drama* (Deland, Fla.: Everett/Edwards, 1969), pp. 287–95.

35. As judge of the Yale series during 1951–1957, W. H. Auden bestowed awards on Adrienne Rich for poetic form, W. S. Merwin for the treatment of myth, Daniel Hoffman for the poet's relationship to the natural world, John Ashbery for the surrealist imagination, James Wright for possible subjects for poetry, and John Hollander for poetry's relationship to music. For a discussion of Auden's influence on contemporary American poets, see Daniel Hoffman's essay "Poetry: After Modernism," in Daniel Hoffman, ed., *Harvard Guide to Contemporary American Writing* (Cambridge: Harvard University Press, 1979), p. 460.

36. W. H. Auden, "In Memory of W. B. Yeats," in *The Collected Poetry of W. H. Auden* (New York: Random House, 1954), p. 50.

37. Consider, for example, Atheneum—a subsidiary of Scribner's, whose parent company is Macmillan. Together, Atheneum and Scribner's publish Marvin Bell, Robert Creeley, Robert Duncan, Anthony Hecht, Randall Jarrell, Donald Justice, Philip Levine, James Merrill, W. S. Merwin, and Mark Strand, among others.

38. Bennett Cerf, quoted in J. Kendrick Noble, Jr., "Books," in Benjamin M. Compaigne, ed., *Who Owns the Media? Concentration of Ownership in the Mass Communications Industry* (New York: Crown, 1979), p. 260.

39. Charles Newman quotes these figures in *The Post-Modern Aura: The Act of Fiction in an Age of Inflation* (Evanston, Ill.: Northwestern University Press, 1985), p. 152.

40. Important avant-garde journals and presses in the postwar decades include Cid Corman's *Origin*, Robert Creeley's *Black Mountain Review*, Robert Kelley's *Trobar*, Robert Bly's *The Fifties, Sixties, Seventies,* and *Eighties* magazines, Gilbert Sorrentino's *Neon*, Clayton Eshelman's *Caterpillar*, George Hitchcock's *Kayak*, John Logan's *Choice*, Hoyt Fuller's *Black World*, Adrienne Rich's *Sinister Wisdom*, and Charles Bernstein's and Bruce Andrews' $L=A=N=G=U=A=G=E$ magazine. Presses include Jerome Rothenberg's Hawkswell Press, Kelley's Trobar Press, Bly's Sixties Press, Jonathan Williams' Jargon Press, Lawrence Ferlinghetti's City Lights Press, Dudley Ran-

dall's Broadside Press, Haki Madhubuti's Third World Press, Florence Howe's and Paul Lauter's The Feminist Press, and many others.

41. Robert Bly, *Talking All Morning: Collected Interviews and Conversations* (Ann Arbor: University of Michigan Press, 1979), p. 107.

42. Brooks Thomas, quoted in Edwin McDowell, "Murdock to Buy Harper and Row," *New York Times,* March 31, 1987, p. D34.

43. According to Daniel Bell, from the end of World War II through the mid-1970s, the world economy enjoyed a 5 percent annual growth rate that reached a crescendo only when the OPEC oil cartel quadrupled oil prices, effectively redistributing these substantial revenues to itself. See Bell, *The Winding Passage* (Cambridge, Mass.: ABT Books, 1980), p. 211. This period of high growth fueled what Daniel Bell, B. Bruce-Briggs, Everett Carll Ladd, Jr., Norman Podhoretz, and others have described as the new class of professional managers who administer today's information/service economy. See B. Bruce-Briggs, ed., *The New Class?* (New York: McGraw-Hill, 1979), and Alvin W. Gouldner, *The Future of Intellectuals and the Rise of the New Class* (New York: Oxford University Press, 1979).

44. In advanced industrial society, Marcuse says, "the productive apparatus tends to become totalitarian to the extent to which it determines not only the socially needed occupations, skills, and attitudes, but also individual needs and aspirations. It thus obliterates the opposition between the private and public existence, between individual and social needs." Herbert Marcuse, *One-Dimensional Man: Studies in the Ideology of Advanced Industrial Society* (Boston: Beacon Press, 1964), p. xv.

45. In 1940 less that 15 percent of those in the 18–21 age group entered college, while by 1975 that figure had risen to 50 percent (Bell, *The Winding Passage,* p. 153). According to the National Center for Educational Statistics, nationwide college enrollment more than doubled from 1940 to 1960, moving from 1.5 million to 3.4 million. That constituency grew steadily from 8.5 million in 1965 to an estimated 10 million college students in the mid-1980s. By the mid-1970s, the nation's graduate student population had plateaued at 1.3 million. As a consequence, the number of full-time faculty members swelled from 154,000 in the 1960s to 369,000 in 1970, peaking at 485,000 in 1983.

46. "The professionalization of knowledge," Mills argued, "has thus narrowed the grasp of the individual professor; the means of his success further this trend; and in the social studies and the humanities, the attempt to imitate exact science narrows the mind to microscopic fields of inquiry, rather than expanding it to embrace man and society as a whole. To make his mark he must specialize, or so he is encouraged to believe." C. Wright Mills, *White Collar* (New York: Oxford University Press, 1953), p. 131.

47. In particular, the MLA's corporate bureaucracy was reluctant to de-

fend Louis Kampf and other members arrested for their antiwar protests at the 1968 annual convention. This failure precipitated an internal debate over scholarship's role in cultural change. The ensuing power struggle led to several institutional reforms within the Association and the eventual elevation of Kampf to its presidency in 1971, followed by Florence Howe two years later.

48. Richard Ohmann, *English in America* (New York: Oxford University Press, 1976), pp. 21–22. William V. Spanos offers a meticulous reading of Harvard University's "Report on the Core Curriculum" (1978) as an example of the academy's swerve away from sociopolitical engagement through the guise of liberal humanism. In Spanos' definition, "humanism comes to be understood as an intellectual legitimation of the dominant economic, social, and political power structures, which reproduces the world in its own image, i.e., assimilates and circumscribes the Other to the central proper self of Capitalistic Man. It comes, in short, to be recognized as an ideology that transforms the vital forces of difference in all its specific manifestations—from consciousness through gender and class to nature itself—into a docile but useful and efficient instrument of hegemonic power." William V. Spanos, "The Apollonian Investment of Modern Humanist Education: The Examples of Matthew Arnold, Irving Babbitt, and I. A. Richards," *Cultural Critique* (Fall 1985), 1:9. See also Gerald Graff and Reginald Gibbons, eds., *Criticism in the University, TriQuarterly* Series on Criticism and Culture, no. 1 (Evanston: Northwestern University Press, 1985); and Stanley Aronowitz and Henry A. Giroux, *Education Under Seige: The Conservative, Liberal, and Radical Debate Over Schooling* (New York: Bergin and Garvey, 1985).

49. Edward Said, "Opponents, Audiences, Constituencies, and Community," *Critical Inquiry* (September 1982), 9:22.

50. For a discussion of pedagogical reproduction see Pierre Bourdieu and Jean Claude Passeron, *Reproduction in Education, Society, and Culture* (Beverly Hills: Sage, 1977).

51. Although Charles Olson could not adjust to the state university system of New York, his major protegé and colleague at Black Mountain, Robert Creeley, is now the David Grey Professor of Poetry and Letters at SUNY, Buffalo—John Logan's home institution. The list of such poet-academicians could be extended indefinitely: A. R. Ammons (Godwin Smith Professor of Poetry, Cornell), Marvin Bell (administrator of the Iowa Writers Workshop), James Dickey (University of South Carolina), Richard Hugo (late of the University of Montana), Philip Levine (University of California, Fresno), Louis Simpson (SUNY, Stony Brook), W. D. Snodgrass (University of Delaware), William Stafford (Lewis and Clark College), Mark

Strand (University of Utah), Charles Wright (University of Virginia), James Wright (late of Hunter College), and so on. This is a more universal model for younger poets. Even poets who pursue "alternative" lifestyles outside the academy, such as Gwendolyn Brooks, Robert Bly, W. S. Merwin, or Adrienne Rich, are supported, in part, by visiting appointments and by reading circuits housed within academia.

52. Poets "find the smog of much over-rated writing and the critical nonsense that deifies it," writes David Ray, "as bewildering and noxious as any form of double-think." David Ray, ed., *From A to Z: 200 Contemporary Poets* (Chicago: Swallow Press/Ohio University Press, 1981), p. viii. Such indictments of critical discourse, however accurate, elevate verse writing beyond the material struggle of verbal praxis, thereby repressing poetry's institutional base of formation and dissemination.

53. Stuart Friebert and David Young, eds., *A Field Guide to Contemporary Poetry and Poetics* (New York: Longman, 1980), pp. xv–xvi.

54. Lawrence Lieberman, *Unassigned Frequencies: American Poetry in Review* (Urbana: University of Illinois, 1977), p. ix.

55. In the mid-1970s, for example, the National Federation of State Poetry Societies, Inc. made no fewer than twenty-three awards, while the New York Poetry Forum alone specified twenty-two categories of prizes.

56. For example, volume 5 of the *Dictionary of Literary Biography,* Donald J. Greiner, ed. (Detroit: Gale Research Company, 1980) comprises critical biographies of 125 major contemporary poets with "master" entries devoted to the top 15. Typical of these "masters," James Dickey has racked up an impressive list of awards: Guggenheim, National Book Award, National Institute of Arts and Letters, Prix Medicis, and so on. But James Wright and W. S. Merwin, both of whom have won Pulitzer Prizes in addition to many of the awards Dickey has won and several he has not— the Yale Younger Poets Award is only one example—are not represented as "master" writers. Dickey's selection for this august title, and Wright's and Merwin's exclusion, is attributable arguably to academic politics rather than publications and prizes alone. As it happens, Dickey, like the *Dictionary*'s editors, is a faculty member of the University of South Carolina. Moreover, while academic presses have devoted critical volumes to each of these writers, Gwendolyn Brooks' career has received much less attention even though she has won comparable awards: Guggenheim Fellowship (1946 and 1947), American Academy of Letters Award (1946), *Poetry*'s Eunice Tietjens Memorial Award (1949) and a Pulitzer Prize (1950), among others.

57. James Dickey, *Babel to Byzantium: Poets and Poetry Now* (New York: Farrar, Straus and Giroux, 1968), p. 8.

58. Standard anthologies include Donald Allen's *The New American Po-*

etry (1960) and *The Postmodernists* (1982), Richard Ellman's *Norton Anthology of Modern Poetry* (1973) and *New Oxford Book of American Verse* (1976), Friebert and Young's *The Longman Anthology of Contemporary American Poetry, 1950–80* (1983), A. Poulin's *Contemporary American Poetry* (1985), Mark Strand's *The Contemporary American Poets* (1969), Helen Vendler's *The Harvard Book of Contemporary American Poetry* (1985), and so on. In addition, numerous pulp anthologies proliferate in today's poetry market. Some, such as Lucien Stryk's *Heartland* (1967), Ron Padgett's and David Shapiro's *The New York Poets* (1970), and Philip Dow's *19 New American Poets of the Golden Gate* (1954), are organized by region. Others, such as Michael Lally's *None of the Above* (1976), David Ray's *From A to Z: 200 Contemporary American Poets* (1981), and Hugh Fox's *The Living Underground* (1973), imitate Donald Allen's early anti-academic stance.

59. So outlandishly does Halpern's volume advertise the credentials of its contributors that careers tend to displace the poetry. "These biographical presentations," Kostelanetz writes, "are, like the book itself, colorless and earnestly ambitious, speaking not about poetry but about careers." Richard Kostelanetz, *The Old Poetries and the New* (Ann Arbor: University of Michigan Press, 1981), p. 68.

60. See Robert Pinsky's "The Romantic Persistence," the third chapter of his *The Situation of Poetry* (Princeton: Princeton University Press, 1976), pp. 47–96.

61. Stephen Henderson, ed., *Understanding the New Black Poetry: Black Speech and Black Music as Poetic Reference* (New York: William Morrow, 1973), p. 4. See also Craig Werner, "New Democratic Vistas: Toward a Pluralistic Genealogy," in Joe Weixlmann and Chester J. Fontenot, eds., *Studies in Black American Literature* (Greenwood, Fla: Penkevill, 1986), 2:85–120.

62. Catharine R. Stimpson, "Editorial," *Signs* (Autumn 1975), 1:v.

63. Sandra Gilbert, "'My Name Is Darkness,: The Poetry of Self-Definition," in Donald Hall, ed., *Claims for Poetry* (Ann Arbor: University of Michigan, 1982), p. 118.

64. Ralph Cohen, "Editor's Preface," *New Literary History* (1969), 1(1):3.

65. Sheldon Sacks, "A Chimera for a Breakfast," *Critical Inquiry* (September 1974), 1:iii.

66. See William V. Spanos, "Charles Olson and Negative Capability: A De-structive Interpretation," in *Repetitions: The Postmodern Occasion in Literature and Culture* (Baton Rouge: Louisiana State University Press, 1987), pp. 107–47.

67. Cary Nelson, *Our Last First Poets: Vision and History in Contemporary American Poetry* (Urbana: University of Illinois Press, 1981), pp. xiv, 9. For other cultural approaches to poetry, see James E. Breslin, *From Modern to*

Contemporary (Chicago: University of Chicago Press, 1984); Paul Breslin, "How to Read the Contemporary American Poem," *American Scholar,* (Summer 1978), 47:357–70; Christopher Clausen, *The Place of Poetry: Two Centuries of an Art in Crisis* (Lexington: University Press of Kentucky, 1981); Anthony Easthope, *Poetry as Discourse* (London: Methuen, 1983); Veronica Forrest-Thomson, *Poetic Artifice: A Theory of Twentieth-Century Poetry* (New York: St. Martin's Press, 1978); Richard Kostelanetz, *The Old Poetries and the New;* Charles Molesworth, *The Fierce Embrace;* Patricia Parker and Chaviva Hosek, *Lyric Poetry: Beyond New Criticism* (Ithaca: Cornell University Press, 1985); and Robert Peters, *The Great American Poetry Bake-Off* (Metuchen, N.J.: Scarecrow, 1979).

68. Charles Bernstein, "Interview with Tom Beckett," *The Difficulties: Charles Bernstein Issue* (Fall 1982), 2:41. See also Bruce Andrews and Charles Bernstein, eds., *The Language Book* (Carbondale: Southern Illinois Press, 1981); Bernstein, *Content's Dream, Essays 1975–1984* (College Park, Md: Sun and Moon, 1985); Bernstein, ed., "Language Sampler," *Paris Review* (Winter 1982), 86:75–125; Ron Silliman, *In the American Tree* (Orono, Maine: National Poetry Foundation, 1986); and Silliman, *The New Sentence* (New York: Roof Books, 1987).

69. See Andrew Ross, "The New Sentence and the Commodity Form: Recent American Writing," in Cary Nelson and Lawrence Grossberg, eds., *Marxism and the Interpretation of Culture* (Urbana: University of Illinois Press, 1987), pp. 361–80.

CHAPTER 2

1. Charles Baudelaire, quoted in Walter Benjamin, "Some Motifs in Baudelaire," in *Charles Baudelaire: A Lyric Poet in the Era of High Capitalism,* Harry Zohn, tr. (London: Verso, 1983), p. 152.

2. Theodor Adorno, *Prisms,* Samuel Weber and Shierry Weber, trs. (Cambridge, Mass.: MIT Press, 1982), p. 34.

3. For an account of Heidegger's association with the Nazis while Rector of the University of Freiburg from 1933 to 1934, see Karl A. Moehling, "Heidegger and the Nazis," in Thomas Sheehan, ed., *Heidegger: The Man and the Thinker* (Chicago: Precedent Publishing, 1981), pp. 31–43; and Thomas Sheehan, "Heidegger and the Nazis," *New York Review of Books,* June 16, 1988, pp. 38–47.

4. Martin Heidegger, " . . . Poetically Man Dwells . . . ," in *Poetry, Language, Thought,* Albert Hofstadter, tr. (New York: Harper and Row, 1971), pp. 215, 213–14.

5. Jean Baudrillard, "The Ecstasy of Communication," in Hal Foster,

ed., *The Anti-Aesthetic* (Port Townsend, Wa.: Bay Press, 1985), pp. 127, 133. See also, Baudrillard's *The Mirror of Production,* Mark Poster, tr. (St. Louis: Telos Press, 1975).

6. See Patricia Parker and Chaviva Hosek, *Lyric Poetry: Beyond New Criticism* (Ithaca: Cornell University Press, 1985).

7. James Wright, quoted in Peter Stitt, "The Art of Poetry," *Paris Review* (January 1975), 16:53. Hereafter cited in the text as PR.

8. W. H. Auden, preface to *The Green Wall* (New Haven: Yale University Press, 1957), p. xiii.

9. James Wright, quoted in Joseph R. McElrath, ed., "Something To Be Said for the Light: A Conversation with James Wright," *Southern Humanities Review* (Spring 1972), 6:137. Hereafter cited in the text as SHR.

10. Robert Lowell, "For the Union Dead," *For the Union Dead* (New York: Farrar, Straus and Giroux, 1966), p. 72.

11. James Wright, *Collected Poems* (Middletown, Conn.: Wesleyan University Press, 1971), p. 21; hereafter cited as CP. Other volumes of Wright's poetry are cited in the text as follows: *Two Citizens* (New York: Farrar, Straus and Giroux, 1973), as TC; and *To A Blossoming Pear Tree* (New York: Farrar, Straus and Giroux, 1977), as BPT.

12. "Ontologically this means that when Dasein maintains itself in idle talk, it is—as Being-in-the-world—cut from its primary and primordially genuine relationships-of-Being toward the world, towards Dasein-with, and towards its very Being-in." Martin Heidegger, *Being and Time,* John Macquarrie and Edward Robinson, trs. (New York: Harper and Row, 1962), p. 214.

13. Dave Smith, "James Wright: The Pure Clear Word, an Interview," in David Smith, ed., *The Pure Clear Word* (Urbana: University of Illinois Press, 1982), p. 22. Hereafter cited in the text as PCW.

14. Theodore Roethke, *The Collected Poems of Theodore Roethke* (Garden City, N.Y.: Anchor/Doubleday, 1975), p. 58.

15. Peter A. Stitt, "The Poetry of James Wright," *Minnesota Review* (Winter 1962), 11:17.

16. James Wright, "The Delicacy of Walt Whitman," in R. W. B. Lewis, ed., *The Presence of Walt Whitman* (New York: Columbia University Press, 1962), p. 173. Hereafter cited in the text as DWW.

17. For example, in his reading of *The Green Wall* in "Five Young Poets," *Poetry* (August 1959), 94:335, Dudley Fitts suggests that the aesthetic inconsistency of Wright's first volume "becomes obstrusive." Similarly, Anthony Hecht, in "That Anguish of the Spirit and the Letter," *Hudson Review* (Winter 1959–1960), 12:599, criticizes *Saint Judas'* tendency "to regard the event as no more than an occasion for meditation." Thom Gunn, in "Ex-

cellence and Variety," *Yale Review* (Winter 1960), 49:297, likewise notices the development of style as a moral instrument, but adds, "at times it is done a bit too overtly for us to be really persuaded." More recently, William Saunders has called attention to Wright's awkward moral tags. See "Indignation Born of Love: James Wright's Ohio Poems," *The Old Northwest* (December 1978), 4:358.

18. Theodore Roethke, *On the Poet and His Craft*, Ralph J. Mills, Jr., ed. (Seattle: University of Washington Press, 1965), p. 40.

19. Wright rejected the term "surrealism" as a label for the method of *The Branch Will Not Break*. A more exact description of his technique occurs in his own criticism of Trakl and Whitman, both of whom, he says, rely on an organic pattern of parallelism to accumulate striking juxtapositions of poetic contents: "Trakl is a poet who writes in parallelism, only he leaves out the intermediary, rationalistic explanations of the relation between one image and another" (PR, 48). "Form, in Whitman, is a principle of growth: one image or scene or sound grows out of another. The general device is parallelism, not of grammar but of action or some other meaning" (DWW, 181).

20. Bly himself criticizes these kinds of moments in *The Branch*, claiming that they are overworked and meaningless. See Crunk (pseudonym of Robert Bly), "The Work of James Wright," *The Sixties* (1966), 7:74. Likewise, Geoffrey Hartman in an early review of *The Branch* suggests that there is an unresolved tension between Wright's Virgilian pastoral mode and Theocritan pastoralism. Hartman finds that the clash between native colloquialisms and exotic imagery results in "the absence of one controlled type of continuity." See Geoffrey Hartman, "Beyond the Middle Style," *Kenyon Review* (Autumn 1963), 25:752.

21. James Wright, "I Come To Speak for Your Dead Mouths," *Poetry* (June 1968), 112:191.

22. Heidegger aims to challenge the authority of tradition. He seeks to destroy inauthentic conventions that mask power's investment in cultural domination. The positive moment of destruction opens sites for the emergence of authentic disclosures of primordial existence. "We understand this task as one in which by taking *the question of Being as our clue*, we are to *destroy* the traditional content of ancient ontology until we arrive at those primordial experiences in which we achieved our first ways of determining the nature of Being—the ways which have guided us ever since" (*Being and Time*, p. 44).

23. In "Two Citizens," *New York Times Book Review*, August 11, 1974, p. 6, Calvin Bedient charges Wright with a "defiant, protective incoherency." Edward Butscher has little use for Wright's outspoken criticism of

America; in "The Rise and Fall of James Wright," *Georgia Review* (1974), 28:267, he claims that "from the standpoint of artistic achievement, *Two Citizens* is an almost total failure." Charles Molesworth, in "James Wright and the Dissolving Self," *Salmagundi,* (1973), 22–23:232, also recognizes the dangers of Wright's late style and notices that "the plainness of Wright's feelings threatens to bring a stop to the inventiveness of his words."

24. Martin Heidegger, "The Origin of the Work of Art," in *Poetry, Language, Thought,* p. 74.

25. Martin Heidegger, "Building Dwelling Thinking," in *Poetry, Language, Thought,* p. 151.

26. T. S. Eliot, "Tradition and the Individual Talent," in *Selected Essays* (New York: Harcourt, Brace and World, 1960), p. 6.

27. "However hard [the writer] tries to create a free language, it comes back to him fabricated, for luxury is never innocent: and it is this stale language, closed by the immense pressure of all the men who do not speak it, which he must continue to use. . . . The writers of today feel this; for them the search for a non-style or an oral style, for a zero level or spoken level of writing is, all things considered, the anticipation of a homogeneous social state." Roland Barthes, *Writing Degree Zero,* Annette Lavers and Colin Smith, trs. (New York: Hill and Wang, 1978), p. 87.

28. The author's disciplinary function, argues Foucault, serves to control and unify the chance elements of a discourse. "We tend to see, in an author's fertility," he writes, "in the multiplicity of commentaries and in the development of a discipline so many infinite resources available for the creation of discourse. Perhaps so, but they are nonetheless principles of constraint, and it is probably impossible to appreciate their positive, multiplicatory role without first taking into consideration their restrictive, constraining role." Michel Foucault, "The Discourse on Language," in *The Archaeology of Knowledge,* A. M. Sheridan Smith, tr. (New York: Harper and Row, 1972), p. 224.

29. W. S. Merwin, *The Lice* (New York: Atheneum, 1967), p. 62. Hereafter cited in the text as L. Other volumes by W. S. Merwin are cited in the text as follows: *Carrier of Ladders* (New York: Atheneum, 1970), CL; *The Compass Flower* (Atheneum, 1977), CF; *Finding the Islands* (Berkeley: North Point Press, 1982), FI; *The Miner's Pale Children: A Book of Prose* (Atheneum, 1970), MPC; *The Moving Target* (Atheneum, 1963), MT; *Opening the Hand* (Atheneum, 1983), OH; *Writings to an Unfinished Accompaniment* (Atheneum, 1973), WA.

30. See Martin Heidegger, "Letter on Humanism," in Martin Heidegger, *Basic Writings,* David Farrell Krell, ed. (New York: Harper and Row, 1977), p. 197; Paul A. Bové, *Destructive Poetics* (New York: Columbia Uni-

versity Press, 1980); and William V. Spanos, "Heidegger, Kierkegaard, and the Hermeneutic Circle: Towards a Postmodern Theory of Interpretation," in William V. Spanos, ed., *Martin Heidegger and the Question of Literature: Towards A Post-Modern Literary Hermeneutics* (Bloomington: Indiana University Press, 1979).

31. Martin Heidegger, "The Origin of the Work of Art," in *Poetry, Language, Thought,* pp. 60–61.

32. It is, of course, in Heidegger's valorization of speech over writing—his description of discourse as "saying," "keeping silent," "hearing the peal of stillness," etc.—that Derrida uncovers the trace of metaphysics it is Heidegger's project to overcome. See Martin Heidegger, *Being and Time,* pp. 203–10; "Letter on Humanism," in *Basic Writings,* pp. 210, 213, 221; "Language," in *Poetry, Language, Thought,* pp. 206–10; and "Conversation on a Country Path About Thinking," in Martin Heidegger, *Discourse on Thinking,* John M. Anderson and E. Hans Freund, trs. (New York: Harper and Row, 1966), p. 68.

33. Jacques Derrida, *Of Grammatology,* Gayatri Chakravorty Spivak, tr. (Baltimore: Johns Hopkins University Press, 1976), p. 22. For other discussions of Derrida's relationship to Heidegger, see Joseph N. Riddel, "From Heidegger to Derrida to Chance: Doubling and (Poetic) Language," *Boundary 2* (Winter 1976), 4:571–92; Frances C. Ferguson, "Reading Heidegger: Jacques Derrida and Paul de Man," *Boundary 2* (Winter 1976), 2:593–610; Bové, *Destructive Poetics;* David Couzens Hoy, "Forgetting the Text: Derrida's Critiques of Heidegger," in William V. Spanos, Paul A. Bové, and Daniel O'Hara, eds., *The Question of Textuality* (Bloomington: Indiana University Press, 1982), pp. 223–36; Rodolphe Gasché, "Joining the Text: From Heidegger to Derrida," in Jonathan Arac, Wlad Godzich, and Wallace Martin, eds., *The Yale Critics: Deconstruction in America* (Minneapolis: University of Minnesota Press, 1983); and Vincent Leitch, *Deconstructive Criticism* (New York: Columbia University Press, 1983).

34. J. Hillis Miller describes the word's appropriation of the world through such rhetorical figures as catachresis and metalepsis. His general term for the threshold where experience is transfigured as language is the "linguistic moment." See *The Linguistic Moment: From Wordsworth to Stevens* (Princeton: Princeton University Press, 1985).

35. Ferdinand de Saussure, *Course in General Linguistics,* Charles Bally and Albert Sechehaye, eds., Wade Baskin, tr. (New York: Philosophical Library, 1959), p. 120. Derrida's radical extension of Saussure to critique all "transcendental signified" meaning has helped to shed new light on Merwin's poetry in two recent essays. The most rigorous Derridean reading of Merwin's career to date is Cary Nelson's "The Resources of Failure: W.

S. Merwin's Deconstructive Career," in his *Our Last First Poets: Vision and History in Contemporary American Poetry,* pp. 177–215. Again, in Charles Altieri's chapter on Merwin in his *Enlarging the Temple* (Lewisburg, Pa.: Bucknell University Press, 1979), we find a similar Derridean moment: "For language is no longer referential, but, as Jacques Derrida puts it, a process of 'supplementation.' . . . Language tries to make things present, but it leaves only an absence requiring more words, ad infinitum" (215).

36. This supplanting of the author as origin of the text by the agency of writing resembles Foucault's analytic critique of the author's traditional role: "[T]he author does not precede the works, he is a certain functional principle by which, in our culture, one limits, excludes, and chooses; in short, by which one impedes the free circulation, the free manipulation, the free composition, decomposition, and recomposition of fiction." Michel Foucault, "What Is an Author?," in Josué V. Harari, ed., *Textual Strategies: Perspectives in Post-Structural Criticism* (Ithaca: Cornell University Press, 1979), p. 159. See also Roland Barthes, "The Death of the Author," in *Image— Music—Text,* Stephen Heath, tr. (London: Fontana, 1977).

37. L. Edwin Folsom and Cary Nelson, "'Fact Has Two Faces': An Interview with W. S. Merwin," *Iowa Review* (Winter 1982), 13:51. Hereafter referred to as Fact.

38. The "whole work," Merwin has said, "*is* one large book" (Fact, 33).

39. Dating from *The Moving Target,* Merwin has abandoned punctuation in order to exploit syntactic ambiguity. This rhetorical strategy, according to Jarold Ramsay, invites the reader into a plural act of interpretation. See his "The Continuities of W. S. Merwin: 'What Has Escaped Us We Bring With Us,'" *Massachusetts Review* (1973), 14(3):573. In addition, the dramatic quality of engagement that these lines demand transforms Merwin's poems into verbal objects, which seem to have an almost autonomous aesthetic life. "Punctuation," Merwin has said, "nails the poem down on the page; when you don't use it the poem becomes more a thing in itself, at once more transparent and more actual"; in "A Portrait of W. S. Merwin" (interview with Frank MacShane), *Shenandoah* (Winter 1970), 21:12.

40. Indeed, Merwin's text so invites these kinds of phenomenological readings of his "otherness" that it is the major preoccupation of most of his critics. For John Vogelsang, Merwin's poetry becomes "an art of recognition, an art that conveys the unsoundable quality of experience, the silence and the divine, in the sounding human voice"; "Toward the Great Language: W. S. Merwin's *The Lice,*" *Modern Poetry Studies* (1972), 3(3):99. In contrast, I find Anthony Libby's discussion of nothingness less hopeful, yet still mystified; in "W. S. Merwin and the Nothing That Is," *Contemporary Literature* (1975), 16:35, Libby writes, "With unusual specificity Mer-

win locates the emptiness that receives mystical truth at the heart of the experience of the various senses, but truth remains as unattainable as it is immediate." In his illuminating contrast of Merwin and Whitman, "Approaches and Removals: W. S. Merwin's Encounter with Whitman's America," *Shenandoah* (Spring 1978), 29:66, L. Edwin Folsom resists that mystification of the void as truth: "It is not a creative void that Merwin faces, not something he expands into and absorbs; rather it is a destructive void which opens its dark abyss, ready to swallow the poet and all of life with him."

41. Stephen Spender, for example, points to the "animistic" quality of the verse, while Denis Donoghue says that in contrast to the fragmented and eruptive language Roland Barthes finds in modernism, Merwin attempts a "natural" syntax in which "relations between one thing and another are given." Stephen Spender, "Can Poetry Be Reviewed?," *New York Review of Books,* September 20, 1973, p. 10; and Denis Donoghue, "Objects Solitary and Terrible," *New York Review of Books,* June 6, p. 22.

42. Moreover, in his own discussions of his verse, Merwin suggests an almost inevitable, even fated quality to his writing's rhetorical base. For example, concerning Whitman's rhetorical excesses, Merwin has said: "When you're trying to avoid that one kind of rhetoric, of course you're developing a different kind of rhetoric" (Fact, 36).

43. Merwin, in MacShane, "Portrait," p. 12.

44. Carol Kyle, "A Riddle for the New Year: Affirmation in W. S. Merwin," *Modern Poetry Studies* (1973), 4:296.

45. This image becomes even more repulsive as a war souvenir in "The Dachau Shoe," MPC, 15–16.

46. Merwin described New York as the archetypal city in a prefatory remark to his reading of "The River of Bees," during a reading given as part of the Fall 1982 Literary Festival sponsored by Southern Methodist University, Dallas, Texas.

47. See Heidegger, *Being and Time,* pp. 317–25.

48. W. S. Merwin, "Notes for a Preface," in William F. Martz, ed., *The Distinctive Voice* (Glenview, Ill.: Scott, Foresman, 1966), pp. 269–70.

49. Laurence Lieberman, "Recent Poetry in Review: Risks and Faiths," *The Yale Review* (1968), 57:597.

50. W. H. Auden, preface to *A Mask for Janus* (New Haven: Yale University Press, 1952).

CHAPTER 3

1. Robert von Hallberg, *Charles Olson: The Scholar's Art* (Cambridge: Harvard University Press, 1978), p. 1. "Olson's design was to undermine this functional division between poetry and prose: his verse is willfully prosaic, both metrically and thematically, because he hoped to destroy the category of Poetry itself" (181).

2. Charles Altieri, "Olson's Poetics and the Tradition" *Boundary 2* (Fall 1973–Winter 1974), 2:182.

3. Marjorie Perloff, "Charles Olson and the 'Inferior Predecessors' 'Projective Verse' Revisited," *Journal of English Literary History* (1973), 40:295–96.

4. Michael Bernstein, *The Tale of the Tribe: Ezra Pound and the Modern Verse Epic* (Princeton: Princeton University Press, 1980), p. 14. In defining *Maximus* as epic, Bernstein locates "a clearly defined 'plot,' an 'epic theme' limited in time and geographical extent, at the core of his work to which the other aspects of the poem can be related and from which they rightfully take their meaning" (249). This privileging of epic, however, leads Bernstein to reject the later volumes as "only peripherally relevant to an analysis of his contribution to the modern verse epic" (265).

5. Charles Olson, *Selected Writings of Charles Olson,* Robert Creeley, ed. (New York: New Directions, 1966), p. 15. Hereafter cited as SW. Charles Olson's other works are cited as follows: *Additional Prose: A Bibliography on America, Proprioception, and Other Notes and Essays,* George F. Butterick, ed. (Bolinas: Four Seasons Foundation, 1974), AP; *Call Me Ishmael* (San Francisco: City Lights, 1967), CMI; *The Maximus Poems* (Berkeley: University of California Press, 1983), M; *The Special View of History,* Ann Charters, ed. (Berkeley: Oyez, 1970), SVH.

6. For a discussion of dialogic form, see M. M. Bakhtin, *The Dialogic Imagination,* Michael Holquist, ed. (Austin: University of Texas Press, 1981), pp. 269, 271–72. Although the phrase COMPOSITION BY FIELD (Olson's upper case format) seems to suggest the kind of spatial form Joseph Frank attributes to the modernist aesthetic, William V. Spanos has argued cogently that Olson understands Field Composition as a wholly temporal mode. See William V. Spanos, "Charles Olson and Negative Capability: A Phenomenological Interpretation," *Contemporary Literature* (Winter 1980), 21:38–80.

7. Quoted in Hugh Kenner, *The Pound Era* (Berkeley: University of California Press, 1971), p. 313.

8. Georg Lukács, *History and Class Consciousness: Studies in Marxist Dialectics,* Rodney Livingstone, tr. (Cambridge: MIT Press, 1971), p. 83.

9. The phrase "marginal utility" was coined in the writings of Elizabeth Hoyt, Hezel Kyrk, and Paul Nystrom. See Stuart Ewen, *Captains of Consciousness* (New York: McGraw-Hill, 1976), pp. 89–90. Hereafter cited in the text as CC.

10. Martin Heidegger, *The Question Concerning Technology and Other Essays,* William Lovitt, tr. (New York: Harper and Row, 1977), p. 134.

11. See Guy Debord, *Society of the Spectacle* (Detroit: Black and Red, 1983). Hereafter cited in the text as SS.

12. Marty Jezer, *The Dark Ages: Life in the United States from 1945–1960* (Boston: South End Press, 1982), pp. 130–32.

13. See Ewen, *Captains of Consciousness,* pp. 208–10.

14. Theodor W. Adorno, "Television and the Patterns of Mass Culture," in Bernard Rosenberg and David Manning White, eds., *Mass Culture* (New York: Free Press, 1957), p. 484.

15. "We speak of an abyss," says Heidegger, "where the ground falls away and a ground is lacking to us, where we seek the ground and set out to arrive at a ground, to get to the bottom of something. But we do not ask now what reason may be; here we reflect immediately on language and take as our main clue the curious statement, 'Language is language.' This statement does not lead us to something else in which language is grounded. Nor does it say anything about whether language itself may be a ground for something else. The sentence, 'Language is language,' leaves us to hover over an abyss as long as we endure what it says." Martin Heidegger, "Language," in *Poetry, Language, Thought,* Albert Hofstadter, tr. (New York: Harper and Row, 1971), p. 191.

16. Paul Bové, for example, employs a Heideggerean rhetoric of disclosure to valorize a more "natural" seeing, an "immediate sensual perception," leading to "the natural vision of [the] thing" itself. Bové somewhat domesticates the "forwarding" of Olson's textuality through the modernist poetics of experience in Pound and Williams that he further joins to Husserlian phenomenology. See *Destructive Poetics* (New York: Columbia University Press, 1980), p. 238. Similarly, William V. Spanos argues that the poet's fascination with Keats' theory of negative capability allows Olson to overcome what Heidegger dismisses as the onto-theological tradition of Western metaphysics. Like Bové, however, Spanos reads Olson's understanding of negative capability through a phenomenological reduction that privileges experience, nature, and world. "The negative capability of Olson's Man of Achievement, in other words, is a generosity in the face of the be-ing of being . . . a meditative openness that, in letting be, lets being be, that is, brings man into the neighborhood of being where we *receive as a gift* a new knowledge or, rather, a new measure from things-as-are (*physics*), the *es gibt* ('there is') of the mysterious earth (*die Erde*)" ("Charles Olson and Neg-

ative Capability," p. 69). This kind of happy dwelling in the neighborhood of the mysterious earth is precisely what Olson fails to achieve, however, in a key text of negative capability: "Maximus, to himself."

17. Bové argues that Olson "gets through the veil of words and images to the things themselves and thus breaks through to the beginning of the circuit of creativity" (*Destructive Poetics,* p. 241).

18. Olson's early "destructive" polemic is grounded in modernism. But through a more radical interrogation of the modernist aesthetic, he occupies the site of its historical closure. Thus, in 1950 Pound and Williams are allies whose open-form imagist/vorticist poetics prepares for his own second wave of projective verse. But later, as Olson works through the modern verse epic, he comes to read the epics of Pound and Williams as complementary "HALVES" (SW, 82–83). Here Pound's revisions of Confucius and Dante are overshadowed by his political entanglements in fascism. Similarly, though Williams is not afflicted with Pound's inflated ego, his approach to the long poem remains derivative (from Joyce) and shallow in its engagement with history:

> the primary contrast for our purposes is, BILL: his Pat
> is exact opposite of Ez's, that is, Bill HAS an
> emotional system which is capable of extensions &
> comprehensions the ego system (the Old Deal, Ez as Cento
> Man, here dates)
> is not. Yet
>
> by making his substance historical of one city (the
> Joyce deal), Bill completely licks himself, lets time
> roll him under as Ez does not
>
> (SW, 82–83)

In this critique of the modern verse epic's aesthetic limits, Olson's strategy is to master his precursors' failures.

19. This passage from Olson's unpublished essay "Projective Verse II" (Charles Olson Archive) is quoted in von Hallberg, *Charles Olson,* p. 34.

20. See Jacques Derrida, "Signature Event Context," in *Margins of Philosophy,* Alan Bass, tr. (Chicago: University of Chicago Press, 1976), pp. 307–30. Hereafter cited in text as Margins.

21. George F. Butterick, *A Guide to the Maximus Poems of Charles Olson* (Berkeley: University of California Press, 1978), p. 102. Hereafter cited in the text as Guide to Maximus.

22. Jacques Derrida, *Writing and Difference,* Alan Bass tr. (Chicago: University of Chicago Press, 1978), p. 200; see also *Of Grammatology,* Gayatri

Chakravorty Spivak, tr. (Baltimore: Johns Hopkins University Press, 1976), pp. 107–08.

23. Bakhtin, *The Dialogic Imagination,* p. 278.

24. Roy Harvey Pearce's *The Continuity of American Poetry* was one of the first postwar studies to promote the modern verse epic as a narrative of cultural history. Pearce regarded the canon of American long poetry, stretching back to Whitman through Williams, as a productive, not mimetic, enterprise. The "inside narrative" of poetry, he held, generates history, not the other way around. "These are meant to be poems not of a new order," he said, "but rather of a new ordering"; *The Continuity of American Poetry* (Princeton: Princeton University Press, 1961), p. 61. For his part, James E. Miller, Jr. sees a dialectic tension at work in the American long poem between the personal lyricism of individual poets and Whitman's more expansive, democratic American vision. Miller notes the utopian didacticism shaping the historical vision of American poets. Each, he argues, adopts a version of Whitman's redemptive hope for America envisioned in *Democratic Vistas*—whether Pound's vision of aristocratic Paradise, Eliot's God of Thunder, Crane's Atlantis, Stevens' Supreme Fiction, Williams' Beautiful Thing, or Charles Olson's Polis. See *The American Quest for a Supreme Fiction* (Chicago: University of Chicago Press, 1979), p. 324. But the limits of such theorizings about the modern verse epic tradition become apparent when we turn to Olson's textuality. What eludes Pearce and Miller as we move toward the contemporary American long poem is poetry's textual dimension. Olson's discursive long poems depart from the modern verse epic's didactic political mission and its narratives of cultural order. Instead, Olson dramatizes a contradictory jostling of linguistic systems, which defines our moment's projective play of mythic language games. His understanding of linguistic difference resists too Whitman's utopian impulse that leads to residual, totalizing myths of cultural order in the American epic tradition.

25. Von Hallberg, *Charles Olson,* p. 181.

26. M. M. Bakhtin, "Epic and Novel," in *The Dialogic Imagination,* p. 18.

27. "Projective Verse II" (Charles Olson Archive), quoted in von Hallberg, *Charles Olson,* p. 34.

28. "Polyphony" is Henri Frankfort's term for the multiple mythic associations through which Egyptians conceived of place in Memphite Theology (see Guide to Maximus, 437).

29. Mark Taylor, "Text as Victim," in Thomas Altizer, ed., *Deconstruction and Theology* (New York: Crossroad, 1982), pp. 70, 73.

CHAPTER 4

1. James Merrill, *The Changing Light at Sandover* (New York: Atheneum, 1982), p. 3. Cited hereafter as CLS.

2. "Unfortunately," writes Barthes, "nothing is more fickle than a colourless writing; mechanical habits are developed in the very place where freedom existed, a network of set forms hem in more and more the pristine freshness of discourse, a mode of writing appears afresh in lieu of an indefinite language. The writer, taking his place as a 'classic,' becomes the slavish imitator of his original creation, society demotes his writing to a mere manner, and returns him a prisoner to this own formal myths." Roland Barthes, *Writing Degree Zero,* Annette Lavers and Colin Smith, trs. (New York: Hill and Wang, 1978), p. 78.

3. James Merrill, in Ross Labrie, "James Merrill at Home: An Interview," *Arizona Quarterly* (1982), 38:32–33. Hereafter cited in the text as JMH.

4. T. S. Eliot, *Four Quartets* (New York: Harcourt Brace Jovanovich, 1971), p. 43.

5. W. B. Yeats, "The Symbolism of Poetry," Hazard Adams, eds., *Critical Theory Since Plato* (New York: Harcourt Brace Jovanovich, 1971), p. 724.

6. Robert Pinsky, *The Situation of Poetry* (Princeton: Princeton University Press, 1976), pp. 47–96.

7. The phrase is from W. B. Yeats, "Sailing to Byzantium," in *The Variorum Edition of the Poems of W. B. Yeats,* Peter Allt and Russell K. Alspach, eds. (New York: Macmillan, 1957), p. 407. Hereafter cited as YVE.

8. Susan Sontag, "Some Notes on Camp," in *The Susan Sontag Reader,* Elizabeth Hardwick, ed. (Farrar, Straus and Giroux, 1982), p. 112.

9. Robert K. Martin, *The Homosexual Tradition in American Poetry* (Austin: University of Texas Press, 1979), p. 202.

10. M. M. Bakhtin, *The Dialogic Imagination,* Michael Holquist, ed. (Austin: University of Texas Press, 1981), p. 163.

11. Peter Sacks, "The Divine Translation: Elegiac Aspects of *The Changing Light at Sandover,*" in David Lehman and Charles Berger, eds., *James Merrill: Essays in Criticism* (Ithaca: Cornell University Press, 1983), p. 162. Seduced by the poem's mystifications, Sacks' enthusiasm waxes beyond his critical judgment, as he asserts, "We, ourselves, have thus become admitted, or perhaps translated, to the celestial ballroom and its guests" (185).

12. Arguing for "The Broken Home" as the prototype for *Scripts,* Spiegelman writes: "'The Broken Home' traces what M. H. Abrams, showing how the romantics appropriated biblical tropes, terms 'the circuitous jour-

ney,' whereby a secular modern artist can refuse to relinquish the myth of unity, division, pilgrimage, and restitution at the heart of biblical narrative." Spiegelman, "Breaking the Mirror: Interruption in Merrill's Trilogy," in Lehman and Berger, eds., *James Merrill: Essays in Criticism,* p. 189.

13. David Lehman, "Elemental Bravery: The Unity of James Merrill's Poetry," in Lehman and Berger, eds., *James Merrill: Essays in Criticism,* p. 35.

14. While acknowledging Merrill's affinity for Blake, Wordsworth, Keats, and Whitman, a few of his critics note the poet's ironic distance from such romantics. Thus Helen Vendler argues for Merrill's Keatsian fusion of the aesthetic and sensual, but also points out the more Stevensian tension between imagination and mortality at work in the trilogy. See *Part of Nature, Part of Us* (Cambridge: Harvard University Press, 1980), pp. 212, 227. The tension between *Ephraim*'s romantic and modern modes is also the guiding theme of Henry Sloss' reading. In "James Merrill's 'Book of Ephraim,'" *Shenandoah* (1976), 27:64, he writes, "The basic strategy of the poem is Romantic . . . but the terms of the enchantment are distinctly modern: what is asked of the reader, as if exemplified by the poet, is both submersion in and resistance to the otherworldly revelation in the poem." Similarly, both David Kalstone and Samuel E. Schulman notice the struggle between what Wordsworth calls "the growth of a poet's mind" and the intrusive force of other voices challenging the poet's unity of identity. In "Persisting Figures: The Poet's Story and How We Read It," in Lehman and Berger, eds., *James Merrill: Essays in Criticism,* p. 129, Kalstone cites Wordsworth's autobiographic impulse in *The Prelude* as a prototype of the modernist long poem only to qualify their generic resemblance. Although essentially lyric in origin, the long poems of this century, Kalstone argues, depart from the straightforward representation of the self's evolution in *The Prelude*. See also Samuel E. Schulman, "Lyric Knowledge in *The Fire Screen* and *Braving the Elements,*" in Lehman and Berger, eds., *James Merrill: Essays in Criticism,* p. 98. Such readings resist the mystical allure of Merrill's text. They share common doubts about the trilogy's thematic and generic unity.

15. Martin Heidegger, "On the Essence of Truth" (*Vom Wesen der Wahrheit*), John Sallis, tr., in Heidegger, *Basic Writings,* David Farrell Krell, ed. (New York: Harper and Row, 1977), pp. 125, 129.

16. Errancy, moreover, is not extrinsic to our nature, but part of our ek-sistence: "Man errs. Man does not merely stray into errancy. He is always astray in errancy, because as ek-sistent he insists and so already is caught in errancy" (Heidegger, *Basic Writings,* p. 135). Only in acknowledging the inevitability of errancy can we escape the delusive idealism of the onto-theological or humanistic tradition of Western metaphysics.

17. As a foundational metaphor, Oedipus, for Lacan, authorizes the sub-

ject's accession to the "symbolic" order of language, speech, and indeed all social forms. The oedipal situation is the deep structure *par excellence* underwriting human culture. Drawing on Melanie Klein's research into child psychology, Lacan argues that prior to the oedipal phase, the infant experiences itself as suspended, fragmented, uncoordinated, and dispersed in time and space. But between the ages of six and eighteen months it matures beyond this disintegrated and disjointed register into the horizon of what Lacan describes as the "imaginary" or "mirror" stage. Here the baby grasps the integrity of its body as an image of wholeness and totality. The child attains the "jubilant assumption of his specular image" by identifying with the unified, Gestalt patterns of dual relationships. As in a mirror, the infant variously internalizes its own specular unity, or that of another child, or the unified form of the mother's body. Such visual identification takes the form of aggressivity toward its counterpart or reflected double, which Lacan reads as a victorious mapping and mastery of what was a fragmented *corps morcelé*. The baby's specular coordination of the previously dispersed body, however, is only a passing moment on the way to the essentially differential character of language's symbolic order.

The child accedes to the "symbolic" stage by way of the oedipal phase. Following Freud, Lacan reads the Oedipus myth as a triangular relationship among the mother, father, and infant. In the imaginary stage, the child invests wholly in the mother, identifying with or "being" the subject of her desire: the phallus. The father breaks this primary identification by instituting the prohibition against incest and inaugurating the Law of the Father which, for Lacan, *is* the order of language: the name of the father (*nom-du-père*). Then the child completes the oedipal circuit not by "being" the phallus for the mother but by having access to it; that is, through identification with the phallic signifier of the symbolic father's discourse. The "successful" outcome of the oedipal phase, then, culminates in the subject's primary repression of imaginary, maternal investments in favor of the symbolic economy of the *nom-du-père*. In sum, the child moves from the register of the specular "I" to that of the sociolinguistic "I." See Jacques Lacan, *Ecrits: A Selection*, Alan Sheridan, tr. (New York: Norton, 1977), pp. 30–113.

18. Helen Vendler writes: "The ouija board is a symbol system that offers potentially unlimited combinations of letters and numbers, affirmations and denials; it can stand, we might say, for language itself" (*Part of Nature, Part of Us*, p. 220).

19. Lehman, "Elemental Bravery," p. 50.

20. Charles Olson, *Selected Writings of Charles Olson*, Robert Creeley, ed. (New York: New Directions, 1966), p. 24.

21. Lehman's resistance to the radical implications of Merrill's role as scribe is particularly acute: "One of the most pernicious developments in recent critical theory is the rise of the doctrine that authors do not exist: not only are their intentions deemed irrelevant, but their authority in every sense has been questioned" ("Elemental Bravery," p. 19).

22. See T. S. Eliot, "Henry James," *Little Review* (August 1918), 4:76.

23. Clara Claireborne, "Where 'The Waste Land' Ends," *Nation* (May 3, 1980), 230:533.

24. Herbert Marcuse, *The Aesthetic Dimension: Toward a Critique of Marxist Aesthetics* (Boston: Beacon Press, 1978), pp. 34–35.

25. "The writerly text," says Barthes, "is a perpetual present, upon which no *consequent* language (which would inevitably make it past) can be superimposed; the writerly text is ourselves writing, before the infinite play of the world (the world as function) is traversed, intersected, stopped, plasticized by some singular system (Ideology, Genus, Criticism) which reduces the plurality of entrances, the opening of networks, the infinity of languages." Roland Barthes, *S/Z*, Richard Miller, tr. (New York: Hill and Wang, 1974), p. 5.

26. "This structure of the *double mark* (caught—both seized and entangled—in a binary opposition, one of the terms retains its old name so as to destroy the opposition to which it no longer quite belongs, to which in *any* event it has *never* quite yielded, the history of this opposition being one of incessant struggles generative of hierarchical configurations) works the entire field within which these texts move." Jacques Derrida, *Dissemination*, Barbara Johnson, tr. (Chicago: University of Chicago Press, 1982), p. 4.

27. A notable exception is Charles Berger, who, employing Frank Kermode's "The Modern Apocalypse," offers a definitive reading of Merrill's thematics of the End. See "Merrill and Pynchon: Our Apocalyptic Scribes," in Lehman and Berger, eds., *James Merrill: Essays in Criticism*, pp. 282–97.

28. See Paul Feyerabend, *Against Method* (Atlantic Highlands, N. J.: Humanities Press, 1975); Thomas S. Kuhn, *The Structure of Scientific Revolutions* (Chicago: University of Chicago Press, 1962); and Jean-François Lyotard, *The Postmodern Condition: A Report on Knowledge,* Geoff Bennington and Brian Massumi, trs. (Minneapolis: University of Minnesota Press, 1984).

29. Lyotard, *The Postmodern Condition*, pp. 60, 64.

CHAPTER 5

1. Robert Bly, "A Wrong Turning in American Poetry," *Choice* (1963), 3:47. Hereafter cited in the text as WT.

2. See Ronald Moran and George S. Lensing, *Four Poets and the Emotive Imagination* (Baton Rouge: Louisiana State University Press, 1976).

3. Charles Altieri, *Enlarging the Temple* (Lewisberg, Pa: Bucknell University Press, 1979), p. 83. Whether Bly has crafted a rhetoric that can stage the meaning of his "deep" vision is open to interpretation. Since *Enlarging the Temple,* Altieri has gone on to argue the limitations of Bly's "immanent" aesthetic contrasted with the more discursive modes of the younger poets of the 1970s. See Charles Altieri, "The Dominant Poetic Mode of the Late Seventies," chapter 2 of his *Self and Sensibility in Contemporary American Poetry* (New York: Cambridge University Press, 1984), pp. 32–51.

4. Theodor W. Adorno, "Lyric Poetry and Society," Bruce Mayo, tr., *Telos* (1974), 20:58.

5. Earl Butz, quoted in Marty Jezer, *The Dark Ages: Life in the United States from 1945–1960* (Boston: South End Press, 1982), p. 162.

6. Robert Bly, *Silence in the Snowy Fields* (Middletown, Conn.: Wesleyan University Press, 1962), p. 37. Hereafter cited in the text as S. Other volumes of Robert Bly's poetry are cited as follows: *The Light Around the Body* (New York: Harper and Row, 1967), L; *Sleepers Joining Hands* (New York: Harper and Row, 1973), SJH.

7. Whether the phenomenon of repetition compulsion, described by Freud in *Beyond the Pleasure Principle* (1920), represents the ego's attempt to master and discharge unconscious tensions or reveals the force of a more radical death instinct which challenges the dominance of the pleasure principle has been a source of heated debate in post-Freudian theory. For a full discussion of repetition compulsion, death instincts, and the pleasure principle, see Sigmund Freud, *Beyond the Pleasure Principle,* in vol. 18 of *The Standard Edition of the Complete Psychological Works of Sigmund Freud,* James Strachey, ed. and tr. (London: The Hogarth Press, 1968), pp. 38–40, 44–45. 55; J. Laplanche and J. B. Pontalis, *The Language of Psycho-Analysis,* Donald Nicholson-Smith, tr. (New York: Norton, 1973), pp. 78–80, 97–103, 322–25; and Samuel Weber, *The Legend of Freud* (Minneapolis: University of Minnesota Press, 1982), pp. 121–25, 130–35.

8. See Peter Lyon, *Eisenhower: Portrait of the Hero* (New York: Little, Brown, 1974), pp. 591–92.

9. Henry David Thoreau, *Walden,* J. Lyndon Shanley, ed. (Princeton: Princeton University Press, 1971), p. 115.

10. Robert Bly, *Talking All Morning: Collected Interviews and Conversations* (Ann Arbor: University of Michigan Press, 1979), p. 78.

11. Robert Bly, "Leaping Up Into Political Poetry," in Robert Bly, ed., *Forty Poems Touching on Recent American History* (Boston: Beacon Press, 1970), p. 10.

12. James F. Mersmann, *Out of the Vietnam Vortex* (Lawrence, Kans.: University Press of Kansas, 1974), p. 124. Discussing Bly's shift to a political poetics, George S. Lensing and Ronald Moran, in *Four Poets and the Emotive Imagination*, note that "the temperate poem becomes baldly topical" (77).

13. An early model for Bly's thoughts on the struggle between unconscious death instincts and civilization is Freud's *Civilization and Its Discontents* (1930): "The fateful question for the human species seems to me to be whether and to what extent their cultural development will succeed in mastering the disturbance of their communal life by the human instinct of aggression and self-destruction." Sigmund Freud, *Civilization and Its Discontents*, vol. 21 of *The Standard Edition*, p. 145.

14. Charles Molesworth, *The Fierce Embrace: A Study of Contemporary American Poetry* (Columbia: University of Missouri Press, 1979), p. 118.

15. Louis Althusser, *Lenin and Philosophy*, Ben Brewster, tr. (Bristol: Western Printing Services, 1971), p. 153. In his chapter "Ideology and the State" Althusser describes this process as an act of "hailing" which transforms individuals into subjects through a process of "interpellation" (162).

16. See Bly's article "Hopping," *The Seventies* (Spring 1972), 1:72.

17. Robert Bly, quoted in Kevin Power, "Conversation with Robert Bly," *Texas Quarterly* (Autumn 1976), 19:93.

18. Adrienne Rich, *Of Woman Born* (New York: Bantam, 1977), pp. 62–63. Hereafter cited as OWB.

19. Joan Bamberger, "The Myth of Matriarchy: Why Men Rule in Primitive Society," in Michelle Zimbalist Rosaldo and Louise Lamphere, eds., *Woman, Culture, and Society* (Stanford: Stanford University Press, 1974), p. 265.

20. Simone de Beauvoir, *The Second Sex*, H. M. Parshley, tr. (New York: Knopf, 1957), p. 70. Both Bamberger and de Beauvoir rely on Claude Lévi-Strauss' distinction between matrilineal descent and matriarchal rule to show that even in quasi-matriarchal societies, such as the Iroquois, women are still reduced to exchange objects and subjected to the guardianship of the ruling father or brother of the extended kinship group. Sarah B. Pomeroy summarizes their point, stating that "there is absolutely no evidence, even in realms where queens were powerful, that women were the dominant class throughout the society." Sarah B. Pomeroy, "A Classical Scholar's

Perspective on Matriarchy," in Bernice A. Carroll, ed., *Liberating Women's History* (Urbana: University of Illinois Press, 1976), p. 219. See also Michelle Zimbalist Rosaldo, "Woman, Culture, and Society: A Theoretical Overview," and Sherry B. Ortner, "Is Female to Male as Nature Is to Culture?," in Rosaldo and Lamphere, eds., *Woman, Culture, and Society*, pp. 17–42 and 67–89. Support for the historical existence of matrifocal societies comes from Helen Diner, *Mothers and Amazons: The First Feminine History of Culture* (Garden City, N. Y.: Anchor/Doubleday, 1973), and Elizabeth Gould Davis, *The First Sex* (New York: Putnam, 1971). Margot Alder, in her review of matriarchal thought, makes the point that apart from the historical controversy over matriarchy, it is "important to stress that, contrary to many assumptions, feminists are viewing the idea of matriarchy as a complex one and that their creative use of matriarchy as *vision* and *ideal* would in no way be compromised if suddenly there were 'definite proof' that few matriarchies ever existed." Margot Adler, "Meanings of Matriarchy," in Charlene Spretnak, ed., *The Politics of Women's Spirituality* (Garden City, N. Y.: Anchor/Doubleday, 1982), p. 130.

21. J. J. Bachofen, *Myth, Religion, and Mother Right*, Ralph Manheim, tr. (Princeton: Princeton University Press, 1967), p. 207.

22. Bachofen, *Myth, Religion, and Mother Right*, p. 144. Anne Dickason emphasizes that Bachofen's conception of the feminine is characterized by a passive, maternal role. She argues that in the first stage women are the victims of male aggression, while in the second "mother right" serves merely as a nurturing phase which is finally superseded by the birth of the third, patriarchal culture. See "The Feminine as a Universal," in Mary Vetterling-Braggin, Frederick A. Elliston, and Jane English, eds., *Feminism and Philosophy* (Totowa, N.J.: Rowman and Littlefield, 1977), pp. 82–84. Similarly, "like many other Victorians," writes Adrienne Rich, "Bachofen is given to sentimental generalizations about women" (OWB, 73). Of Neumann, Rich writes, "However, like Jung, he is primarily concerned with integrating the feminine into the masculine psyche . . . and his bias is clearly masculine" (OWB, 82–83).

23. Feminist writers such as Shulamith Firestone, Kate Millett, and Juliet Mitchell have criticized Engels' economic model for not addressing women's oppression in terms of biological, sexual, and psychodynamic factors. Radical feminist stances such as Firestone's locate patriarchy's origins in the masculine subjugation of women through their biology. Arguing from a psychoanalytic perspective, Juliet Mitchell theorizes Freud's oedipal situation as a universal unconscious complex underlying patriarchy's oppression of women. See Juliet Mitchell, *Woman's Estate* (New York: Random House, 1971), p. 169. More recently, Zillah R. Eisenstein has attempted to fuse

radical and socialist feminist critiques of Engels to show how patriarchy reinforces differences in biological sex with specific ideological and economic forces: "Patriarchy precedes capitalism through the existence of the sexual ordering of society which derives from ideological and political interpretations of biological difference. . . . Today, the sexual division of society is based on real differences that have accrued from years of ideological pressure." Zillah R. Eisenstein, "Developing a Theory of Capitalist Patriarchy and Socialist Feminism," in Zillah R. Eisenstein, ed., *Capitalist Patriarchy and the Case for Socialist Feminism* (New York: Monthly Review Press, 1979), p. 25.

24. Bachofen's myth of the struggle between matriarchal and patriarchal societies not only influenced Engels' economic analysis of the evolution of the family, but was a forerunner to Freud's psychological interpretation of history. Bachofen's identification of femininity with natural, biological determinants tended to define matriarchal psychology in terms of material, irrational, and passive characteristics. Similarly, in the representative terms of *Moses and Monotheism,* Freud's mythic description of the origins of patriarchy echoed the Victorian bias of Bachofen's earlier sexism. In Freud's words: "This turning from the mother to the father points . . . to a victory of intellectuality over sensuality—that is, an advance in civilization, since maternity is proved by the evidence of the senses while paternity is an hypothesis, based on an inference and a premise. Taking sides in this way with a thought-process in preference to a sense perception has proved to be a momentous step." Sigmund Freud, *Moses and Monotheism,* in vol. 23 of *The Standard Edition,* p. 114; quoted in Peggy Kamuf, "Writing Like a Woman," in Sally McConnell-Ginet, Ruth Borker, and Nelly Furman, eds., *Women and Language in Literature and Society* (New York: Praeger, 1980), p. 289.

25. C. G. Jung, "Woman in Europe," in *Civilization in Transition,* vol. 10 of *The Collected Works of C. G. Jung,* Sir Herbert Read, ed., R. F. C. Hull, tr. (New York: Pantheon, 1964), p. 123.

26. Although Neumann rejected the historical inaccuracies of the Bachofen problematic, he nevertheless affirmed the usefulness of Bachofen's scheme as a psychological model: "Hence our repeated references to Bachofen, for although his historical evaluation of mythology may be out of date, his interpretation of the symbols has been largely confirmed by modern depth psychology." Erich Neumann, *The Origins and History of Consciousness,* R. F. C. Hull, tr. (Princeton: Princeton University Press, 1970), pp. 265–66.

27. Neumann, *Origins and History,* p. 125.

28. As Marianne Hirsch points out in her article "Mothers and Daughters," *Signs: Journal of Women in Culture and Society* (Autumn 1981), 7:205,

even feminist projects based in Jung and Neumann must recognize that in these methodologies "we find not only a male theorist but a developed androcentric system, which, even if deconstructed and redefined, still remains a determining and limiting point of departure." Moreover, as Karen F. Rowe and Susan Gubar have argued, many of the traditional folk tales and myths that Jung and Neumann work with reflect the masculine bias of patriarchal culture to begin with. See Karen F. Rowe, "Feminism and Fairy Tales," and Susan Gubar, "Mother, Maiden, and the Marriage of Death: Women Writers and an Ancient Myth," in *Women Studies* (1979), 6(3):237–57; 301–15.

29. De Beauvoir, *The Second Sex*, p. 132.

30. See Herbert Marcuse, *Eros and Civilization: A Philosophical Inquiry into Freud*, 2d ed. (Boston: Beacon Press, 1966).

31. "Mother consciousness," Bly writes, "was in the world first, and embodied itself century after century in its favorite images: the night, the sea, animals with curving horns and cleft hooves, the moon, bundles of grain. Four favorite creatures of the Mother were the turtle, the owl, the dove, and the oyster—all womb-shaped, night, or ancient round sea creatures. Matriarchal thinking is intuitive and moves by associative leaps. Bachofen discovered that it favored the left side (the feeling side) of the body" (SJH, 32).

32. This kind of nostalgia, according to Sally R. Binford, Gayle Rubin, and Joan Bamberger, is not only a historical fantasy but reinforces the status quo of patriarchy's mystification of woman as emotive madonna. "Feminist authors," writes Sally R. Binford, "concerned with demonstrating religions based on the Great Goddess often share the assumption, which is sometimes made explicit, that there are enormous psychological and biological differences between the sexes; women are by nature sensitive, loving, and nurturing, while men are aggressive, brutal and violent. As anthropologist Gayle Rubin points out, this is precisely the assumption of conventional sexists, and it cannot be supported by either biological or social science." Sally R. Binford, "Myths and Matriarchies" in Spretnak, ed., *The Politics of Women's Spirituality*, p. 559. Similarly, "The elevation of woman to deity on the one hand," Bamberger writes, "and the downgrading of her to child or chattel on the other, produce the same result. Such visions will not bring her any closer to attaining male socioeconomic and political status." Joan Bamberger, "The Myth of Matriarchy," p. 280.

33. Luce Irigaray, "When Our Lips Speak Together," Carolyn Burke, tr., *Signs* (1980), 6:75.

34. For readings that argue against my reservations about Bly's feminist representations see Victoria Harris, "'Walking Where the Plows Have Been

Turning': Robert Bly and Female Consciousness," in Richard Jones and Kate Daniels, eds., *Of Solitude and Silence: Writings on Robert Bly* (Boston: Beacon Press, 1981), pp. 153–68; and William Virgil Davis, " 'At the Edges of the Light': A Reading of Robert Bly's *Sleepers Joining Hands,*" in the same collection, pp. 250–67.

CHAPTER 6

1. Herbert Marcuse, "Marxism and Feminism," *Women's Studies* (Old Westbury, N.Y., 1974), 2(3): 282. Hereafter cited in text as Marxism/Feminism.

2. Adrienne Rich, *On Lies, Secrets, and Silence: Selected Prose 1966–1978* (New York: Norton, 1979), p. 130. Hereafter cited in the text as LSS. Quotations from other works by Adrienne Rich are documented as follows: *Diving into the Wreck: Poems 1971–1972* (New York: Norton, 1973), DW; *The Dream of a Common Language: Poems 1974–1977* (Norton, 1978), DCL; *The Fact of a Doorframe: Poems Selected and New, 1950–1984* (Norton, 1984), FD; *Of Woman Born: Motherhood as Experience and Institution* (New York: Bantam, 1976), OWB; *A Wild Patience Has Taken Me This Far: Poems 1978–1981,* (Norton, 1981), WP.

3. W. H. Auden, preface to *A Change of World,* in Barbara Charlesworth Gelpi and Albert Gelpi, eds., *Adrienne Rich's Poetry* (New York: Norton, 1975), p. 126. Hereafter cited in text as Preface.

4. Randall Jarrell, "Review of *The Diamond Cutters and Other Poems,*" in Gelpi and Gelpi, eds., *Adrienne Rich's Poetry,* p. 129. The strategy of legitimating Rich's writing by noting its family resemblance to high modernist patriarchs also marks Helen Vendler's reading with a residual androcentricism. Describing "Necessities of Life," for example, she writes: "This beautiful passage, though it could perhaps not have been written before Stevens' poetry of poverty, has the touch of the physical in it that Stevens' poetry lacked." Helen Vendler, *Part of Nature, Part of Us* (Cambridge: Harvard University Press, 1980), p. 252.

5. Nancy Woloch, *Women and the American Experience* (New York: Knopf, 1984), pp. 485, 487.

6. Betty Friedan, *The Feminine Mystique* (New York: Norton, 1963), p. 43.

7. These titles are mentioned in Friedan, *The Feminine Mystique,* p. 44.

8. Simone de Beauvoir, *The Second Sex,* H. M. Parshley, ed. and tr. (New York: Bantam, 1965), p. 687. See Wendy Martin, *An American Trip-*

tych: Anne Bradstreet, Emily Dickinson, Adrienne Rich (Chapel Hill: University of North Carolina Press, 1984), p. 183.

9. Theodore Roethke, *On the Poet and His Craft*, Ralph J. Mills, Jr., ed. (Seattle: University of Washington Press, 1965), p. 12.

10. See Kenneth Burke, "The Vegetal Radicalism of Theodore Roethke," *Sewanee Review* (Winter 1950), 58:68–108.

11. The sources for these three excerpts are as follows: Adrienne Rich, "Necessities of Life," FD, 55; Theodore Roethke, "Root Cellar," *The Collected Poems of Theodore Roethke*, (Garden City, N.Y.: Anchor/Doubleday, 1975), p. 38; Robert Bly, "When the Dumb Speak," *The Light Around the Body* (New York: Harper and Row, 1967), p. 62.

12. See Annette Kolodny, "Dancing Through the Minefield: Some Observations on the Theory, Practice, and Politics of a Feminist Literary Criticism," *Feminist Studies* (1980), vol. 6; rpt. in Elaine Showalter, ed., *The New Feminist Criticism: Essays on Women, Literature, and Theory* (New York: Pantheon, 1985), pp. 144–67.

13. "Father-right," as Rich defines it, "must be seen as one specific form of the rights men are presumed to enjoy simply because of their gender: the 'right' to the priority of male over female needs" (LSS, 219–20).

14. See Alicia Ostriker, "The Thieves of Language: Women Poets and Revisionist Mythmaking" in Showalter, ed., *The New Feminist Criticism*, pp. 314–38.

15. Margaret Atwood, "Review of *Diving into the Wreck*," in Jane Roberta Cooper, ed., *Reading Adrienne Rich* (Ann Arbor: University of Michigan Press, 1984), p. 238.

16. Albert Gelpi, for example, notes the controversy surrounding Jung's work, but assumes its usefulness as a "descriptive" framework: "Whether initial differences between men and women in psychological character and orientation are inherent or acculturated is a matter for specialists to continue to investigate." See his "Adrienne Rich: The Poetics of Change" in Gelpi and Gelpi, eds., *Adrienne Rich's Poetry*, p. 137. Gelpi's grounding in Jung leads him to endorse "androgynous wholeness" as the goal of feminist individuation. The androcentric etymology of this term, for Rich, is particularly suspect as a descriptive rubric for women's experience.

17. See Adrienne Rich's essay "Compulsory Heterosexuality and Lesbian Experience," *Signs* (Summer 1980). 5:631–60. "My organizing principle is the belief that it is not enough for feminist thought that specifically lesbian texts exist. Any theory of cultural/political creation that treats lesbian existence as a marginal or less 'natural' phenomenon, as mere 'sexual preference,' or as the mirror image of either heterosexual or male homosexual relations, is profoundly weakened thereby, whatever its other contributions" (632).

18. Traditional accounts of gender view the differences between men and women as determined in the oedipal phase when, according to Freud, the child comes to understand that "anatomy is destiny." In Freud's scheme, women assume alienated gender roles in service to the Victorian ideal of childbearing. The male bias of Freud's theory of gender identification is clearly visible in his essay "Femininity," in vol. 22 of *The Standard Edition of the Complete Psychological Works of Sigmund Freud,* James Strachey, ed. and tr. (London: The Hogarth Press, 1968), pp. 112–35. But post-Freudian psychoanalysts such as Karen Horney, Melanie Klein, and Ernest Jones have challenged Freud's subordination of women's sexuality to reproduction.

19. See Nancy Chodorow, *The Reproduction of Mothering: Psychoanalysis and the Sociology of Gender* (Berkeley: University of California Press, 1978). While Rich finds Chodorow's writing appealing, she also critiques Chodorow's blindness to patriarchal oppression: "Chodorow's account barely glances at the constraints and sanctions which, historically, have enforced or insured the coupling of women with men and obstructed or penalized our coupling or allying in independent groups with other women. Adrienne Rich," "Compulsory Heterosexuality," p. 636.

20. Adrian Oktenberg's " 'Disloyal to Civilization': The *Twenty-One Love Poems* of Adrienne Rich" elaborates the same fusion of mind and body at work in Rich's *Twenty-One Love Poems*: "By rejecting the patriarchal dichotomy between mind and passion, and suggesting instead their unification, she has begun to articulate an idea that it is difficult for most of us even to imagine;" in Cooper, ed., *Reading Adrienne Rich,* p. 85.

21. In "It is the Lesbian in Us . . . ," Rich's remarks at the December 28, 1976 MLA Convention, she clarifies her use of the term: "I believe that I failed, in preparing my remarks, to allow for the intense charge of the word *lesbian,* and for all its deliquescences of meaning, ranging from 'man-hater' and 'pervert' to the concepts I was trying to invoke, of the self-chosen woman, the forbidden 'primary intensity' between women, and also the woman who refuses to obey, who has said 'no' to the fathers" (LSS, 202).

22. Women's alienation from patriarchal language is also the subject of Joanne Feit Diehl's " 'Cartographies of Silence': Rich's *Common Language* and the Woman Poet": "Why should the process of image making, using language for one's own ends, be, in Rich's words, 'mined with risks' for women? And how are these pressures different from those confronting men? The poems respond directly to these issues and suggest that women are not only secondary in status, but are also latecomers to a patriarchal world of images": in Cooper, ed., *Reading Adrienne Rich,* p. 94.

23. Hélène Cixous, "The Laugh of the Medusa," in Elaine Marks and Isabelle de Courtivron, eds., *The New French Feminisms* (New York: Schocken, 1981), p. 259.

24. "The semiotic activity, which introduces wandering or fuzziness into language and *a fortiori,* into poetic language is, from a synchronic point of view, a mark of the workings of drives (appropriation/rejection, orality/anality, love/hate, life/death) and, from a diachronic point of view, stems from the archaisms of the semiotic body. . . . Language as symbolic function constitutes itself at the cost of repressing instinctual drive and continuous relation to the mother." Julia Kristeva, *Desire in Language: A Semiotic Approach to Literature and Art,* Leon S. Roudiez, ed., Thomas Gora et al., trs. (New York: Columbia University Press, 1980), p. 136. Hereafter cited in the text as Desire.

25. Associated with the *Tel quel* theorists in Paris during the 1960s, Kristeva's writing bridges the Continental tradition of post-Saussurian structural linguistics with what she describes as Russian "postformalism." Following Bakhtin, Kristeva reads poetic language as a social production—a signifying practice that undermines the authority of ideal knowledge based in transcendental signified meaning.

26. My use of Kristeva might pose problems for some readers who question Kristeva's background in Lacanian psychoanalysis. To begin with, the stereotyping of Lacan as anti-feminist ignores, according to Jane Gallop, his playful and subversive verbal style, highly prized within French feminism. In "Reading the Mother Tongue: Psychoanalytic Feminist Criticism," *Critical Inquiry* (Winter 1987), 13:315, Gallop espouses "the influence of Lacanian psychoanalysis which promotes language to a principle role in the psychoanalytic drama and so naturally offers fertile ground for crossing psychoanalytic and literary concerns." Kristeva, of course, offers a powerful revision of Lacan in valorizing the infant's preoedipal bond to the mother as it persists in language's ludic and somatic body. Moreover, as Susan R. Suleiman has argued, Kristeva is a particularly cogent advocate for feminism for at least three reasons: "she seeks to analyze and show the limitations of Western culture's traditional discourse about motherhood; she offers a theory, however incomplete and tentative, about the relation between motherhood and feminine creation; finally, she *writes* her own maternal text as an example of what such creation might be." Susan R. Suleiman, "Writing and Motherhood," in Shirley Nelson Garner, Claire Kahane, and Madelon Sprengnether, eds., *The (M)other Tongue* (Ithaca: Cornell University Press, 1985), p. 369.

27. Cary Nelson joins Rich's desire for a feminist writing to the larger context of an American Whitmanesque tradition. "The ideal of a language of female sexuality," he says, "linked as it is in Rich's poetry with a disavowal of America's patriarchal history of repression, is inseparable from the 'drive/to connect. The dream of a common language' (DCL, 7) that

so many American poets since Whitman have shared." Cary Nelson, *Our Last First Poets: Vision and History in Contemporary American Poetry* (Urbana: University of Illinois Press, 1981), p. 159. This incorporation is problematic insofar as it homogenizes the differences between women's linguistic communities and those of men.

28. Of Rich's ambivalence toward language, Charles Altieri writes, "The myth that matters is not beyond language but one of language"; *Self and Sensibility in Contemporary American Poetry* (New York: Cambridge University Press, 1984), p. 179.

29. Rich's insistence on the material history of language's "verbal privilege" exceeds Jane Vanderbosch's logocentric privileging of voiced experience over writing's textuality: "Rich's suggestion is quite simple: the oral is more fundamental than the literary. It is the primal whisper behind all speech, the human sound that most approximates the wind"; "Beginning Again," in Cooper, ed., *Reading Adrienne Rich*, p. 132.

30. See Jacques Derrida, "Signature Event Context," in *Margins of Philosophy*, Alan Bass, tr. (Chicago: University of Chicago Press, 1976), pp. 307–30.

31. Emily Dickinson, *The Complete Poems of Emily Dickinson* (Boston: Little, Brown, 1927), p. 126.

32. Alicia Ostriker, *Writing Like a Woman* (Ann Arbor: University of Michigan Press, 1984), p. 117.

33. Julia Kristeva, "Oscillation Between Power and Denial," interview with Xaviere Gauthier in *Tel quel*, Summer 1974; rpt. in Showalter, ed., *The New French Feminisms*, p. 166.

34. My reading contradicts Marianne Whelchel's argument that Rich transcends this historical problematic by retrieving and celebrating the lives of women: "She celebrates individual women and offers them to us for inspiration and models." See "Mining the 'Earth-Deposits': Women's History in Adrienne Rich's Poetry," in Cooper, ed., *Reading Adrienne Rich*, p. 69.

35. See Gerda Lerner, "Placing Women in History: Definitions and Challenges," *The Majority Finds Its Past* (New York: Oxford University Press, 1979); quoted in FD, 333.

36. My point here is that Rich eludes any utopian readings that simplify or homogenize her contradictory attitudes toward feminist precursors. See for example Susan Stanford Friedman's "Adrienne Rich and H.D.: An Intertextual Study," in Cooper, ed., *Reading Adrienne Rich*: "Rich's stance toward women writers is distinctly compassionate and noncompetitive" (172).

37. See Doris Davenport, "The Pathology of Racism: A Conversation with Third World Wimmin," in Cherrie Moraga and Gloria Anzaldua, eds.,

This Bridge Called My Back: Writings of Radical Women of Color (Watertown, Mass.: Persephone Press, 1981), pp. 85–90.

38. Adrienne Rich, "Notes Toward a Politics of Location," in Myriam Diaz-Diocaretz and Iris M. Zavala, eds., *Women, Feminist Identity, and Society in the 1980s: Selected Papers* (Philadelphia: John Benjamins, 1985), pp. 16, 20.

CHAPTER 7

1. Gwendolyn Brooks, *Report from Part One* (Detroit: Broadside Press, 1972), p. 86. Hereafter cited in the text as R. Quotations from Brooks' poetry are taken from *Blacks* (Chicago: The David Company, 1987), hereafter cited in the text as B; *To Disembark* (Detroit: Broadside Press, 1981), cited as TD; and *Mayor Harold Washington* (Chicago: Brooks Press, 1983), cited as MHW.

2. "In black language, methodically fostered by black people today, it strengthens solidarity, the consciousness of identity, and of their repressed or distorted cultural tradition. And because of this function, it militates against generalization." Herbert Marcuse, *Counterrevolution and Revolt* (Boston: Beacon Press, 1930), p. 80.

3. Raymond Williams, *Marxism and Literature* (London: Oxford University Press, 1977), p. 205.

4. For an account of Lowell's ties to New Criticism see James E. Breslin, *From Modern to Contemporary* (Chicago: University of Chicago Press, 1984).

5. Louis Simpson, review of Brooks' *Selected Poems, New York Herald Tribune Book Week*, October 27, 1963, p. 27.

6. John Crowe Ransom, "The Communities of Letters," in *Poems and Essays* (New York: Vintage Books, 1955), pp. 109–18.

7. Beyond scattered journal articles and two book-length studies of Brooks—Harry B. Shaw, *Gwendolyn Brooks* (New York: Twayne, 1980) and D. H. Melhem, *Gwendolyn Brooks: Poetry and the Heroic Voice* (Lexington: University Press of Kentucky, 1987)—there is only one collection of critical essays on Brooks to date: Maria K. Mootry and Gary Smith, eds., *A Life Distilled: Gwendolyn Brooks, Her Poetry and Fiction* (Urbana: University of Illinois Press, 1987). The major critics of contemporary American poetry—James E. Breslin (*From Modern to Contemporary*, 1984); Charles Altieri (*Enlarging the Temple*, 1979; *Self and Sensibility*, 1984); Anthony Libby (*Mythologies of Nothing*, 1984); Charles Molesworth (*The Fierce Embrace*, 1979); Cary Nelson (*Our Last First Poets*, 1981); Marjorie Perloff (*The Poetics of Indeterminacy*, 1981); and Helen Vendler (*Part of Nature, Part of Us*, 1980)— do not even index Brooks, let alone devote a chapter to her writing.

8. In an essay titled "The Black Aesthetic in the Thirties, Forties, and Fifties," Dudley Randall, the influential editor and publisher of Broadside Press, groups Brooks with Robert Hayden and M. B. Tolson as part of a post–Harlem Renaissance generation. Randall describes them as figures who were "familiar with and learned from the modern experimental masters such as Hart Crane, Eliot, Pound, and Yeats"; in Addison Gayle, Jr., ed., *The Black Aesthetic* (Garden City, N.Y.: Doubleday, 1971), p. 231. Randall's judgment repeats Margaret Walker's own 1950 review of black poets in *Phylon*. Walker's analysis of *Annie Allen*'s "neo-classical" style defends Brooks against the charge of being "obscurantist," but Walker, like Randall, finds Brooks' work "less preoccupied with the theme of race as such. Race is rather used as a point of departure toward a global point of view than as the central theme of one obsessed by race." Margaret Walker, "New Poets," in Addison Gayle, Jr., ed., *Black Expression: Essays By and About Black Americans in the Creative Arts* (New York: Weybright and Talley, 1969), p. 65. This general critical line continues throughout the 1960s and 1970s in the readings of a later generation of black poets. Although Gary Smith also reads Brooks as transitional, he details her differences from both the modernist and Harlem Renaissance traditions. See "Gwendolyn Brooks' *A Street in Bronzeville,* the Harlem Renaissance, and the Mythologies of Black Women," *MELUS* (Fall 1983), 10:35.

9. "At this time," Haki Madhubuti says, "Gwendolyn Brooks didn't think of herself as an African or as an African-American. At best she was a 'new negro' becoming black" (quoted in R, 17).

10. Suzanne Juhasz, *Naked and Fiery Forms* (New York: Farrar, Straus and Giroux, 1978), p. 150. For a reading closer to my own sense of Brooks' rich feminist achievement, see Hortense J. Spillers, "Gwendolyn the Terrible: Propositions on Eleven Poems," in Sandra M. Gilbert and Susan Gubar, eds., *Shakespeare's Sisters: Feminist Essays on Women Poets* (Bloomington: Indiana University Press, 1979), pp. 233–244; and Beverly Guy-Sheftall, "The Women of Bronzeville," in Roseann P. Bell et al., eds., *Sturdy Black Bridges: Visions of Black Women in Literature* (New York: Anchor Books, 1979), pp. 157–70. "A major poet," writes Barbara Christian, "Brooks has always written about women. . . . And her work has always focused on the sexist expressions of racism in this country. Yet Brooks would not consider herself a woman poet. . . . Her poetry about women, however, is some of the most poignant in American literature"; *Black Feminist Criticism: Perspectives on Black Women Writers* (New York: Pergamon Press, 1985), p. 123.

11. As Dudley Randall and Margaret Walker point out, Brooks' early writing is everywhere marked by the influence of modernist precursors. She admits the importance of works such as "The Love Song of J. Alfred

Prufrock" and *The Waste Land* for her own poetics. In "Truth," to site only one example, she so internalizes the general angst we associate with modernism that her very language is encoded with Eliot's characteristic rhetoric. Compare, for example, Prufrock's lament, "Though I have wept and fasted. Wept and prayed" with Brooks' "Though we have wept for him, / Though we have prayed." Gwendolyn Brooks, *The World of Gwendolyn Brooks* (New York: Harper and Row, 1971), p. 114.

12. Nathan A. Scott, Jr., "Black Literature," in Daniel Hoffman, ed., *Harvard Guide to Contemporary American Writing* (Cambridge: Harvard University Press, 1979), p. 327.

13. See, for example, Addison Gayle, Jr., "Cultural Strangulation: Black Literature and the White Aesthetic," in Gayle, ed., *The Black Aesthetic,* pp. 39–46. Similarly, in his "Editor's Introduction: Writing 'Race' and the Difference It Makes," Henry Louis Gates, Jr. writes, "Current language use signifies the difference between cultures and their possession of power, spelling out the distance between subordinate and superordinate, between bondsman and lord in terms of their 'race.' These usages develop simultaneously with the shaping of an economic order in which the cultures of color have been dominated in several important senses by Western Judeo-Christian, Greco-Roman cultures and their traditions"; *Critical Inquiry* (Autumn 1985), 12:6.

14. Compare, for example, Addison Gayle, Jr.'s comments concerning the black author's white audience, to Adrienne Rich's focus on women's patriarchal audience. Gayle writes, "The black artist of the past worked with the white public in mind" ("Introduction," in Gayle, ed., *The Black Aesthetic,* p. xxi). Rich has said (as quoted in chapter 6), "No male writer has written primarily or even largely for women, or with the sense of women's criticism as a consideration when he chooses his materials, his theme, his language. But to a lesser or greater extent, every woman writer has written for men even when, like Virginia Woolf, she was supposed to be addressing women." Adrienne Rich, "When We Dead Awaken: Writing as Re-vision," in *On Lies, Secrets, and Silence* (New York: Norton, 1979), pp. 37–38.

15. Mary Helen Washington, "'Taming All that Anger Down': Rage and Silence in Gwendolyn Brooks' *Maud Martha,*" in Henry Louis Gates, Jr., ed.,*Black Literature and Literary Theory* (New York: Methuen, 1984), p. 257.

16. Langston Hughes' well-known metaphor of the "racial mountain" describes the "desire to pour racial individuality into the mold of American standardization, and to be as little Negro and as much American as possible"; "The Negro Artist and the Racial Mountain," in Gayle, ed., *The Black Aesthetic,* p. 175. "From the time of Phillis Wheatley on down to the present," writes Arthur P. Davis, "every Negro poet has protested the color

proscription in America"; "The Black and Tan Motif in the Poetry of Gwendolyn Brooks," *College Language Association Journal* (December 1962), 6:97.

17. Gwendolyn Brooks, "They Call It Bronzeville," *Holiday,* October 1951, p. 62.

18. See Mary Frances Berry and John W. Blassingame, *Long Memory: The Black Experience in America* (New York: Oxford University Press, 1982), pp. 326–27.

19. Larry Neal, "And Shine Swam On," in Leroi Jones (Imamu Amiri Baraka) and Larry Neal, eds., *Black Fire* (New York: William Morrow, 1968), p. 638.

20. Brooks' alignment with feminism is contradictory. On the one hand, her career celebrates women's lives, but on the other, she disavows formal ties to the feminist movement. Although Brooks endorses women's emancipation from patriarchy, she does not venture beyond the domestic sphere to embrace contemporary feminism's lesbian and matriarchal alternatives to the nuclear family. Instead, her feminism is lodged within a panoramic vision of the black community and its vernacular and folk traditions. "I think 'Women's Lib' is not for black women for the time being," she said in a 1971 interview, "because men *need* their women beside them, supporting them in these very tempestuous days." See Ida Lewis, "Conversation: Gwen Brooks and Ida Lewis," *Essence,* April 1971; rpt. in Brooks, *Report from Part One,* p. 179. Later, in 1977, she clarified this earlier subordination of women's role to the supporting of men: "on account of everything that had been done to smash our men down there was this tendency on the part of the women—announced too—to lift the men up, to *heroize* them." See Gloria T. Hull and Posey Gallagher, "Update on *Part One*: An Interview with Gwendolyn Brooks," *College Language Association Journal* (1977), 21:36. In 1983 she still disavowed any feminist agenda that would challenge patriarchy's domestic family unit: "I'm saying, yes, black women have got some problems with black men and vice versa, but these are family matters. They must be worked out within the family. At no time must we allow whites, males or females, to convince us that we should split. . . . It's another divisive tactic dragging us from each other, and it's going to lead to a lot more racial grief"; "Gwendolyn Brooks," in Claudia Tate, ed., *Black Women Writers at Work* (New York: Crossroad/Continuum, 1983), p. 47.

21. George Kent reads "The Mother" as flawed by its failure to unify irony and compassion: " 'The Mother' seems to me to protest too much and to suffer from a labored irony, which fails to convey the attitude of the author toward her subject—the several abortions of the mother"; "The Poetry of Gwendolyn Brooks," part 2, *Black World* (1971), 20(11):38.

22. Berry and Blassingame, *Long Memory,* p. 84.

23. Manning Marable, *Race, Reform, and Rebellion: The Second Reconstruction in Black America, 1945–1982* (Jackson: University Press of Mississippi, 1984), p. 176. See also Reynolds Farley and Walter R. Allen, *The Color Line and the Quality of Life in America* (New York: Russell Sage Foundation, 1987), p. 165.

24. Farley and Allen, *The Color Line*, p. 137.

25. Alphonso Pinkney, *Black Americans* (Englewood Cliffs, N.J.: Prentice-Hall, 1969), p. 94.

26. In that year 260,000 black men were serving terms in federal and state prisons; during this period, over 10,000 were murdered annually (Marable, *Race, Reform, and Rebellion*, p. 174).

27. Pinkney, *Black Americans*, p. 43.

28. Farley and Allen, *The Color Line*, pp. 47, 50.

29. See Brooks, *Report from Part One*, p. 200.

30. Moreover, between 1930 and 1969, 405 of the 455 men executed for rape in America were black (Berry and Blassingame, *Long Memory*, pp. 123, 125).

31. Hazel V. Carby, "'On the Threshold of Woman's Era': Lynching, Empire, and Sexuality in Black Feminist Theory," *Critical Inquiry* (Autumn 1985), 12:270.

32. George Kent views this work as well as Brooks' "The Chicago Defender Sends a Man to Little Rock" as compromised by each poem's sacrifice of aesthetic to political material (see "The Poetry of Gwendolyn Brooks," p. 38). His reading, however, ignores both the subtle portrait of the Mississippi mother's psychic anguish and Brooks' sophisticated depiction of postwar America's political unconscious in "Little Rock."

33. "And indeed," Carmichael writes, "if the ghetto had been formally and deliberately planned, instead of growing spontaneously and inevitably from the racist functioning of the various institutions that combine to make the society, it would be somehow less frightening"; "Toward Black Liberation," in Jones and Neal, eds., *Black Fire*, p. 125.

34. W. E. B. DuBois, *The Souls of Black Folk*, in John Hope Franklin, ed., *Three Negro Classics* (New York: Avon Books, 1965), p. 215. Houston A. Baker, Jr. reads Brooks' poetic style as marked by a "double-consciousness": "Both DuBois and Miss Brooks manifest the duality of their lives in their literary works. . . . The high style of both authors, however, is often used to explicate the condition of the black American trapped behind a veil that separates him from the white world. What one seems to have is 'white' style and 'black' content—'two warring ideals in one dark body.'" See "The Achievement of Gwendolyn Brooks," *College Language Association Journal* (1972), 1:23.

35. Quoted in Godfrey Hodgson, *America in Our Time* (Garden City, N.Y.: Doubleday, 1976), p. 197.

36. Compare, for example, the following statements on the concept of black nationalism: "It is more than a figure of speech to say that the Negro community in America is the victim of white imperialism and colonial exploitation"(Stokley Carmichael, "Toward Black Liberation," in Jones and Neal, eds., *Black Fire*, p. 124). "The American Negro shares with Colonial peoples many of the socio-economic factors which form the material basis for present-day revolutionary nationalism" (Harold Cruse, "Revolutionary Nationalism and the Afro-American," in *Black Fire*, p. 41). "Colonialism, whether in Asia, Africa, Latin America or inside the United States of America, was established by the gun and is maintained by the gun" (James Boggs, "Black Power: A Scientific Concept Whose Time Has Come," in *Black Fire*, p. 118).

37. Malcolm X, "Basic Unity Program, Organization of Afro-American Unity," in Abraham Chapman, ed., *New Black Voices* (New York: Mentor Books, 1972), p. 565.

38. "The new magazine," Fuller said, "sought to reflect the new black spirit wafting gingerly across the land and to provide it room in which to expand and mature." Hoyt Fuller, quoted in Abby Arthur Johnson and Ronald Mayberry Johnson, *Propaganda and Aesthetics: The Literary Politics of Afro-American Magazines in the Twentieth Century* (Amherst: University of Massachusetts Press, 1979), p. 193.

39. Gwendolyn Brooks, *A Capsule Course in Black Poetry Writing* (Detroit: Broadside Press, 1977), p. 4. Hereafter cited in the text as Capsule.

40. Carolyn Rogers, quoted in James A. Emanuel, "Blackness Can: A Quest for Aesthetics," in Gayle, ed., *The Black Aesthetic,* p. 214.

41. Don L. Lee (Haki Madhubuti), "Toward a Definition: Black Poetry of the Sixties (After LeRoi Jones)," in Gayle, ed., *The Black Aesthetic,* p. 240.

42. John Bartlow Martin, "The Strangest Place in Chicago," *Harper's Magazine* (December 1950), 201:87.

43. As R. Baxter Miller points out, Alfred's parodies of Whitman, Baudelaire, Browning, and others resist modernist influences, "Tension," says Baxter, "separates the literary vision of the past from that of the present." See "Define . . . The Whirlwind: *In the Mecca*—Urban Setting, Shifting Narrator, and Redemptive Vision," *Obsidian* (1978), 4(1):24.

44. See T. S. Eliot, "Ulysses, Order, and Myth," *Dial,* November 1923.

45. Gwendolyn Brooks, quoted in Paul M. Engle, *We Asked Gwendolyn Brooks* (Chicago: Illinois Bell Telephone, n.d.); rpt. in Brooks, *Report from Part One,* p. 146.

46. "In contrast to Alfred," writes William H. Hansell, "Lee is certain of his goals and is eager to act. . . . Alfred's symbolic actions, by Lee's standard, are inadequate"; "Gwendolyn Brooks' 'In the Mecca': A Rebirth into Blackness," *Negro American Literature Forum* (Summer 1974), 8:204.

47. In contrast to my reading, George E. Kent argues that *Mecca*'s ending is problematic. See "Aesthetic Values in the Poetry of Gwendolyn Brooks," in R. Baxter Miller, ed., *Black American Literature and Humanism* (Lexington: University of Kentucky Press, 1981), p. 81.

48. Stephen E. Henderson, "'Survival Motion': A Study of the Black Writer and the Black Revolution in America," in Mercer Cook and S. E. Henderson, eds., *The Militant Black Writer in Africa and the United States* (Madison: University of Wisconsin Press, 1969), p. 68. William H. Hansell takes up the role of violence in Brooks' later aesthetic in three essays: "Essence, Unifyings, and Black Militancy: Major Themes in Gwendolyn Brooks' *Family Pictures* and *Beckonings*," *Black American Literary Forum* (1977), 11:63–66; "The Role of Violence in Recent Poems of Gwendolyn Brooks," *Studies in Black Literature* (Summer 1974), 5:21–27; and "The Poet Militant and Foreshadowings of a Black Mystique: Poems in the Second Period of Gwendolyn Brooks," *Concerning Poetry* (1977), 10:37–45.

49. Ron Karenga, "Black Cultural Nationalism," in Gayle, ed., *The Black Aesthetic*, pp. 33–34.

50. Although her major black critics universally approve of this shift toward an Afro-American audience, Dan Jaffe, one of Brooks' white readers, attacks the whole notion of the black aesthetic influence on her recent work: "The label 'black poetry' cheapens the achievement of Gwendolyn Brooks. It recommends that race matters more than artistic vocation or individual voice." Beyond Jaffe's appeal to vague and idealist notions of "vocation" or "voice," however, he lays out an even more improbable criterion: "Can the poet make the white feel black?" See David Jaffe, "Gwendolyn Brooks: An Appreciation from the White Suburbs," in C. W. E. Bigsby, ed., *The Black American Writer* (Deland, Fla.: Everett C. Edwards, 1960), vol. 2, pp. 92, 94. In responding to this kind of reading, Brooks has said: "I believe whites are going to say what they choose to say about us, whether it's right or wrong, or just say *nothing,* which is another very effective way of dealing with us, so far as they are concerned. We should ignore them"; "Gwendolyn Brooks," in Tate, ed., *Black Women Writers at Work,* p. 45.

51. In addition to noting the Greek etymology of "warp" as meaning "to whirl," William H. Hansell also speculates on Brooks' possible intertextual echoes of W. E. B. Dubois' *The Souls of Black Folk.* See Hansell's "The Role of Violence in Recent Poems of Gwendolyn Brooks," *Studies in Black Literature* (Summer 1974), 5:22.

52. Hull and Gallagher, "Update on *Part One*: An Interview with Gwendolyn Brooks," p. 39.

53. Walter Benjamin, "Thesis on the Philosophy of History," quoted in Fredric Jameson, *The Political Unconscious: Narrative as a Socially Symbolic Act* (Ithaca: Cornell University Press, 1981), p. 281.

54. "Gwendolyn Brooks," in Tate, ed., *Black Women Writers at Work*, p. 44.

55. Continuing her work with young Chicago poets, Brooks, as Poet Laureate of Illinois, supplemented the adult laureate awards with prizes for school-age poets, funded with her own money.

56. Addison Gayle, Jr., "Introduction," in Gayle, ed., *Black Expression*, p. xv. Gayle's ethical criterion complements William H. Hansell's description of Brooks' black ideal: "Black life is portrayed in her poetry as having retained the idealistic values white America has neglected or ignored"; "The Role of Violence," p. 26.

57. During the 1970s, the status and fate of the black aesthetic movement was the topic of heated debate among such early proponents as Larry Neal, Amiri Baraka, Stephen Henderson, and such later academic critics as Robert B. Stepto, Dexter Fisher, Henry Louis Gates, Jr., Sherley Anne Williams, Robert Hemenway, and Robert O'Meally. See in particular Dexter Fisher and Robert B. Stepto, eds., *Afro-American Literature: The Reconstruction of Instruction* (New York: MLA of America, 1979), and Houston A. Baker, Jr., "Discovering America: Generational Shifts, Afro-American Literary Criticism, and the Study of Expressive Culture," chapter 2 of *Blues, Ideology and Afro-American Literature: A Vernacular Theory* (Chicago: University of Chicago Press, 1984), pp. 64–112.

Index